Babies! Babies!

We love you so!

Much, much more

than you'll ever know!

Smiling, laughing

and sleeping too!

We just can't get

enough of you!

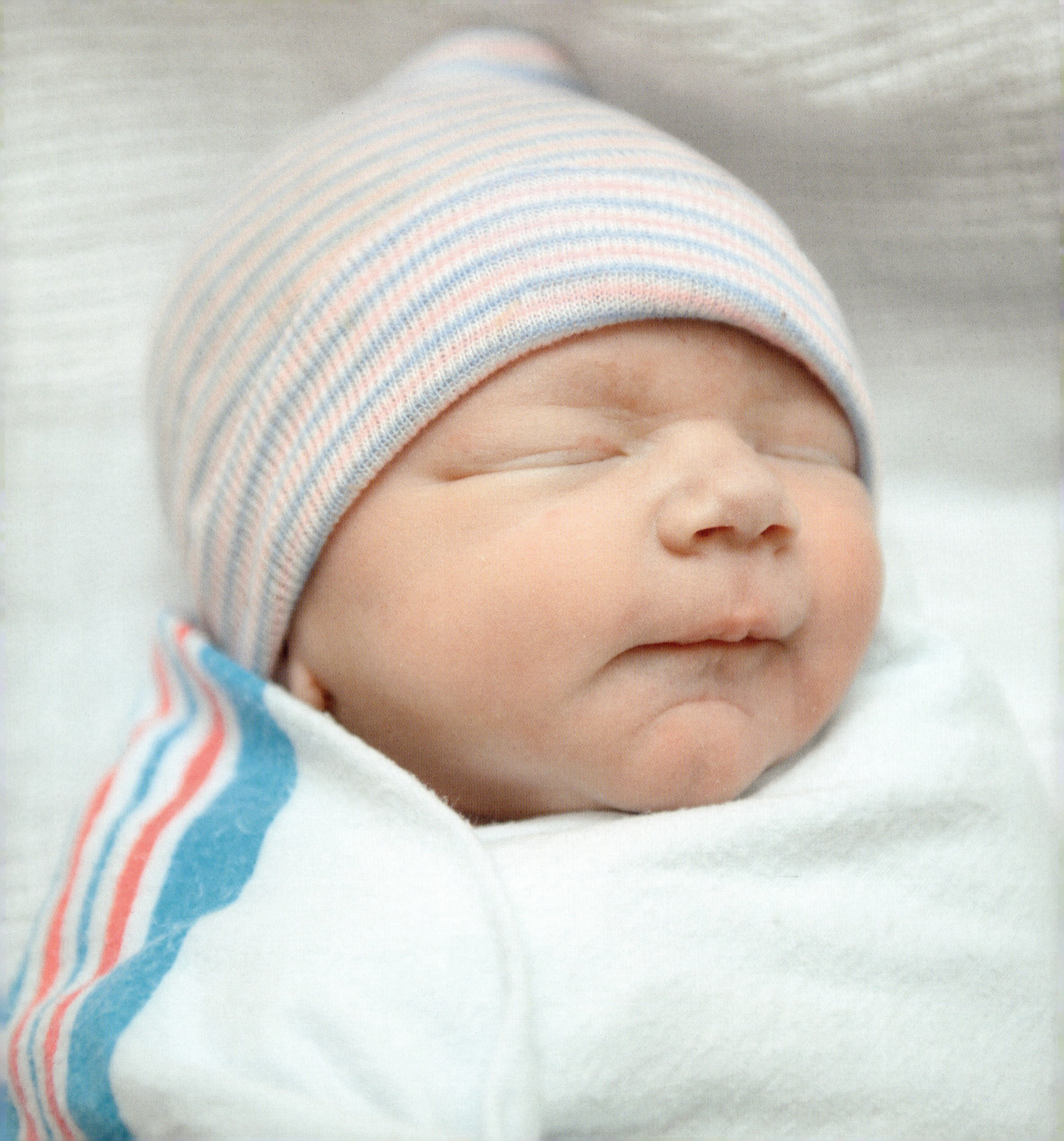

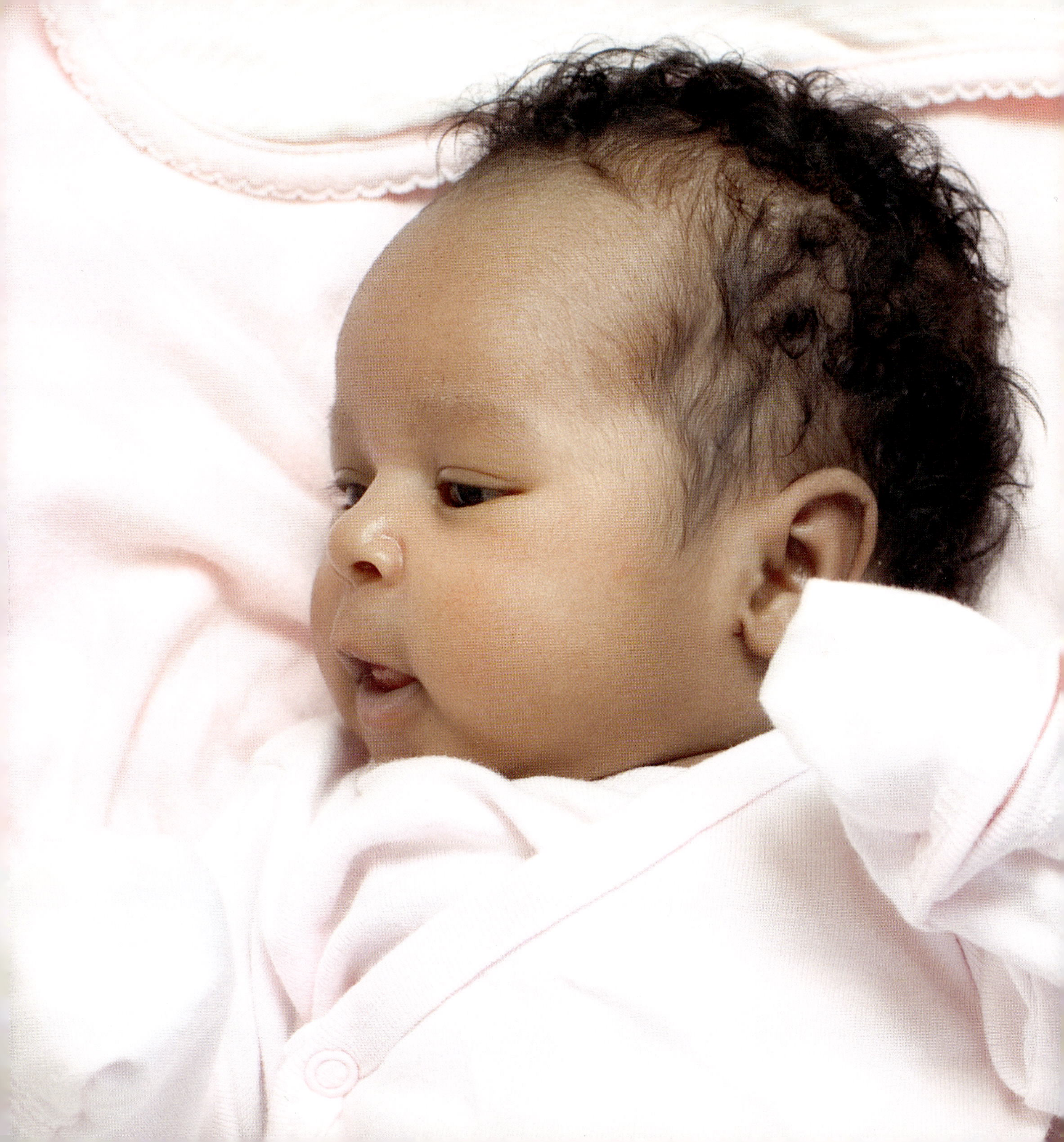

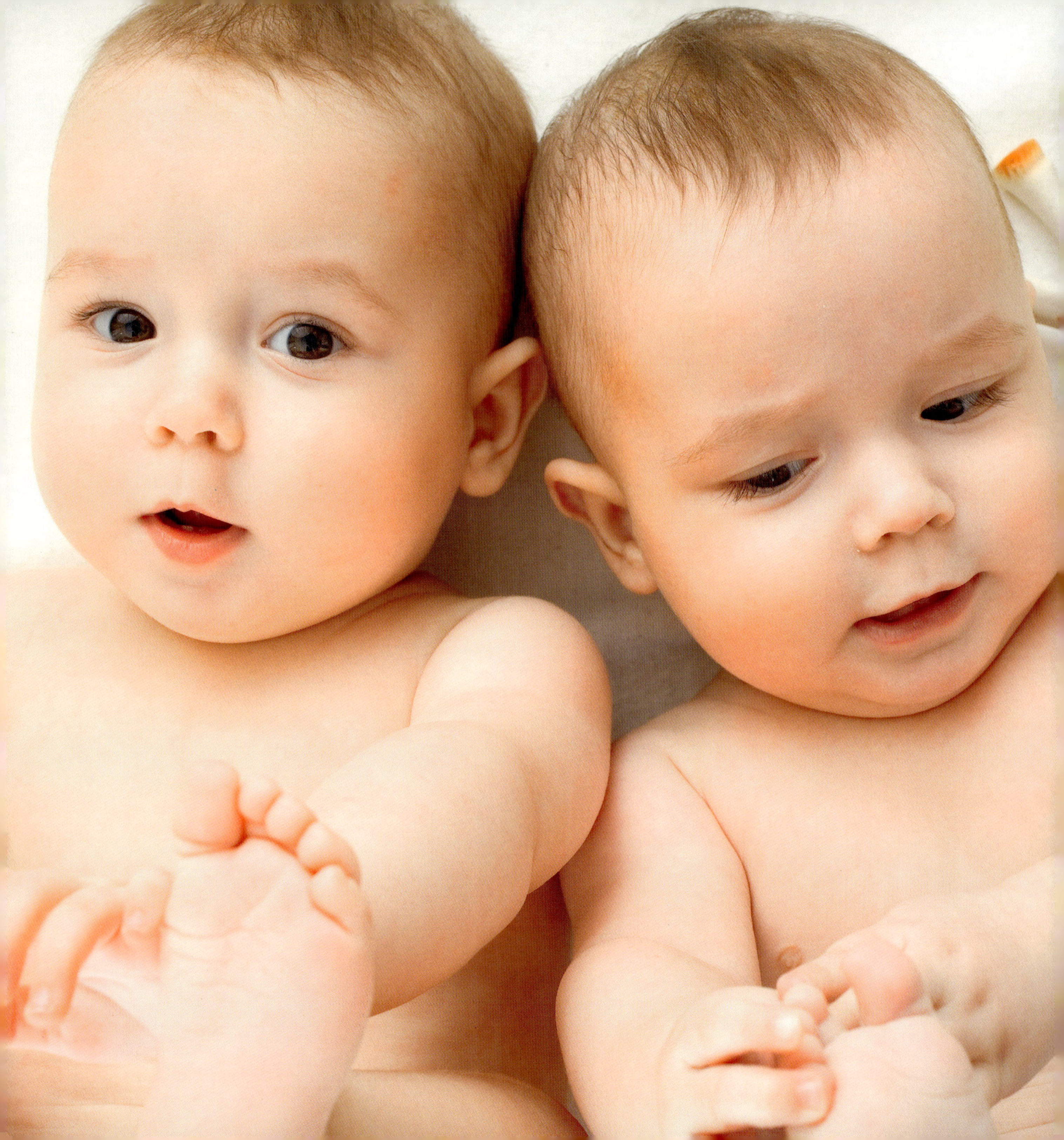

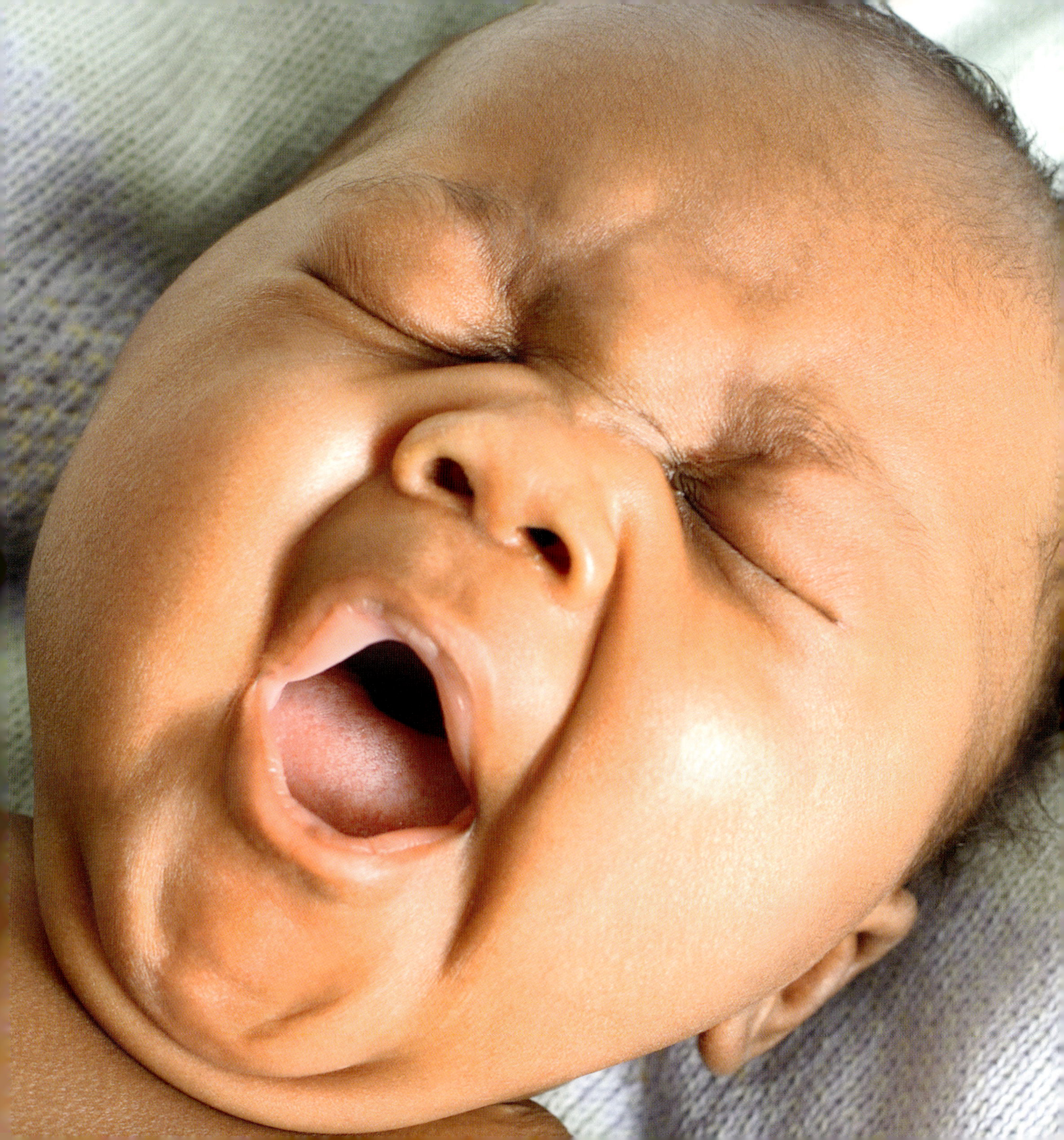

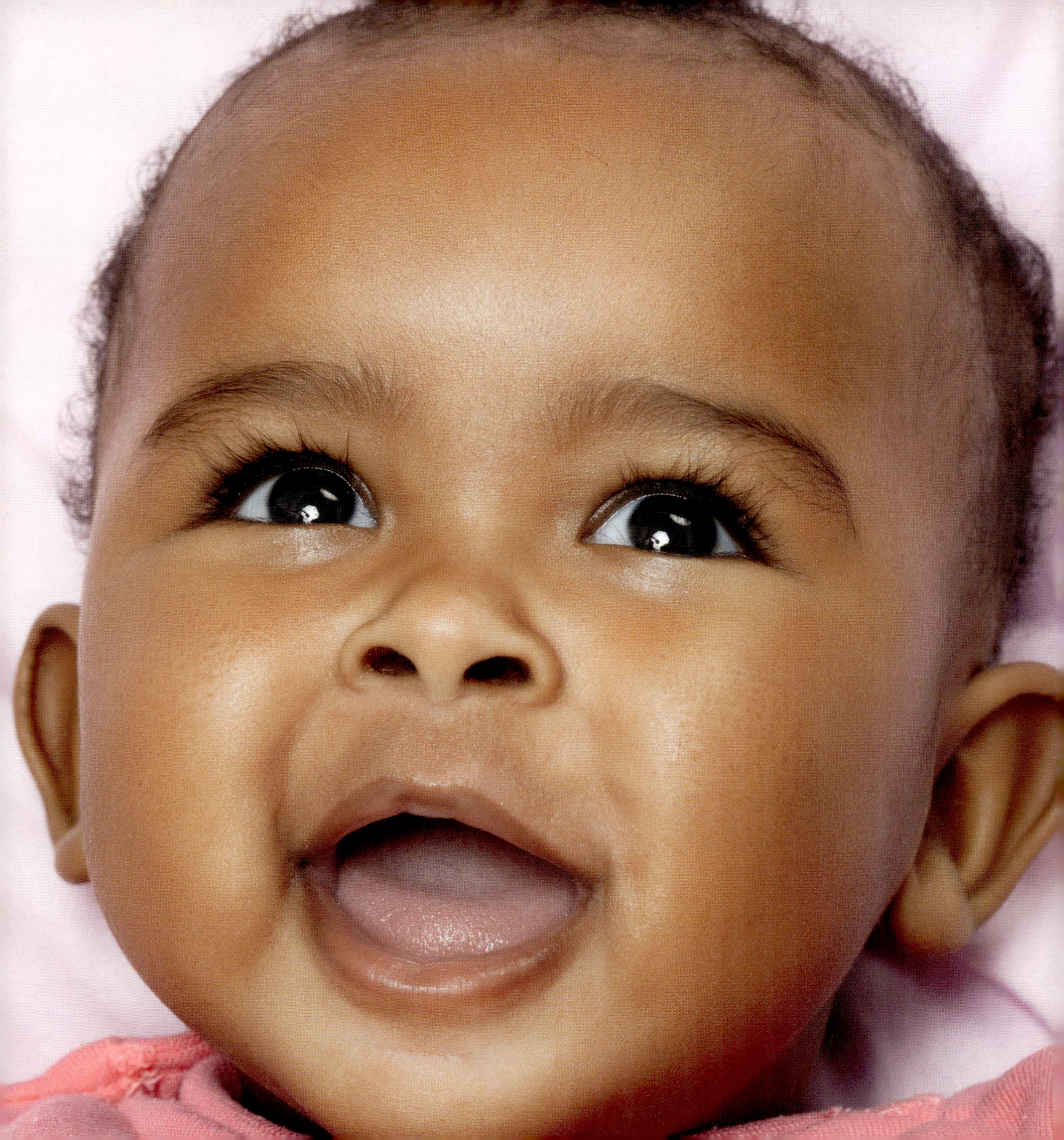

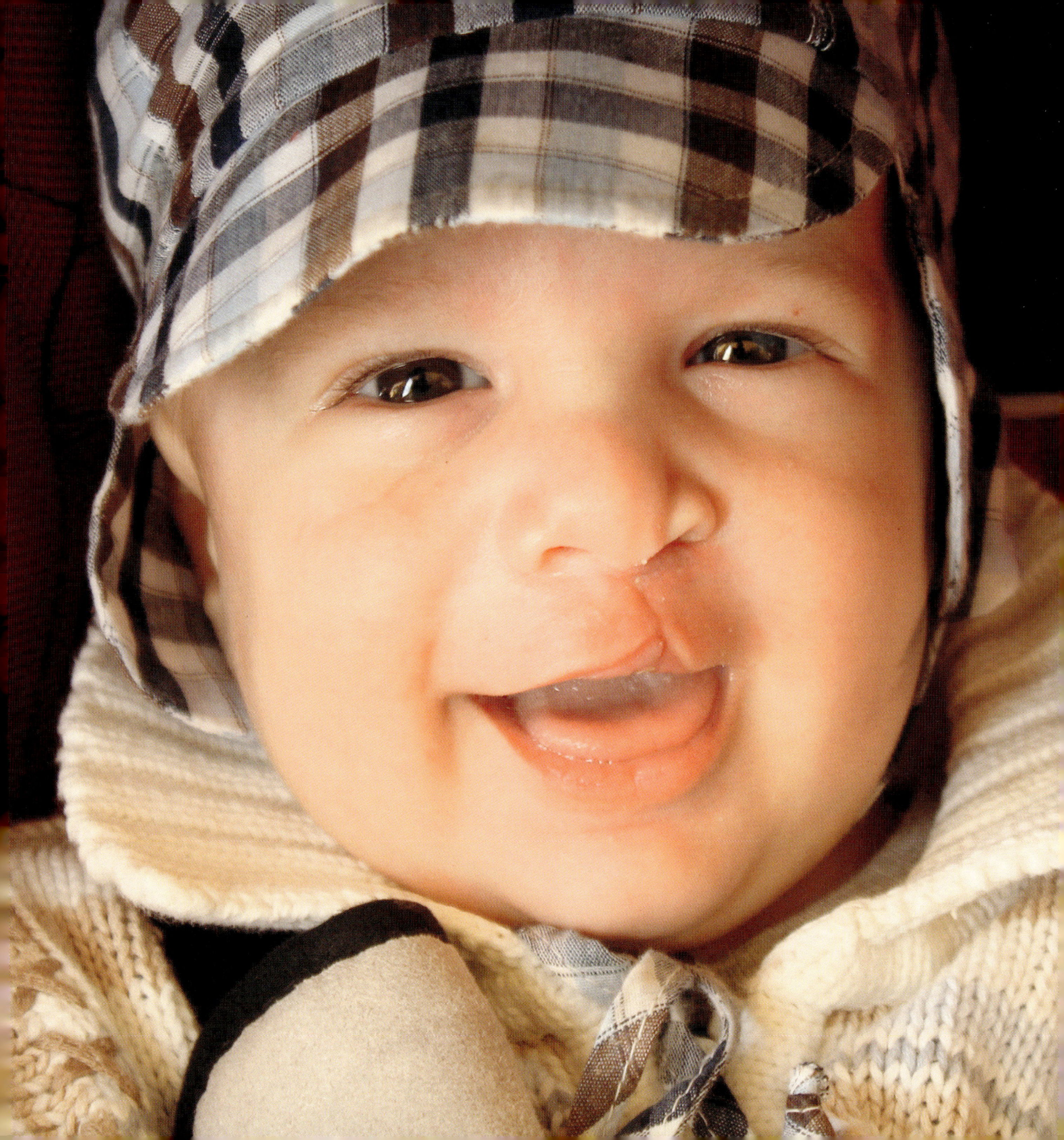

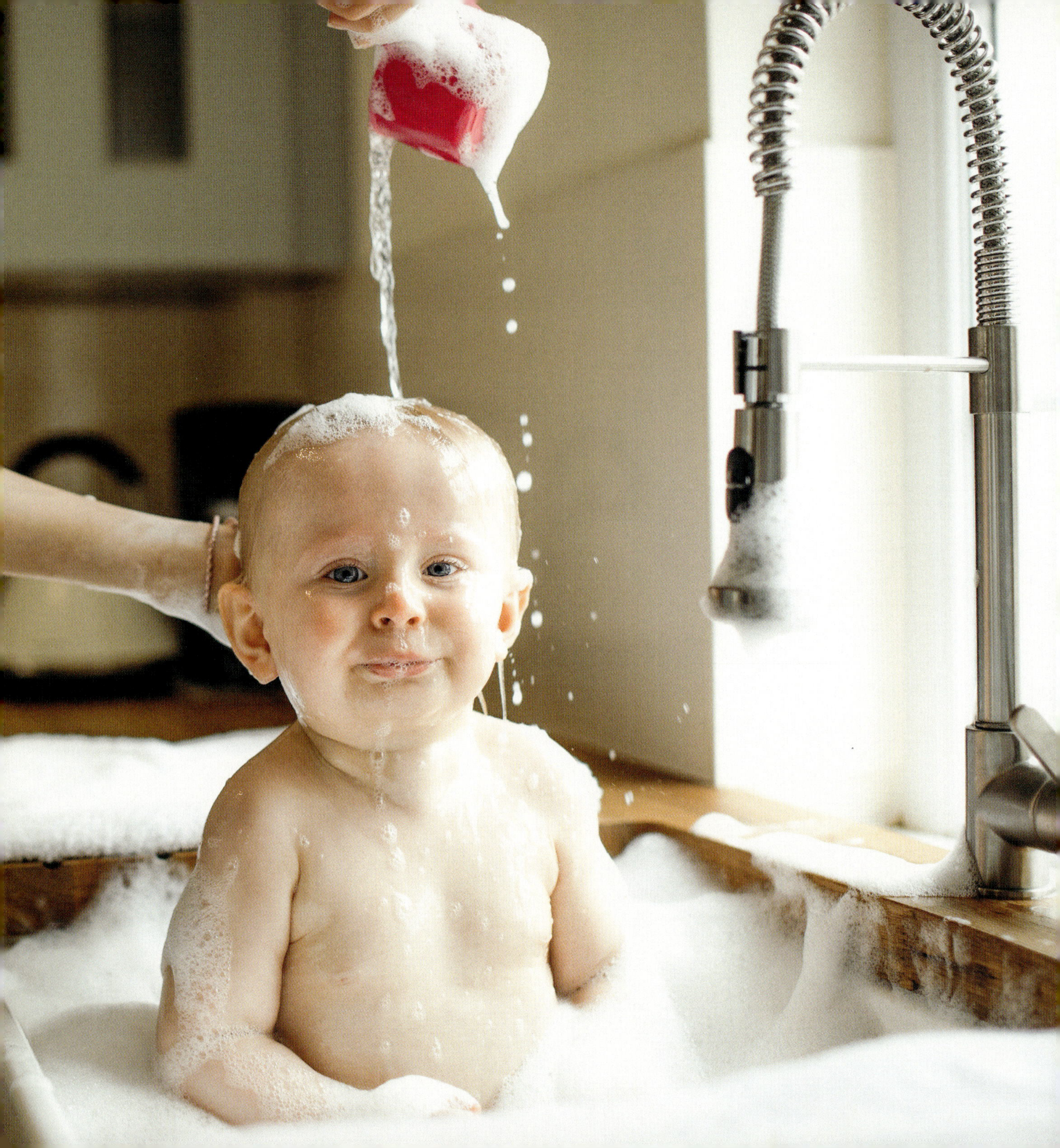

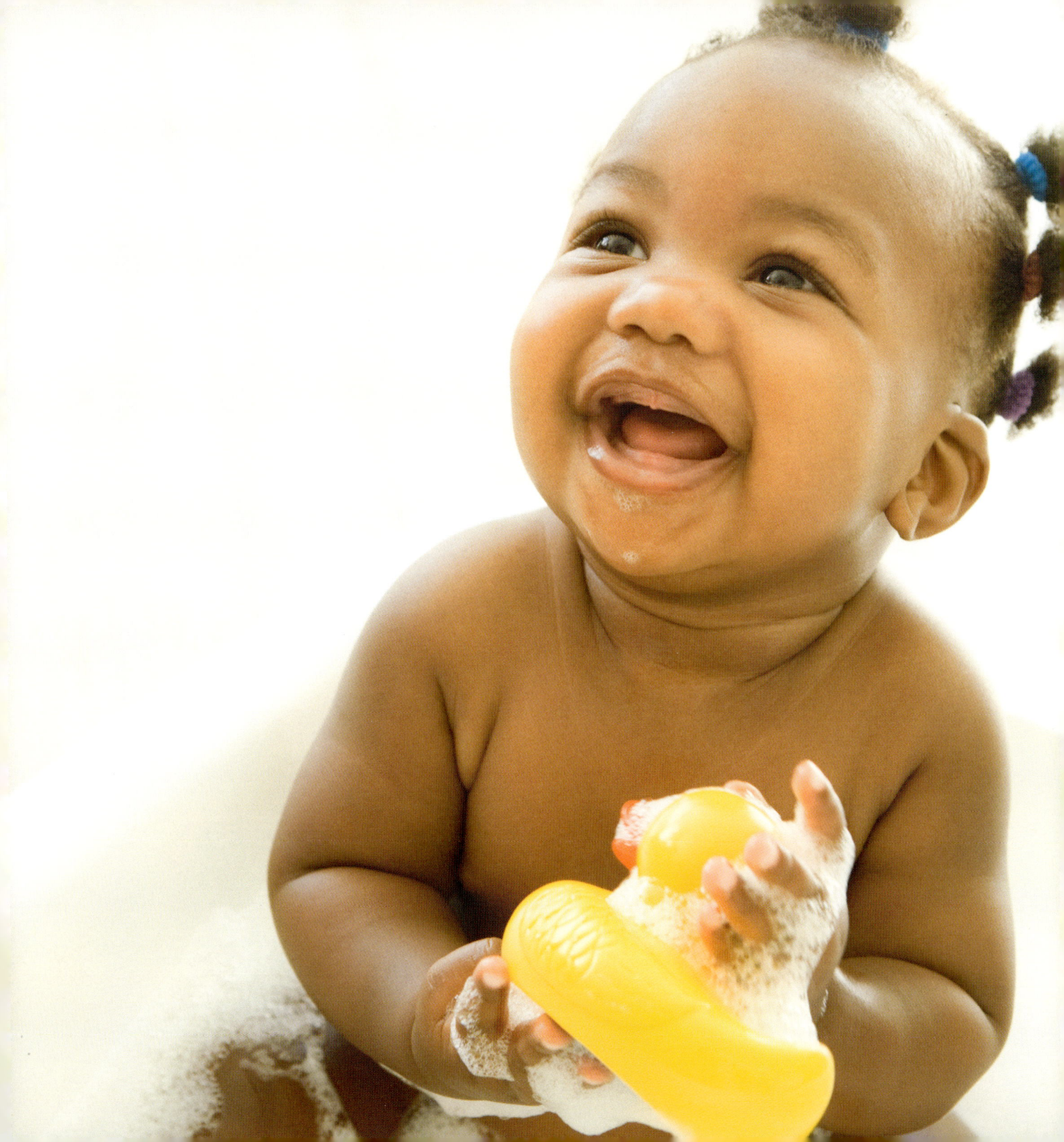

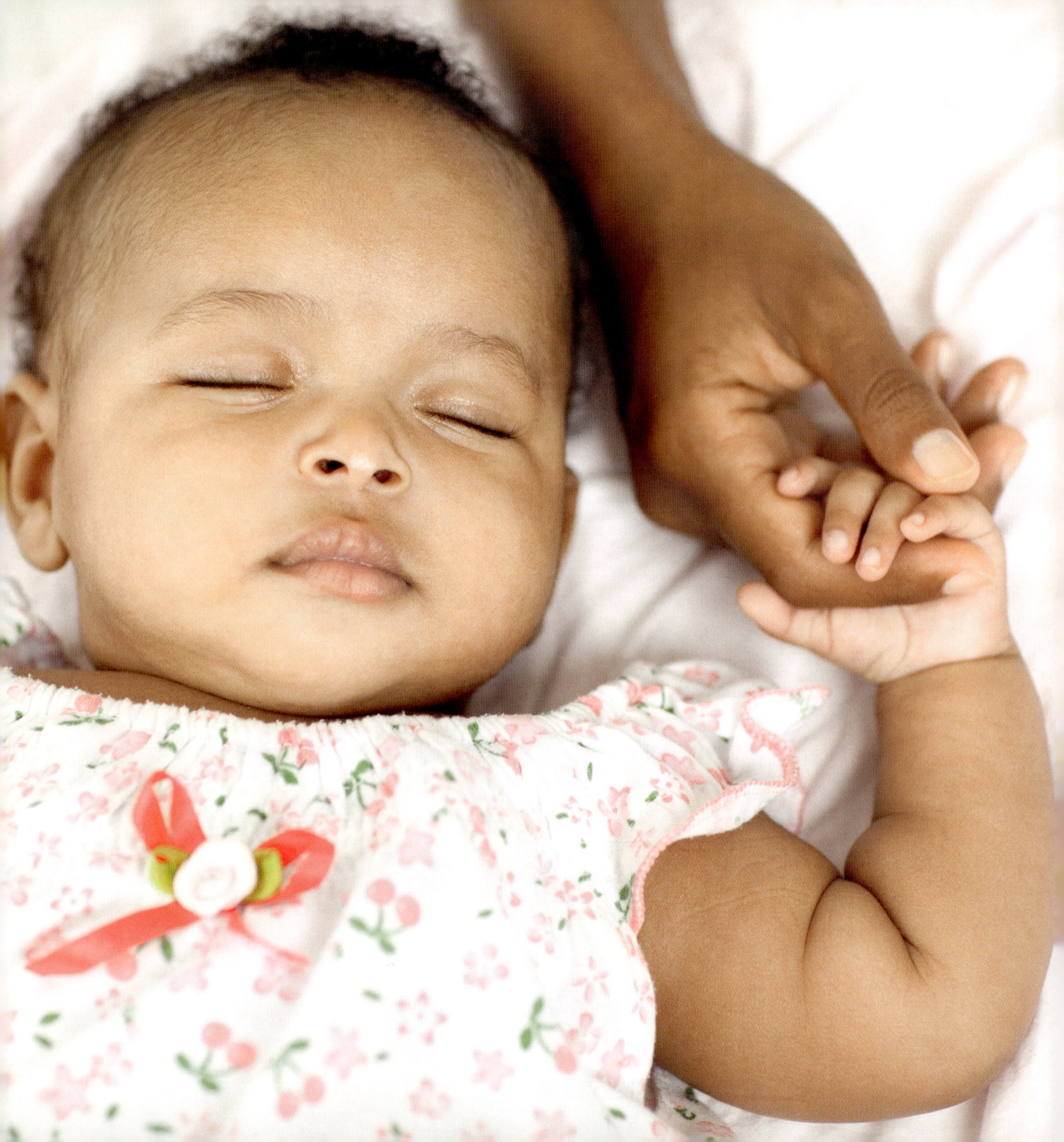

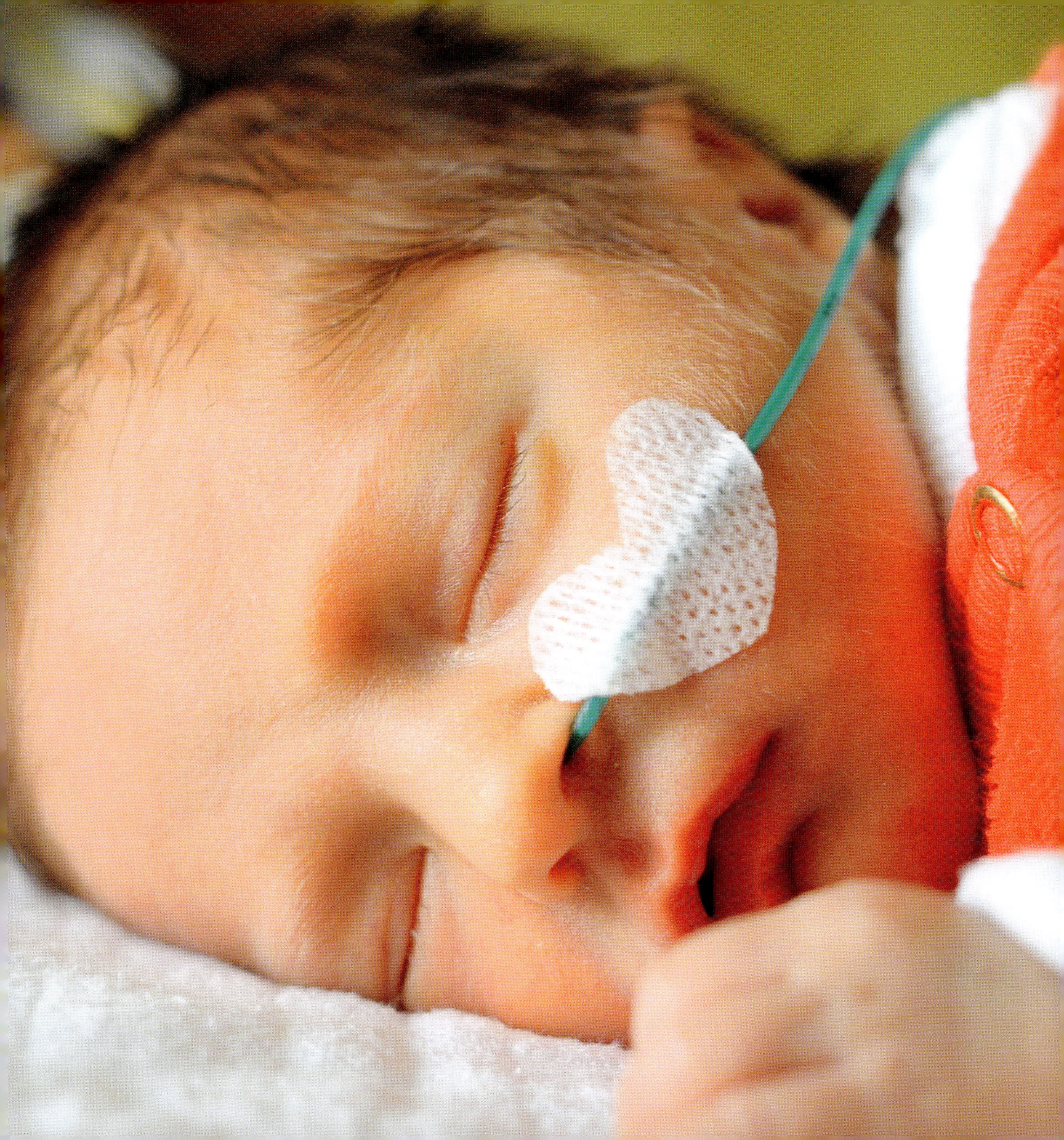

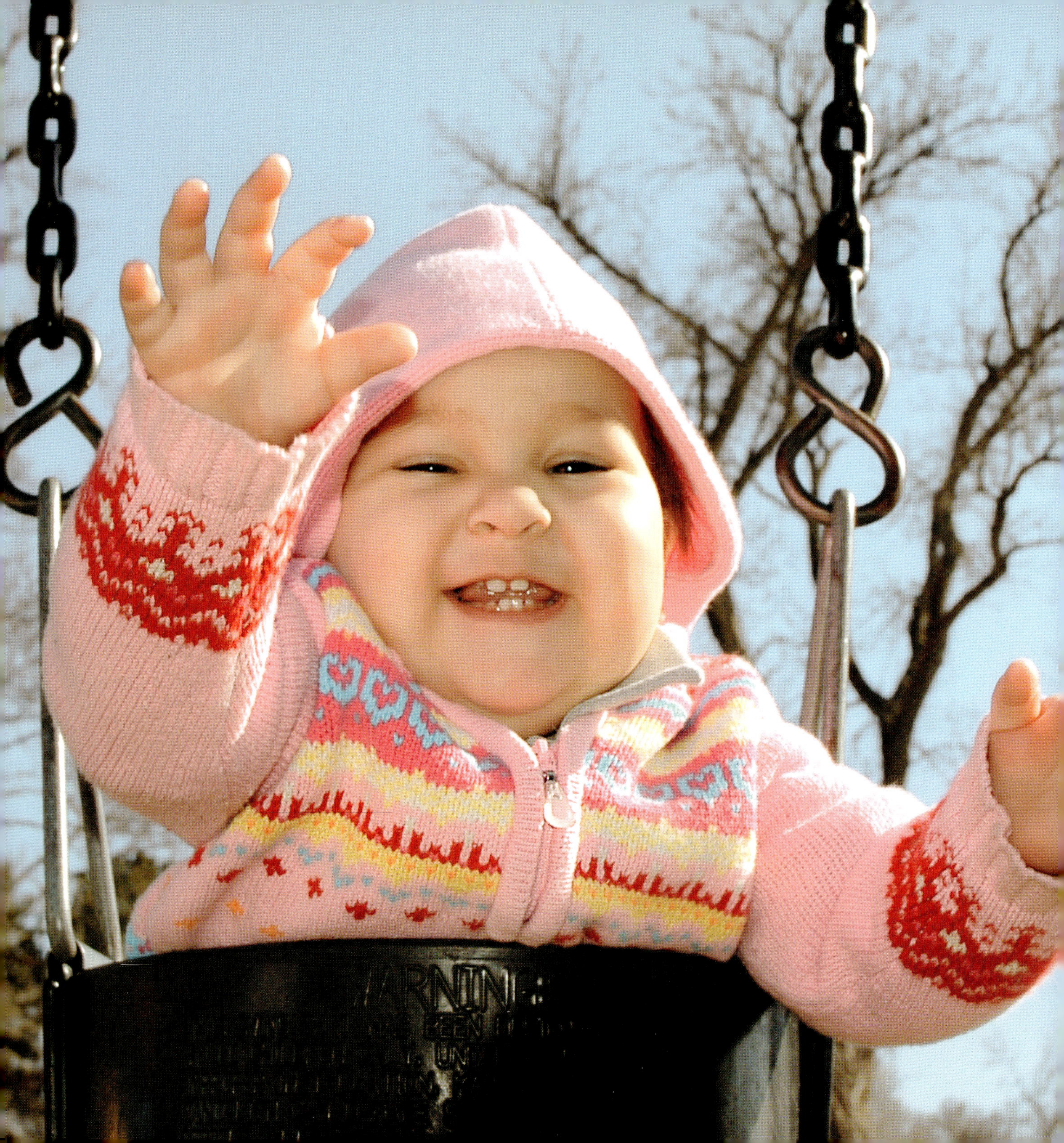

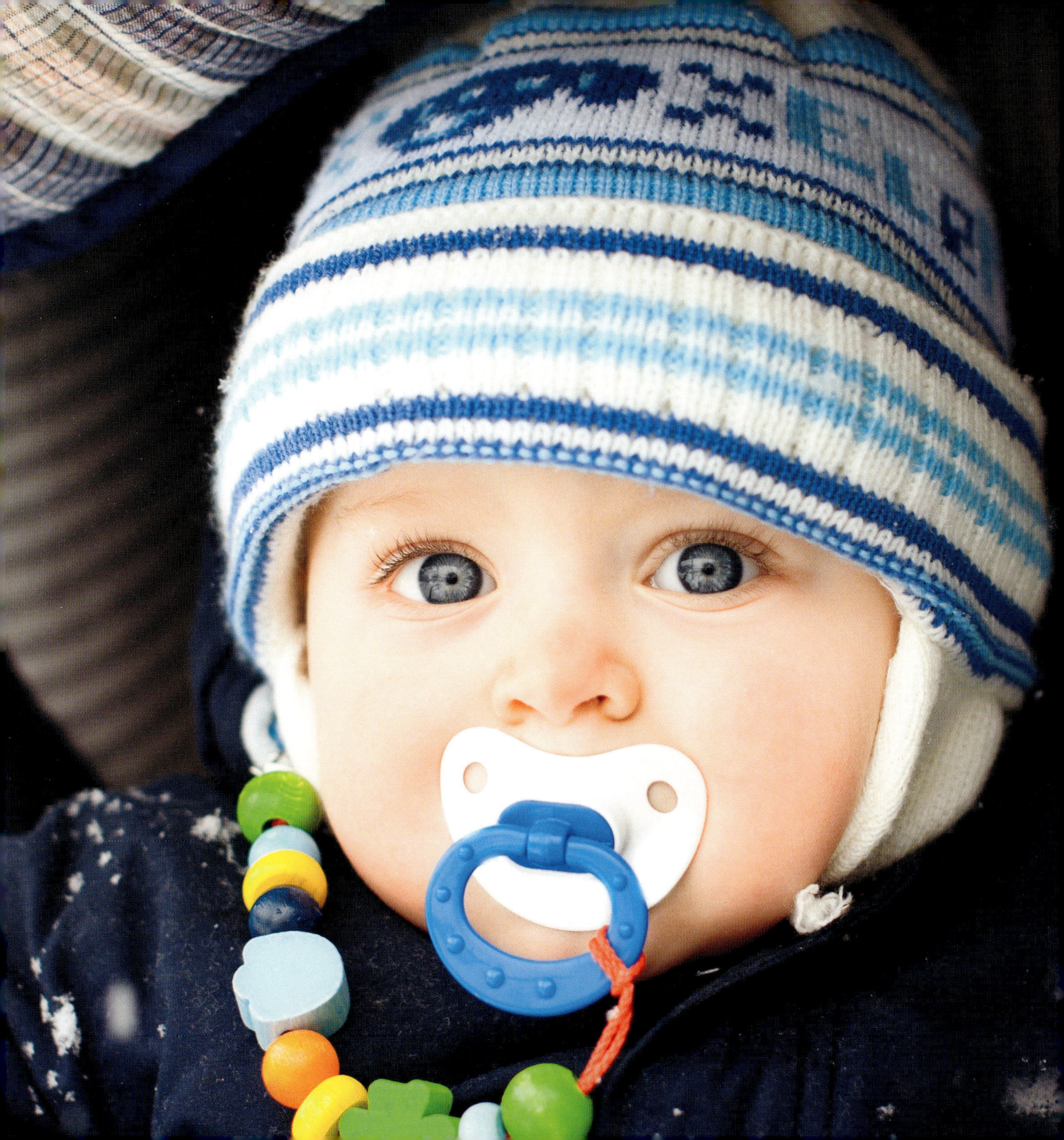

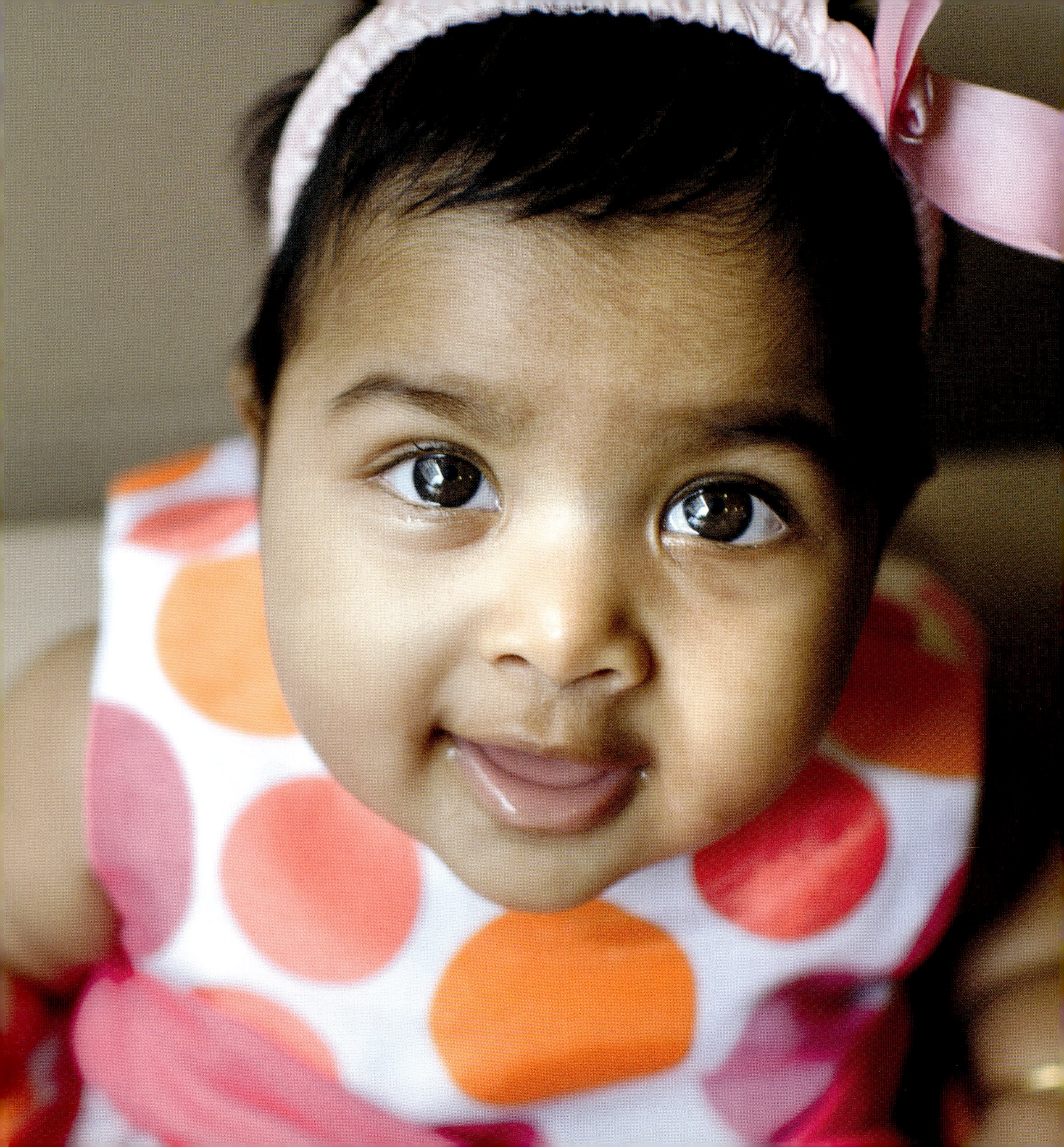

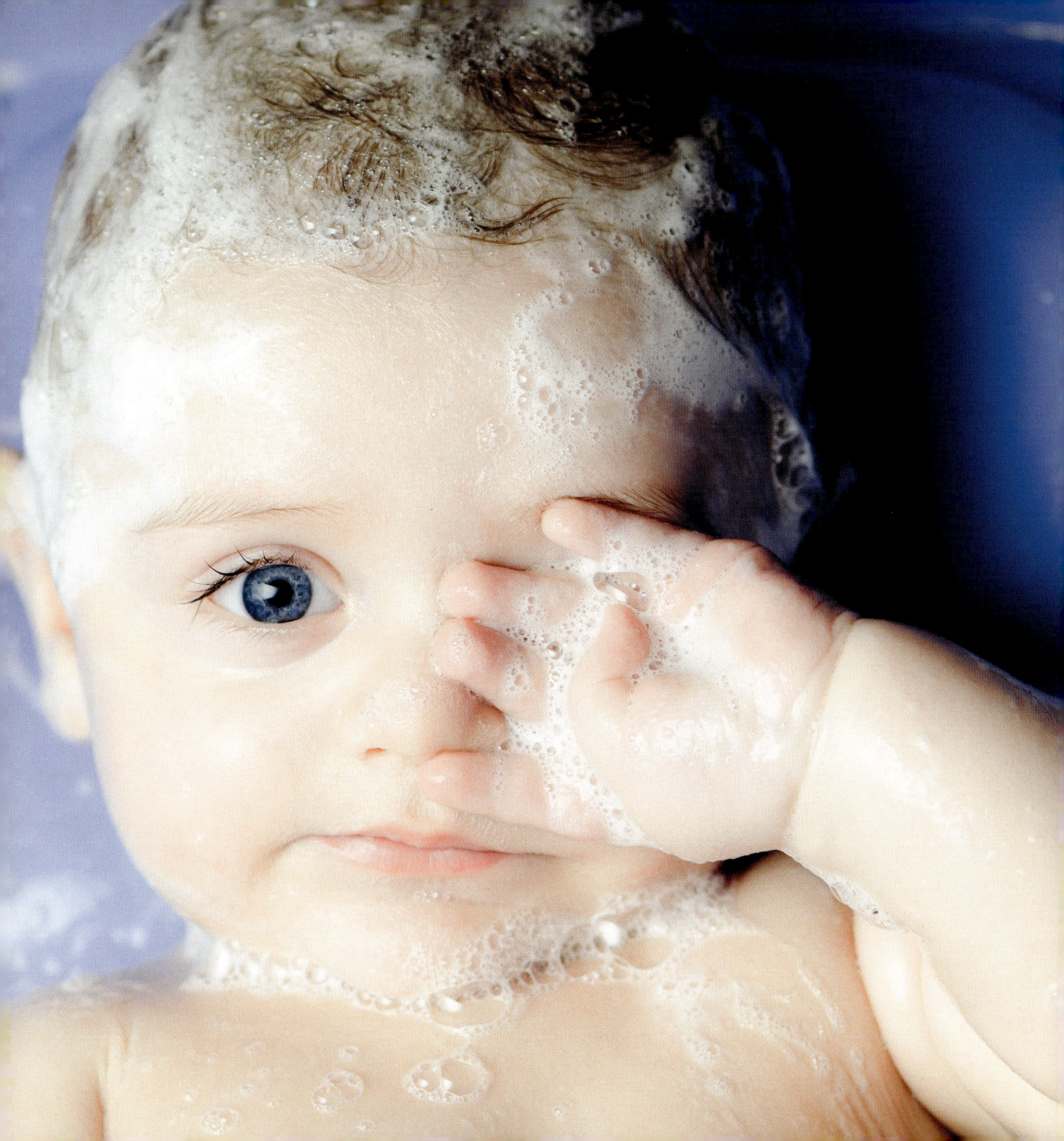

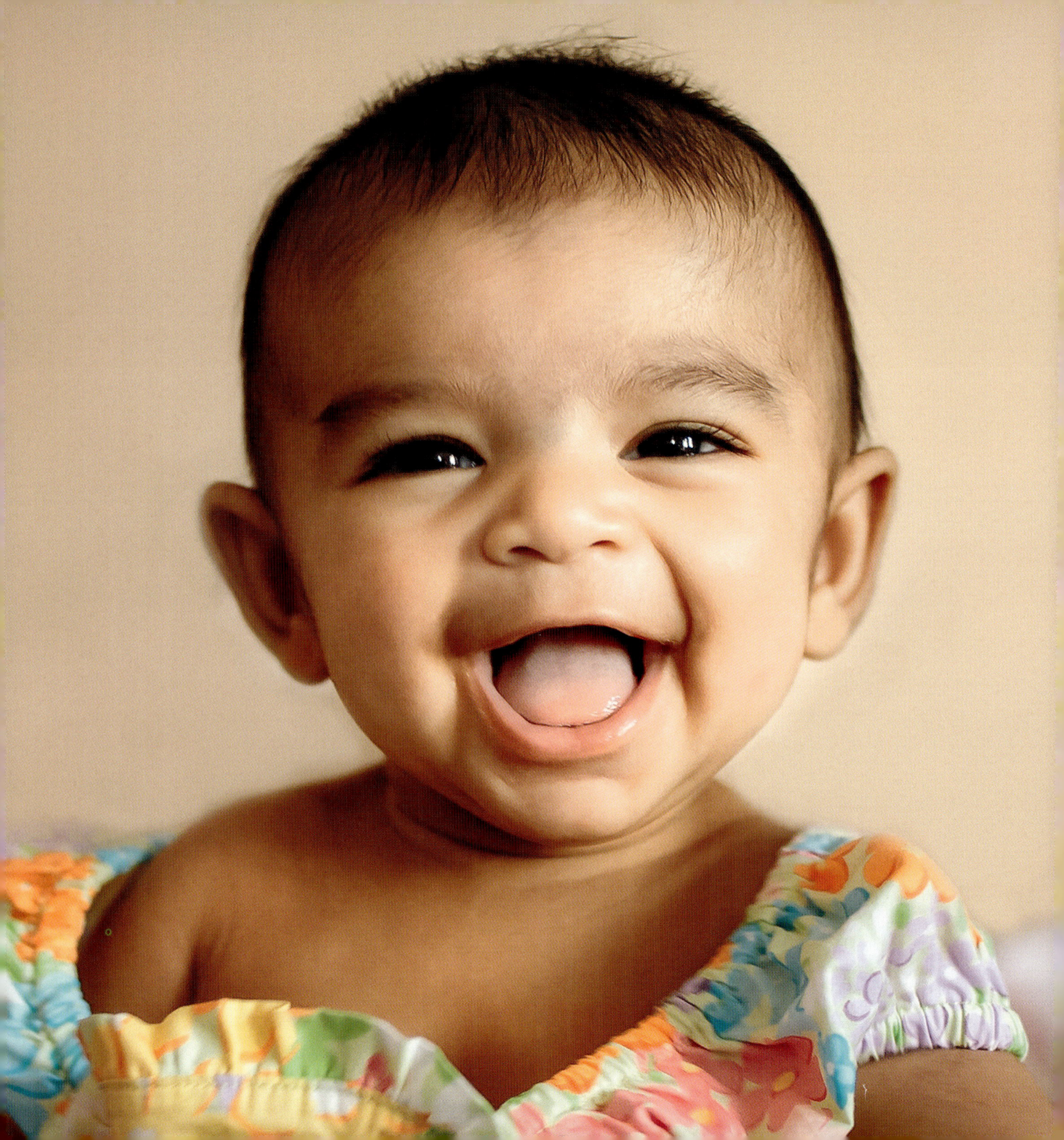

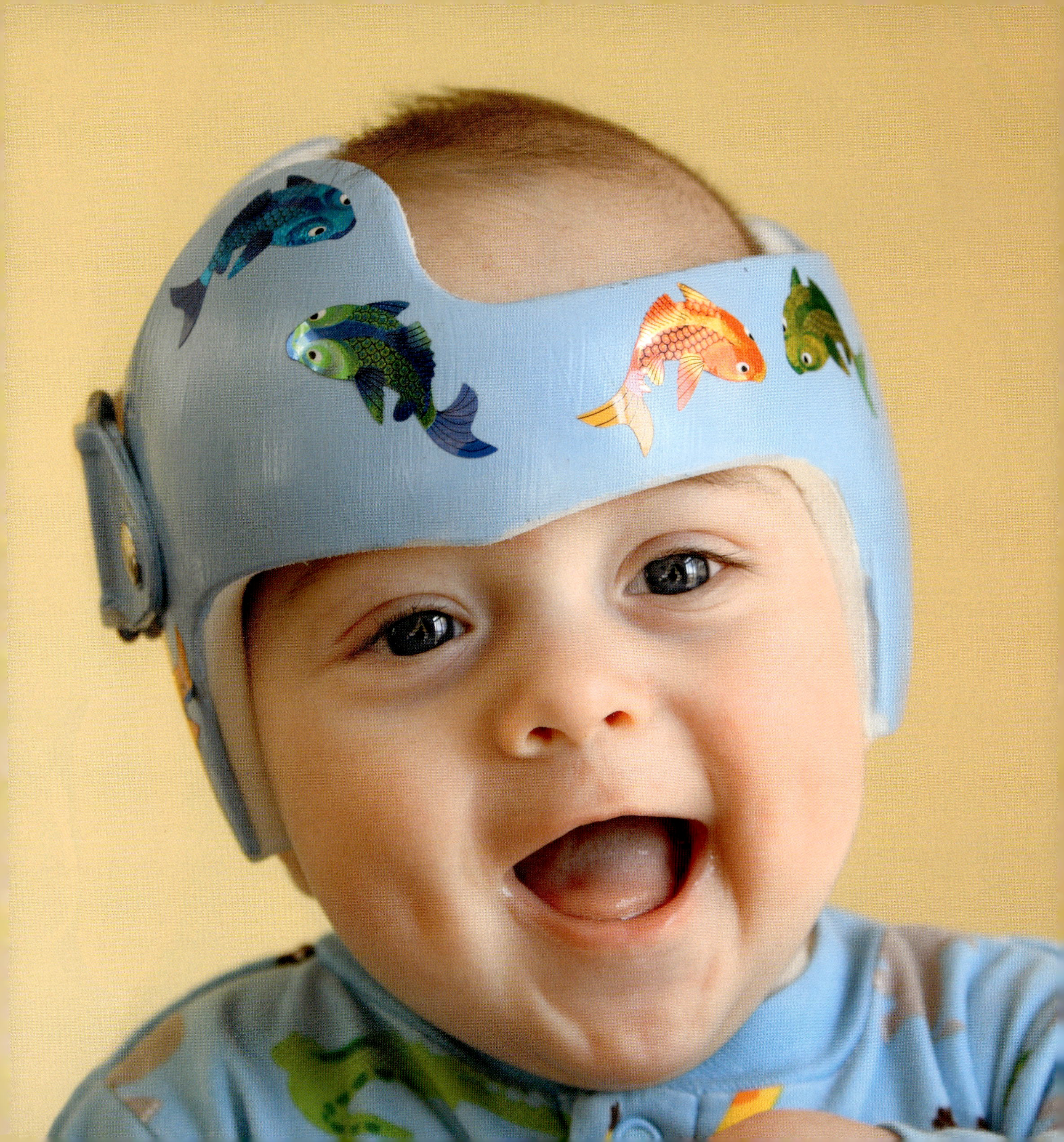

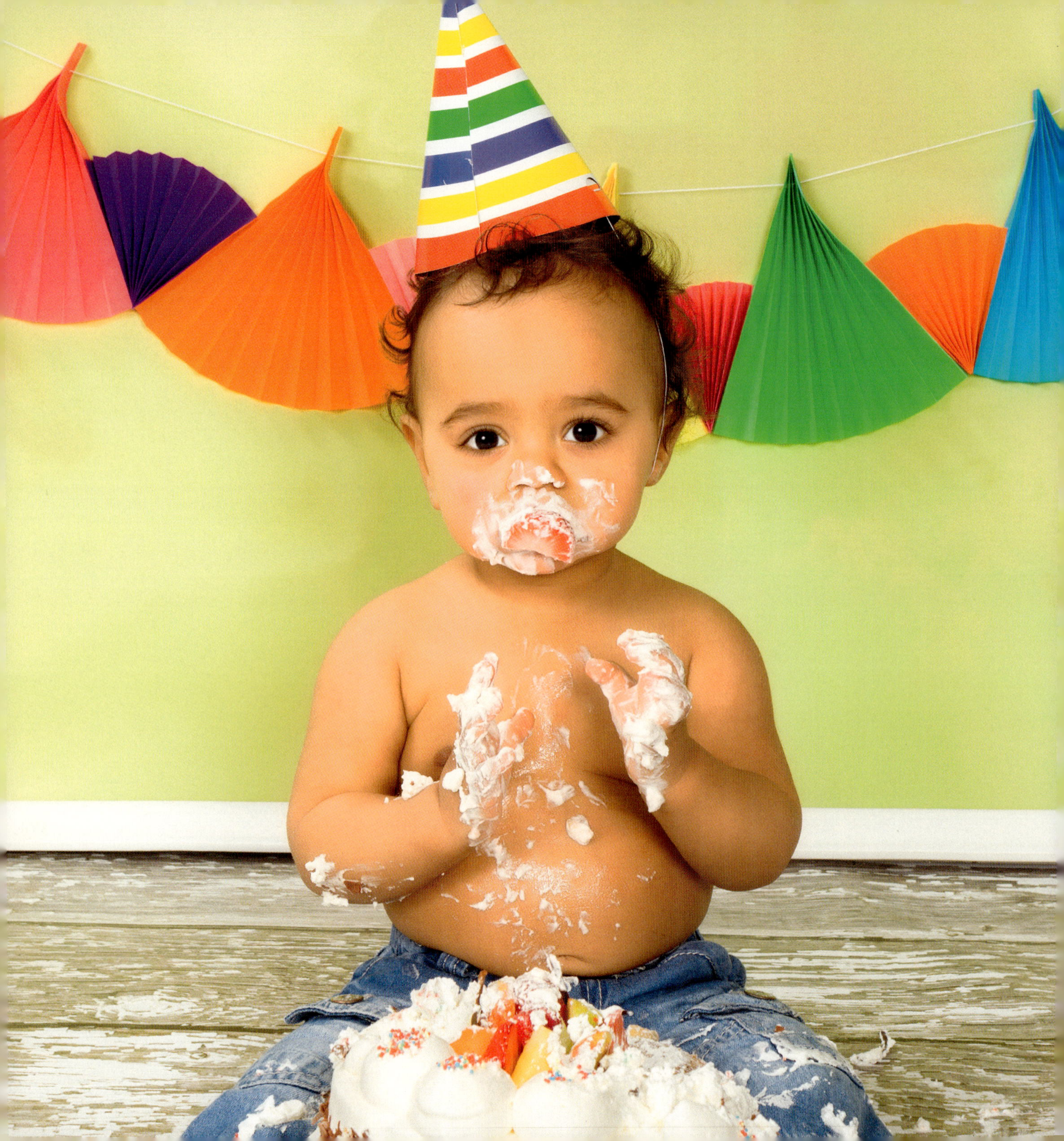

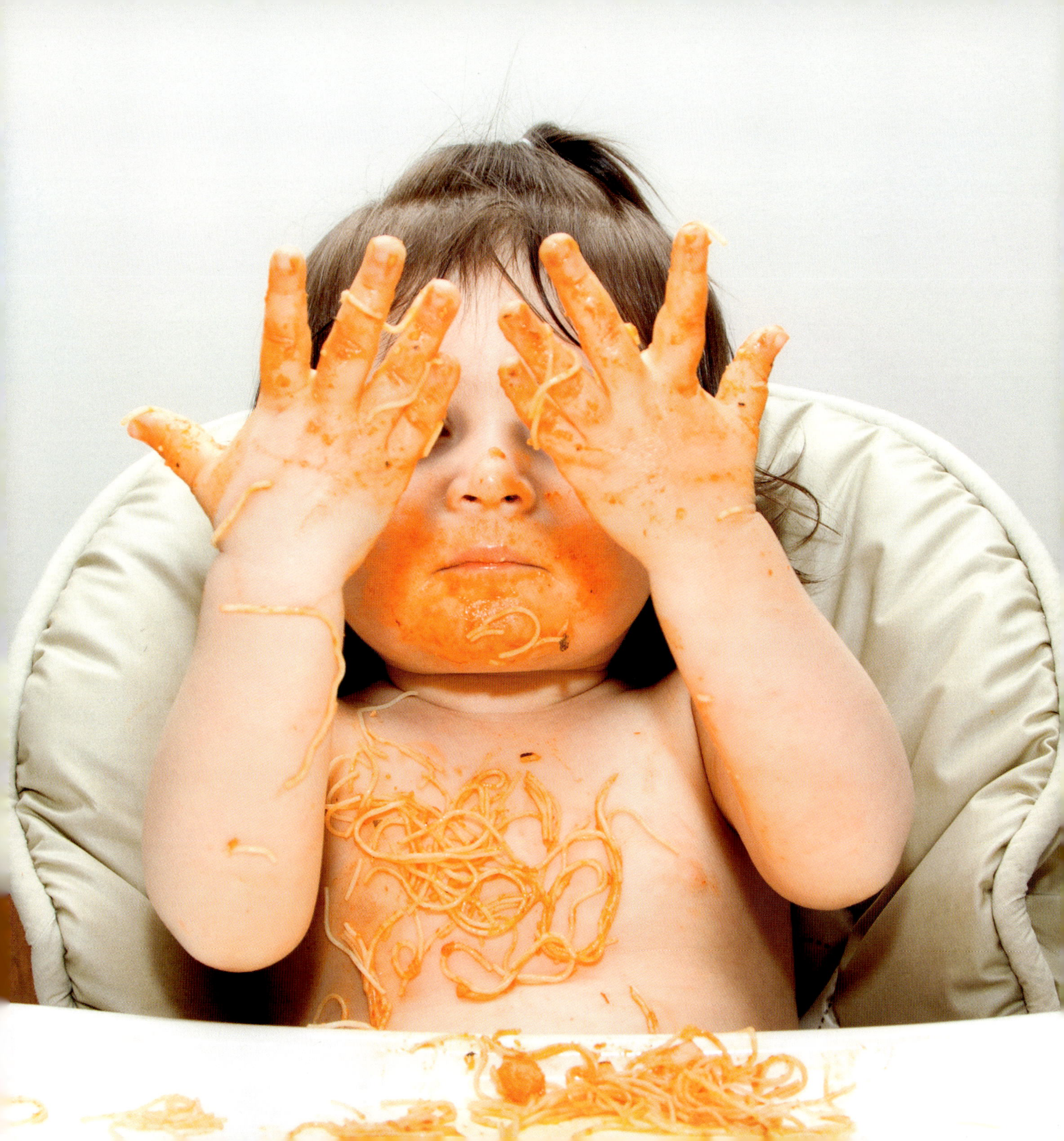

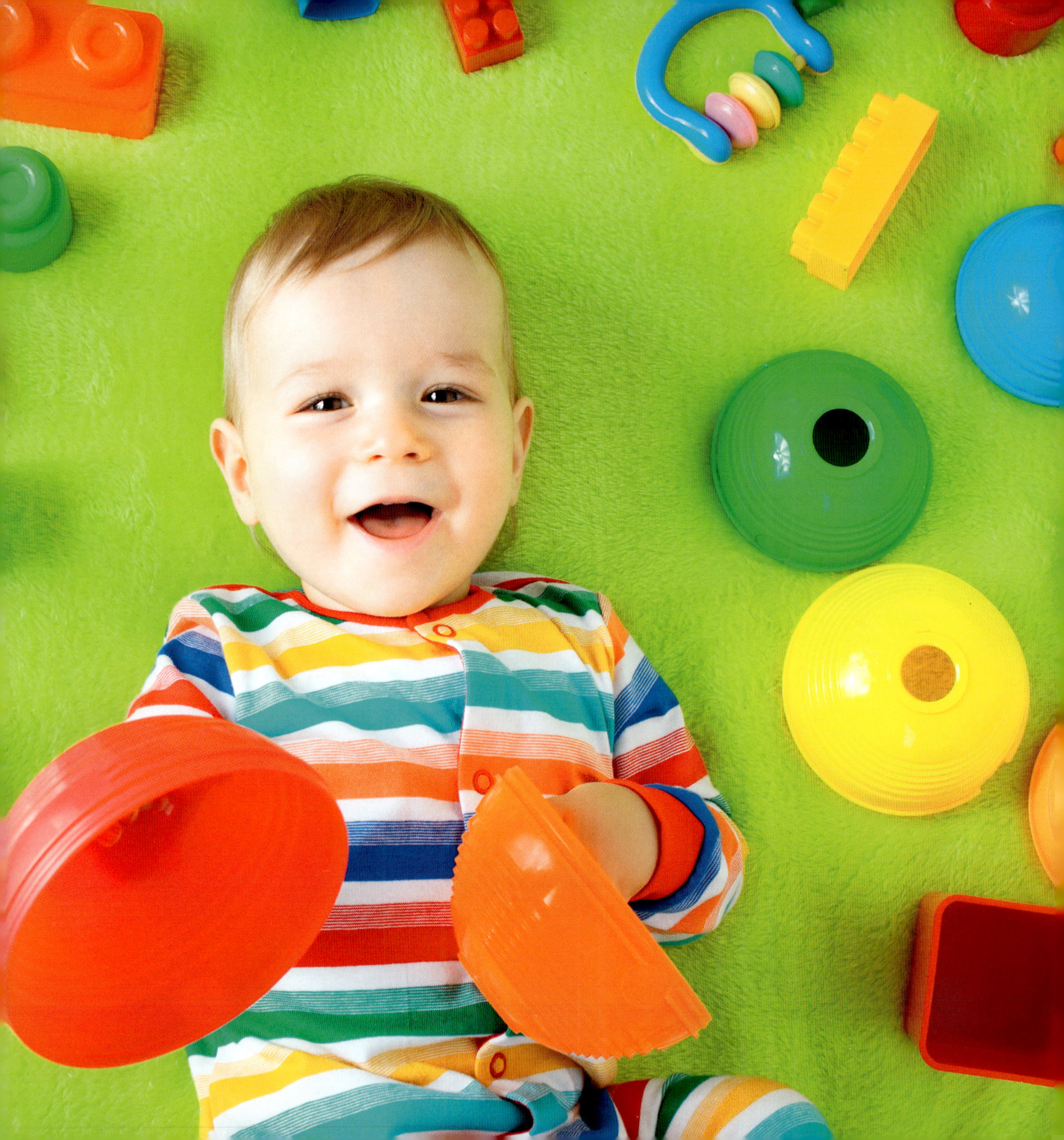

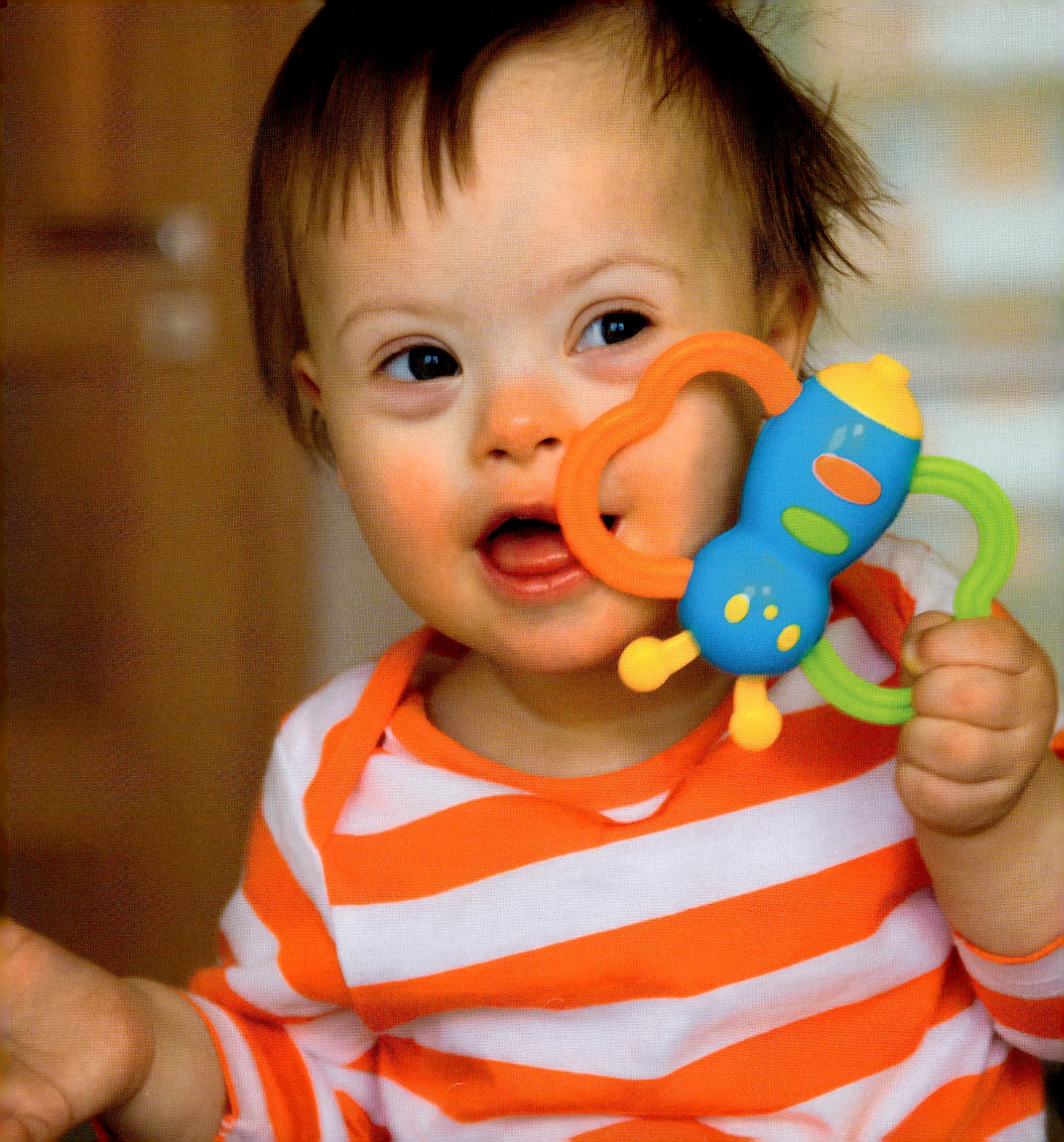

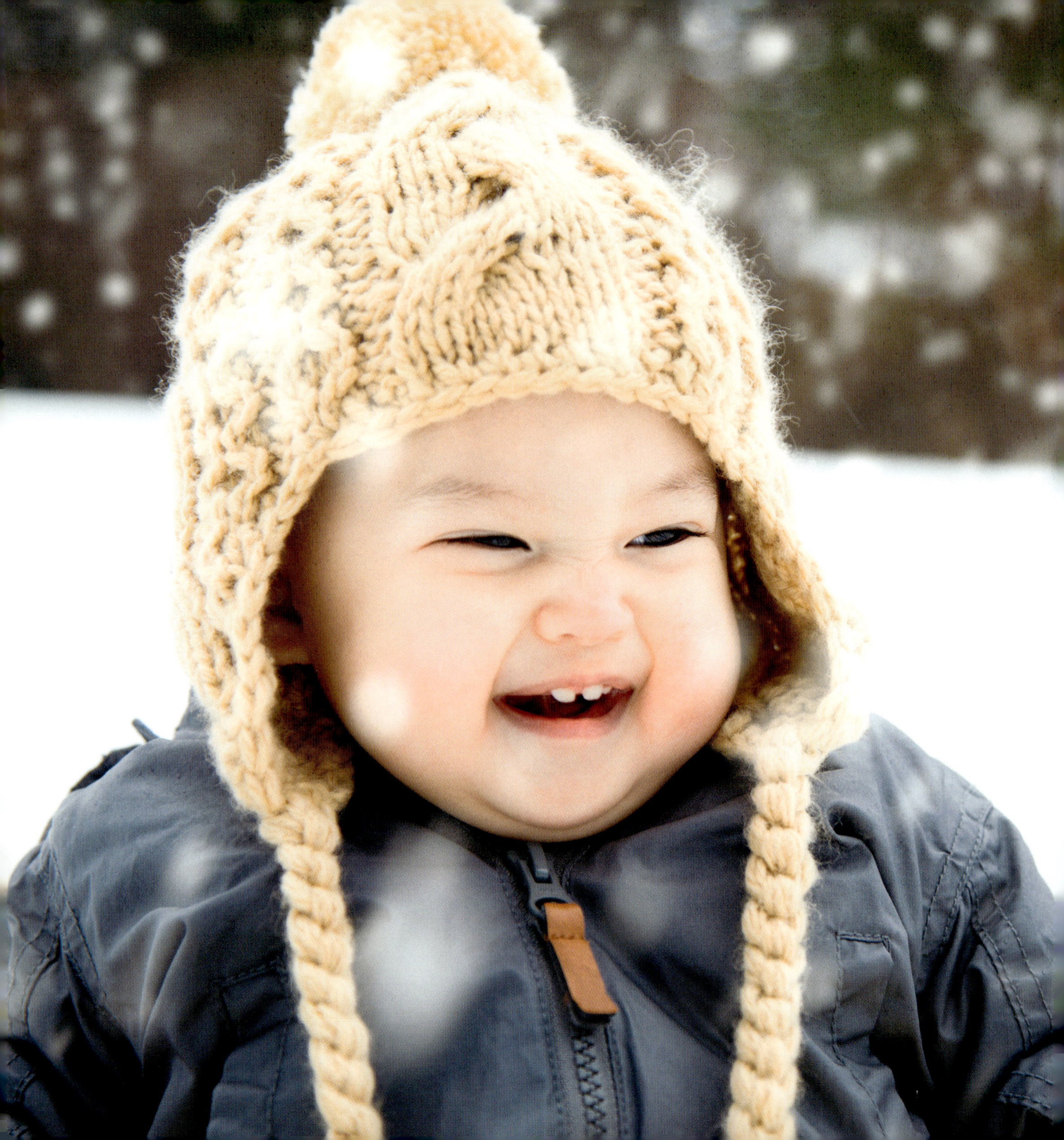

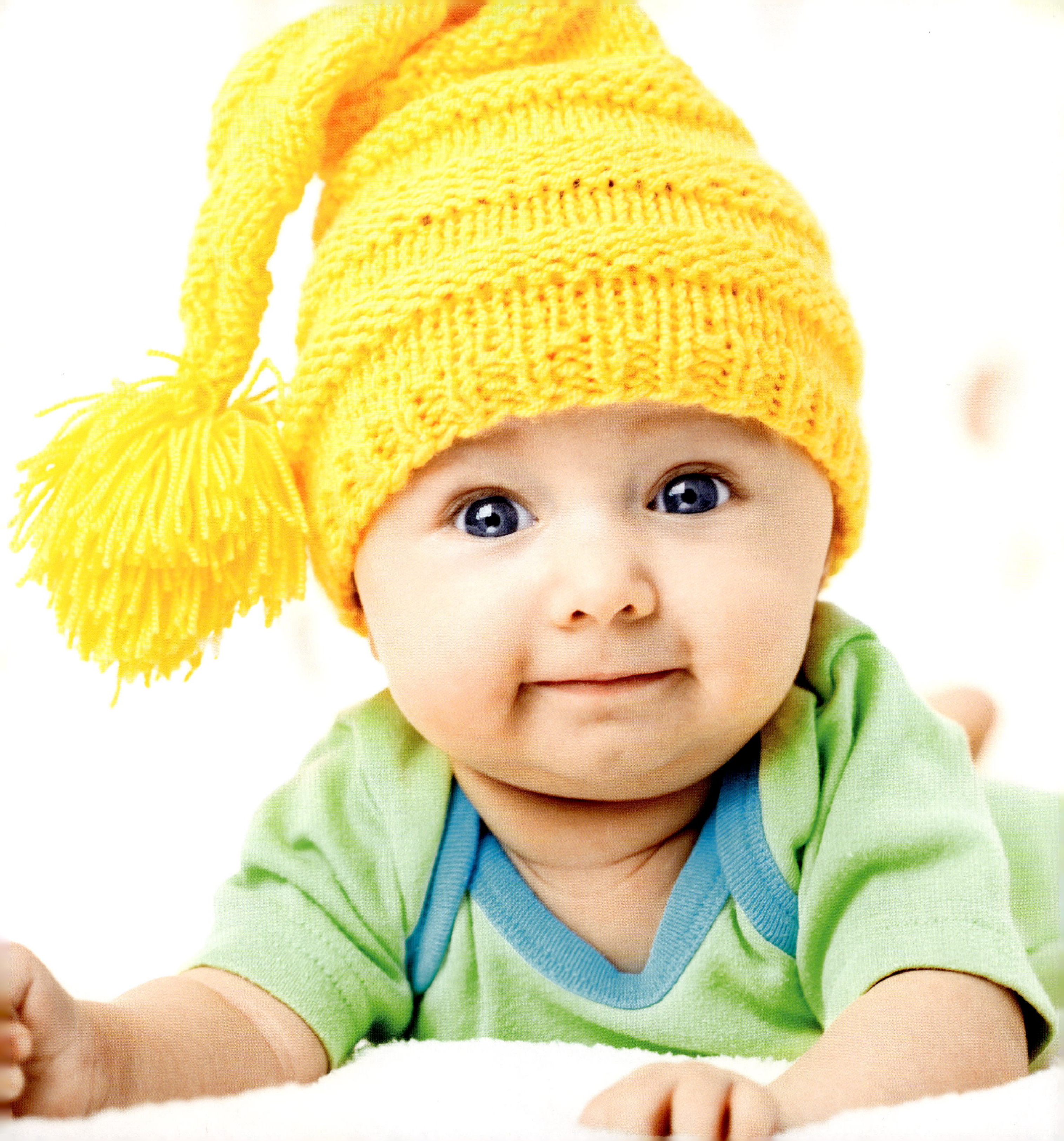

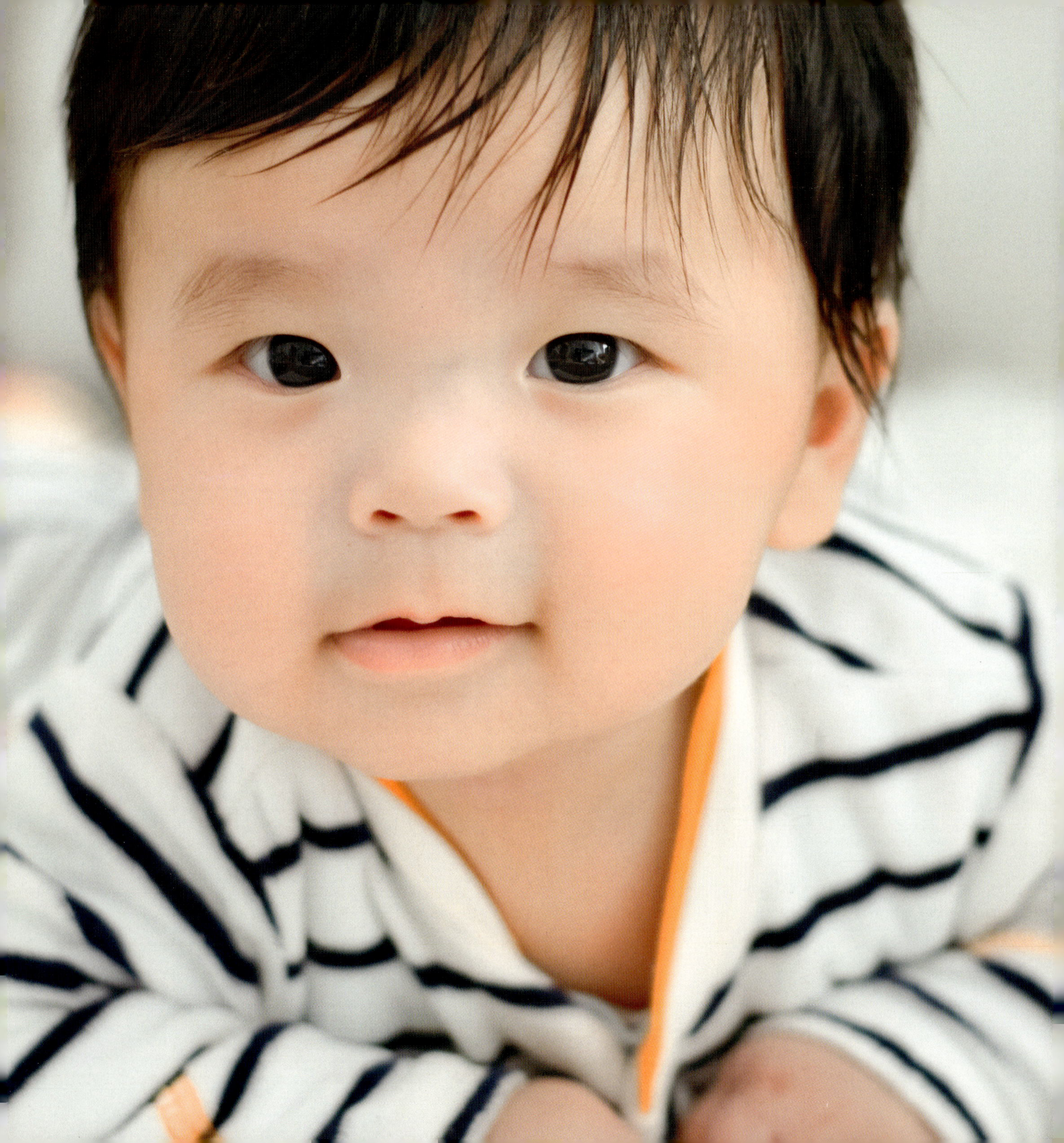

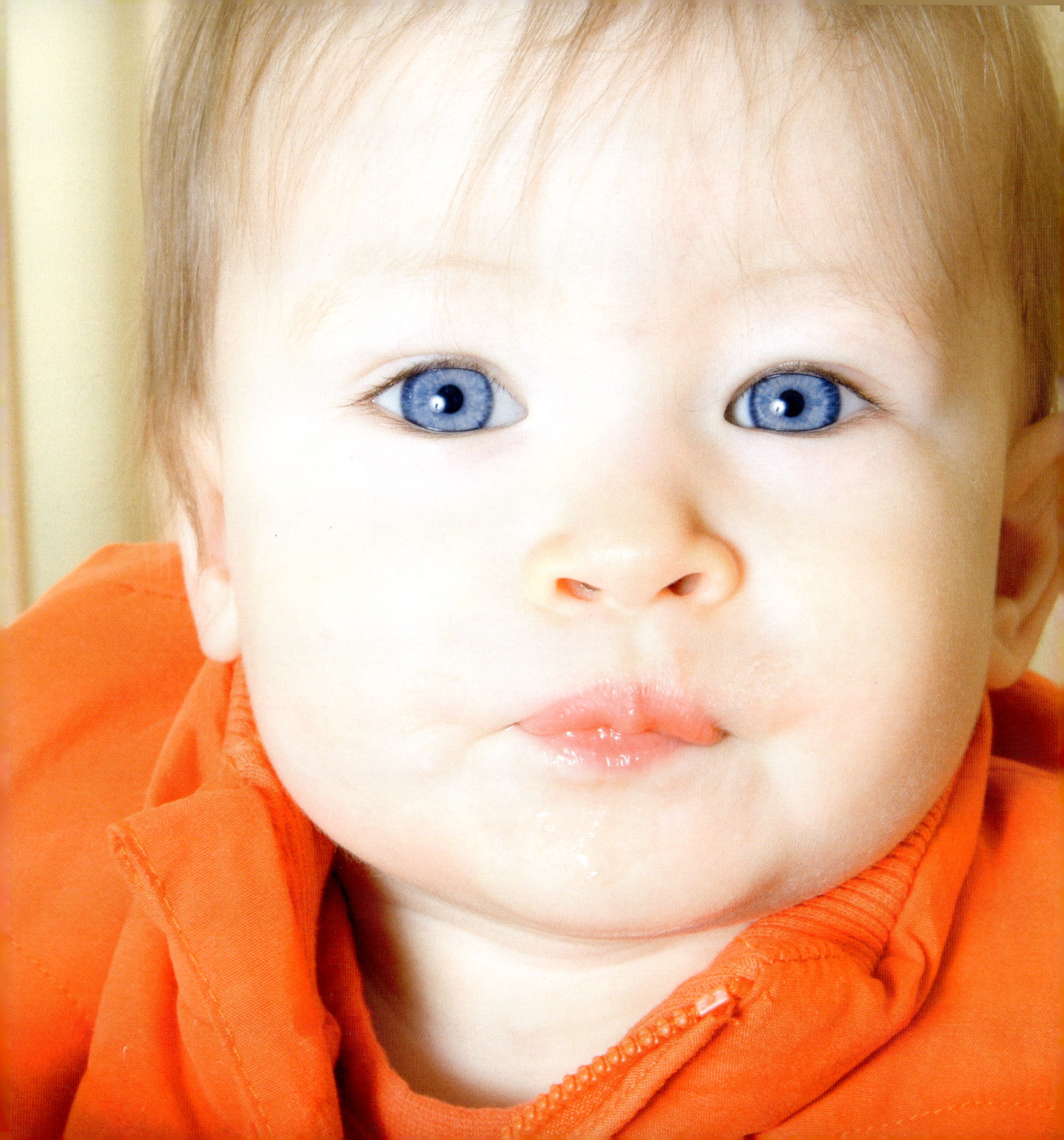

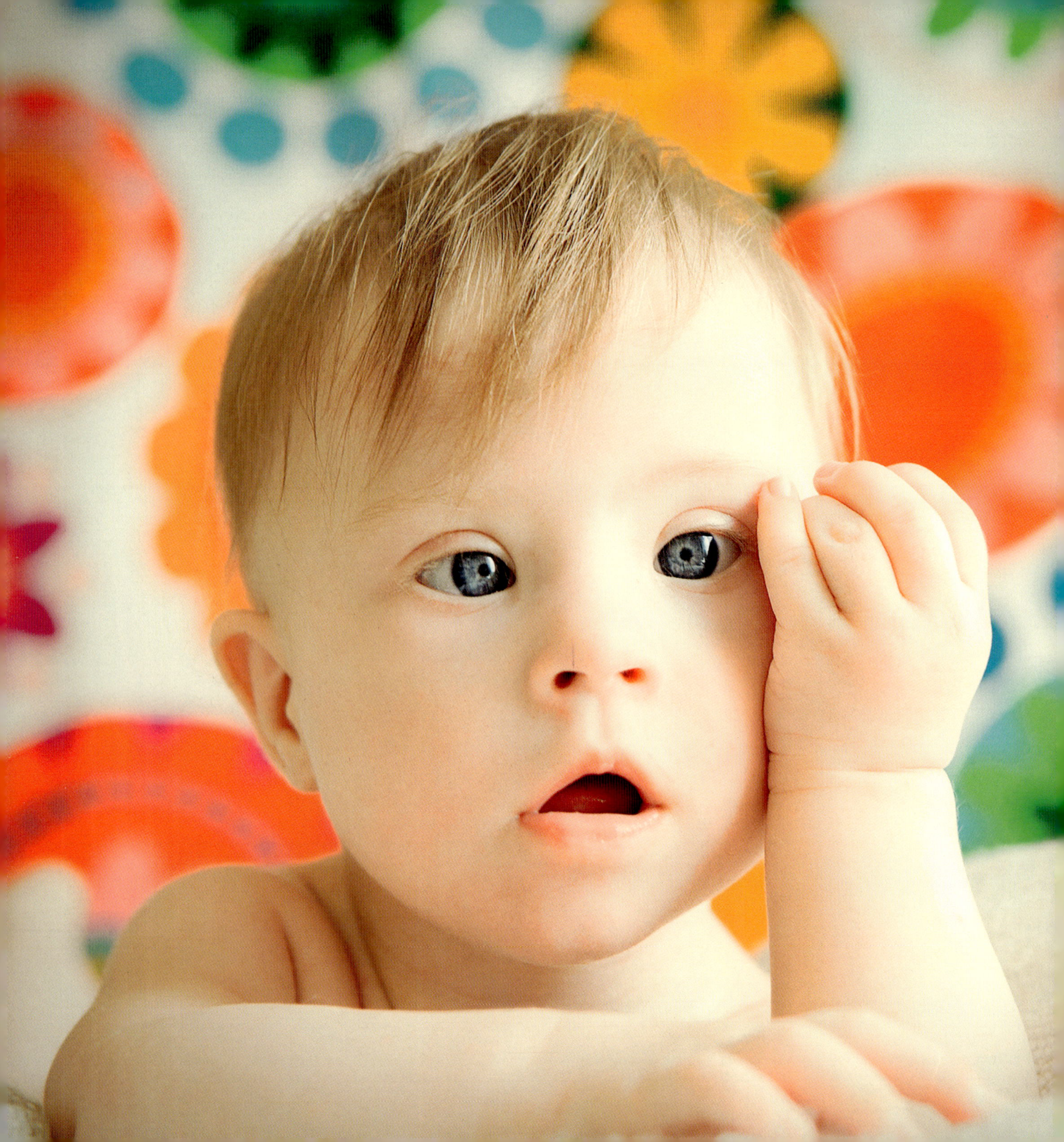

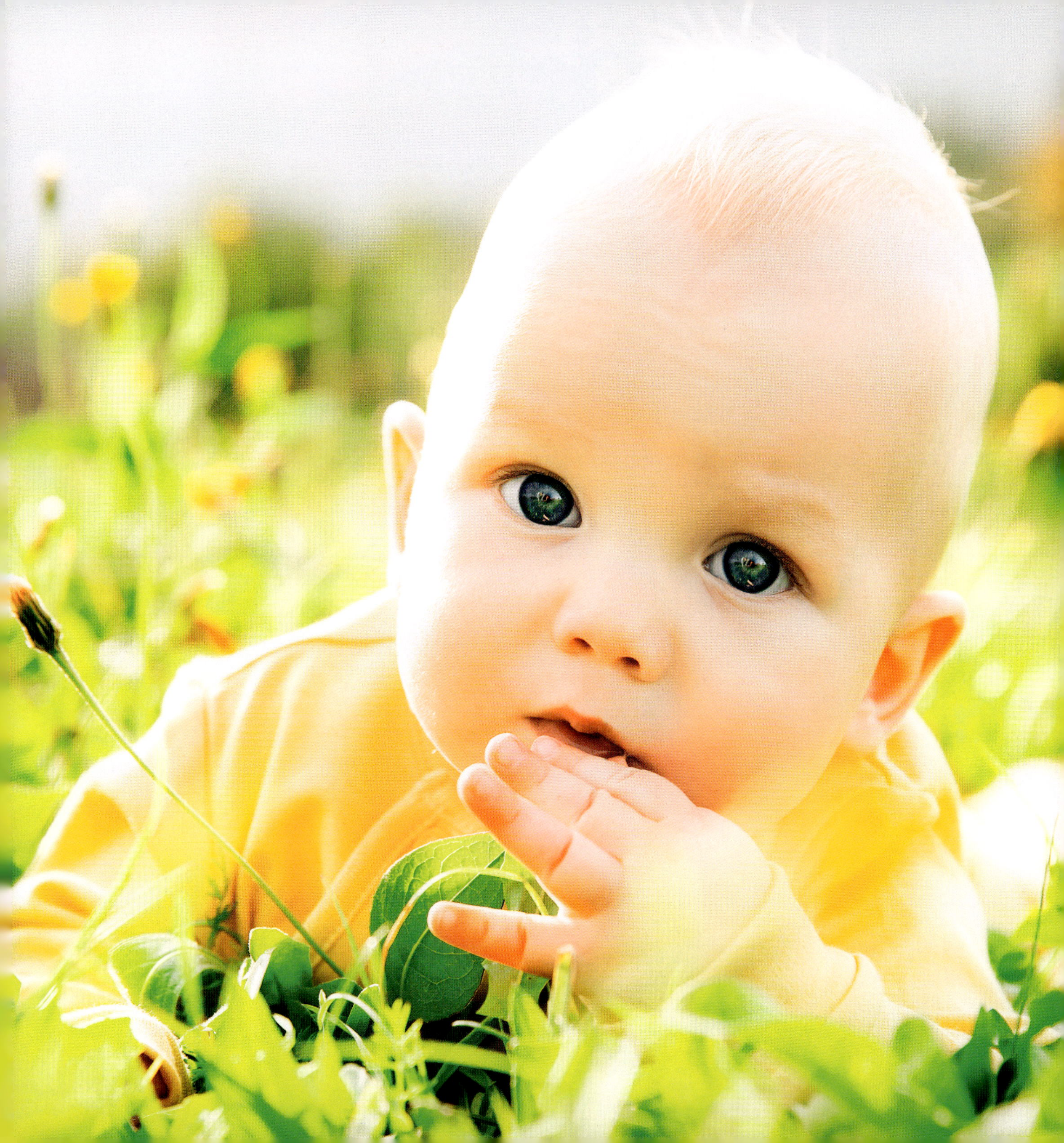

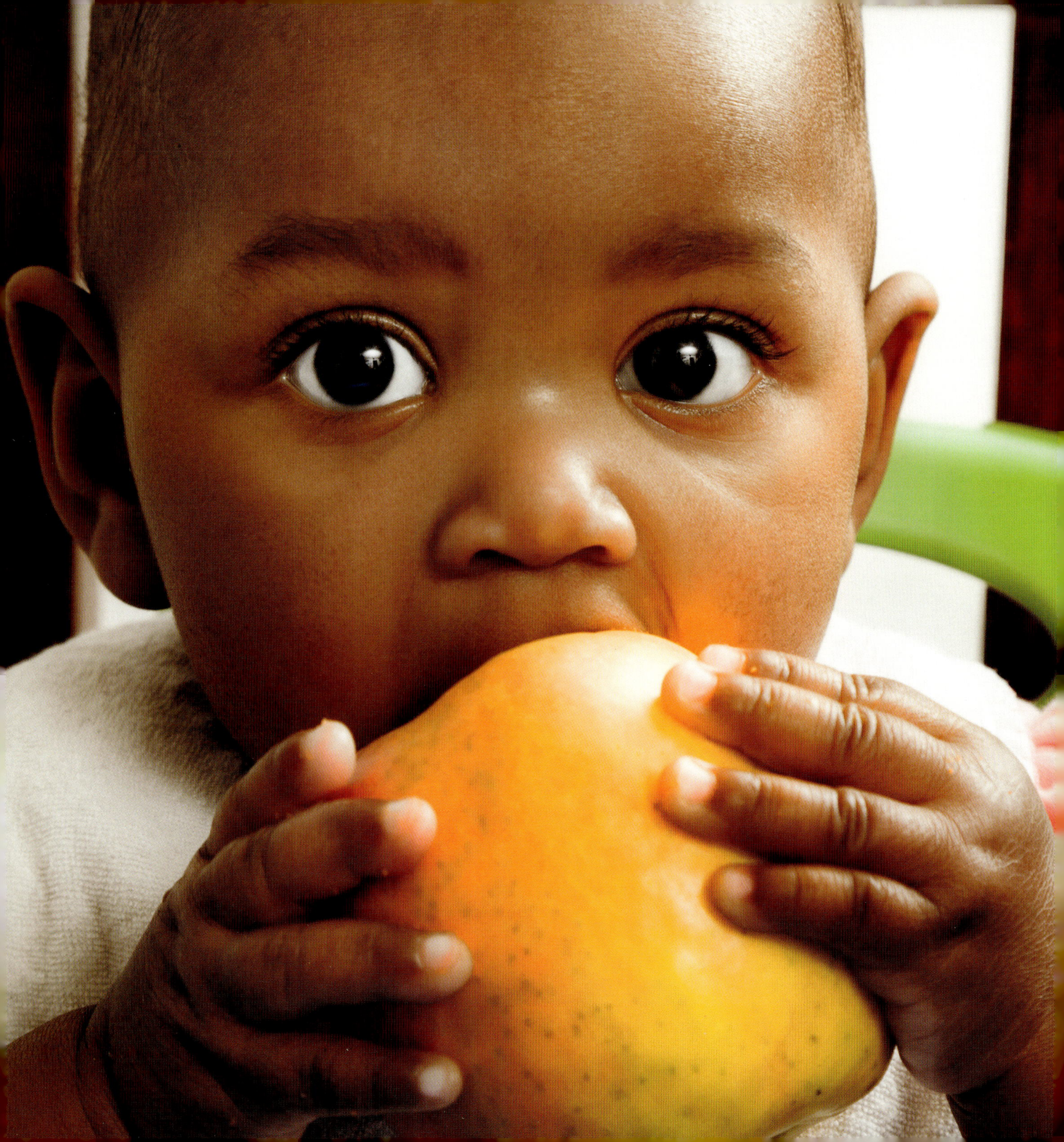

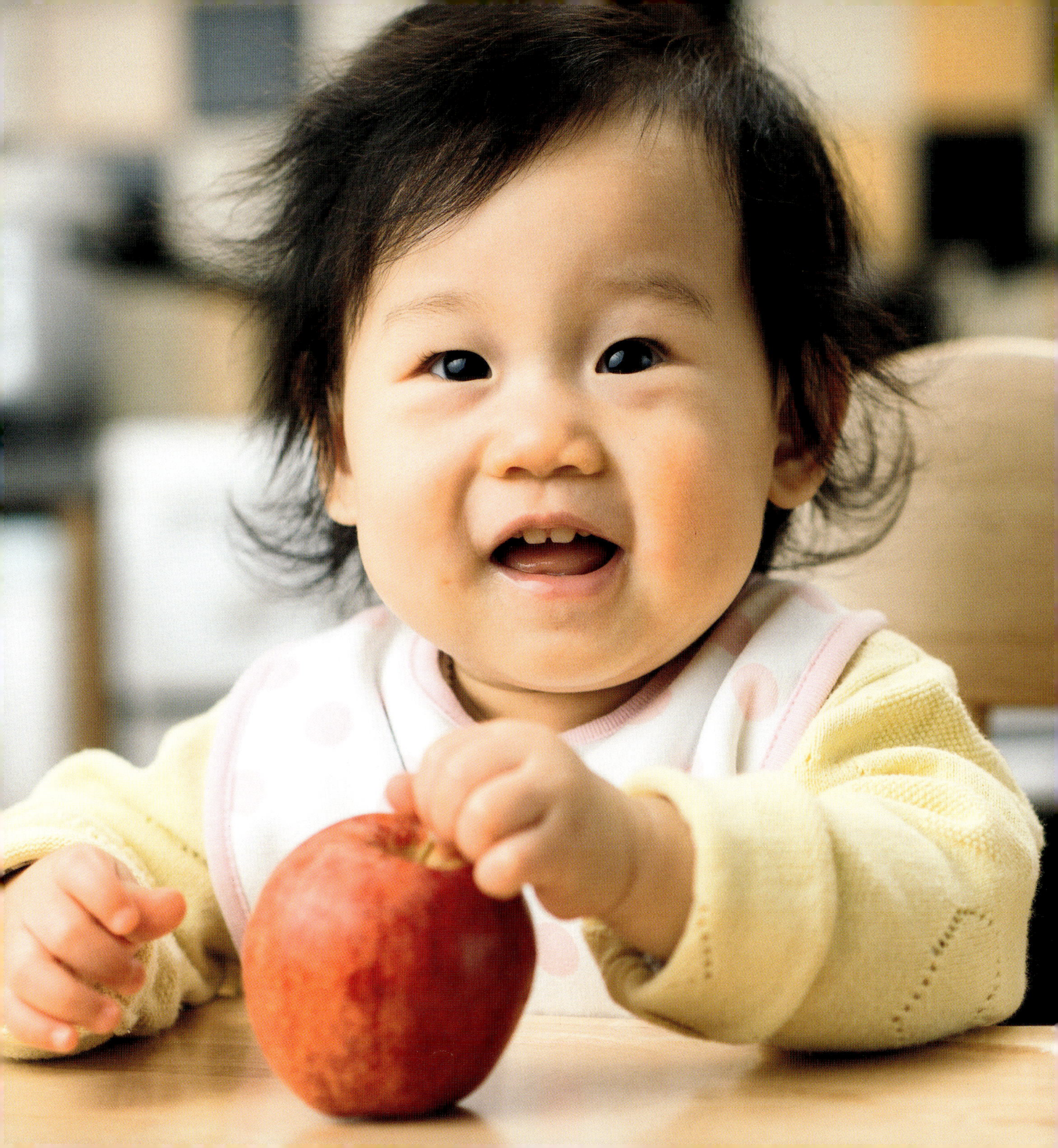

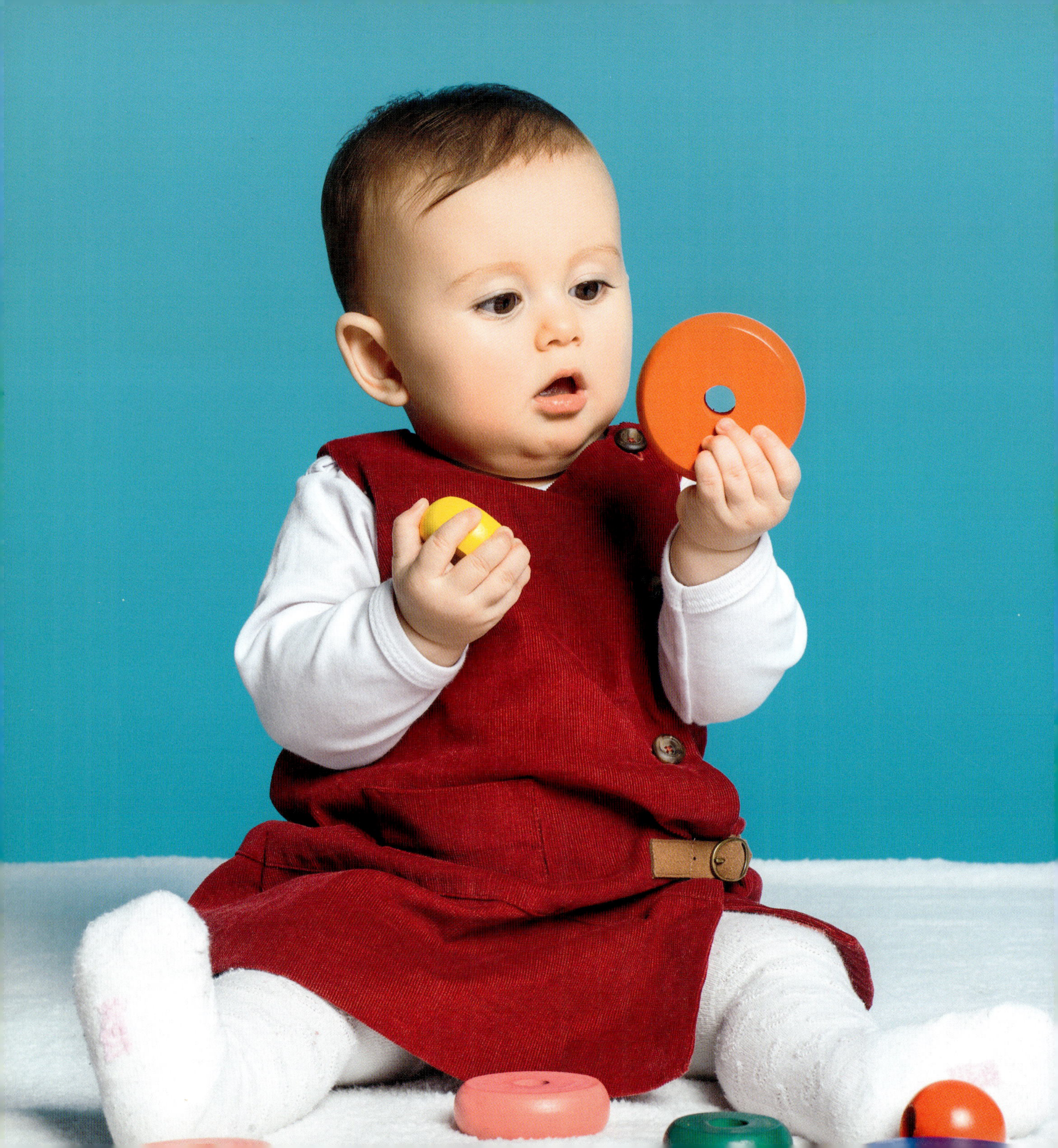

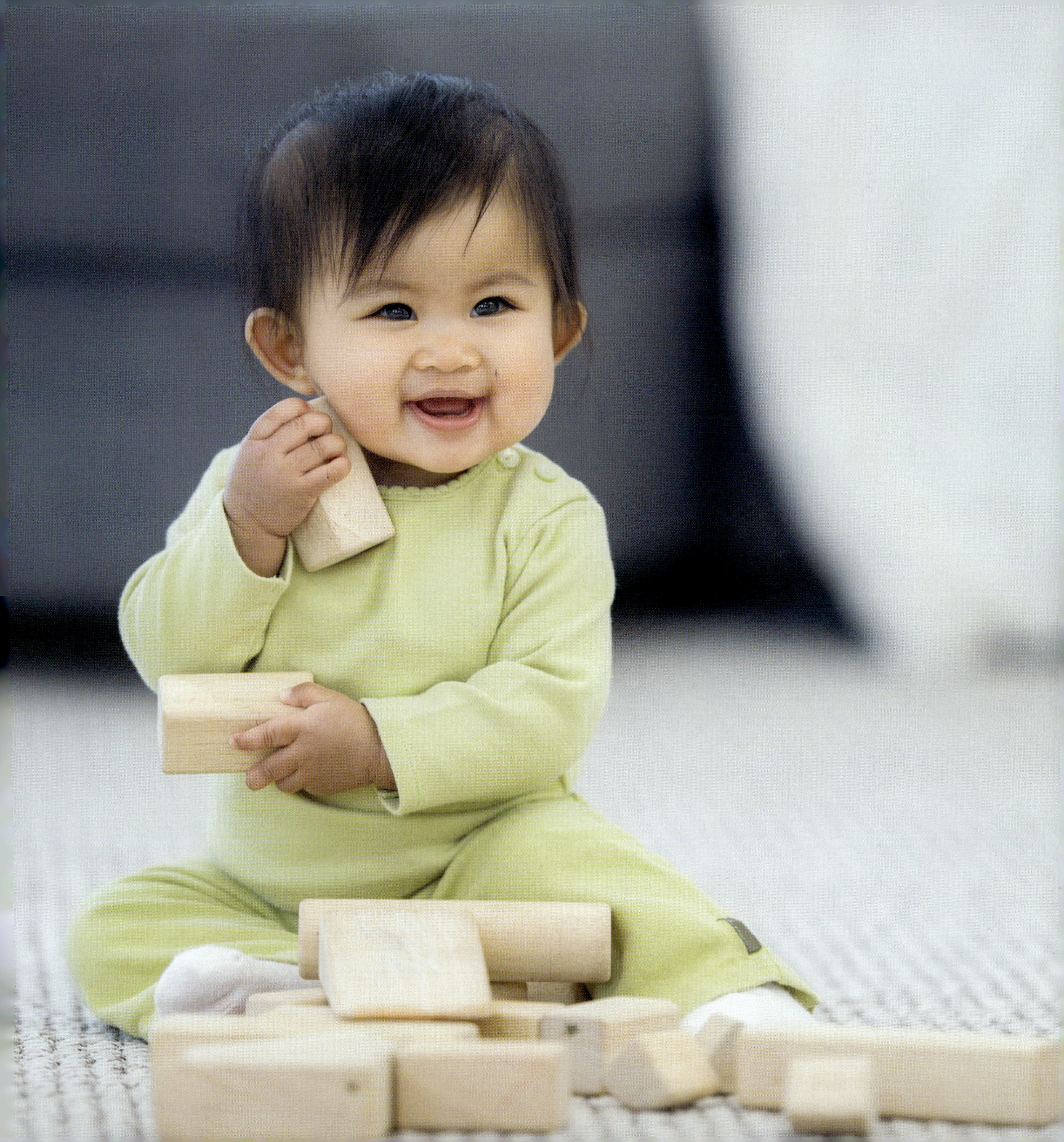

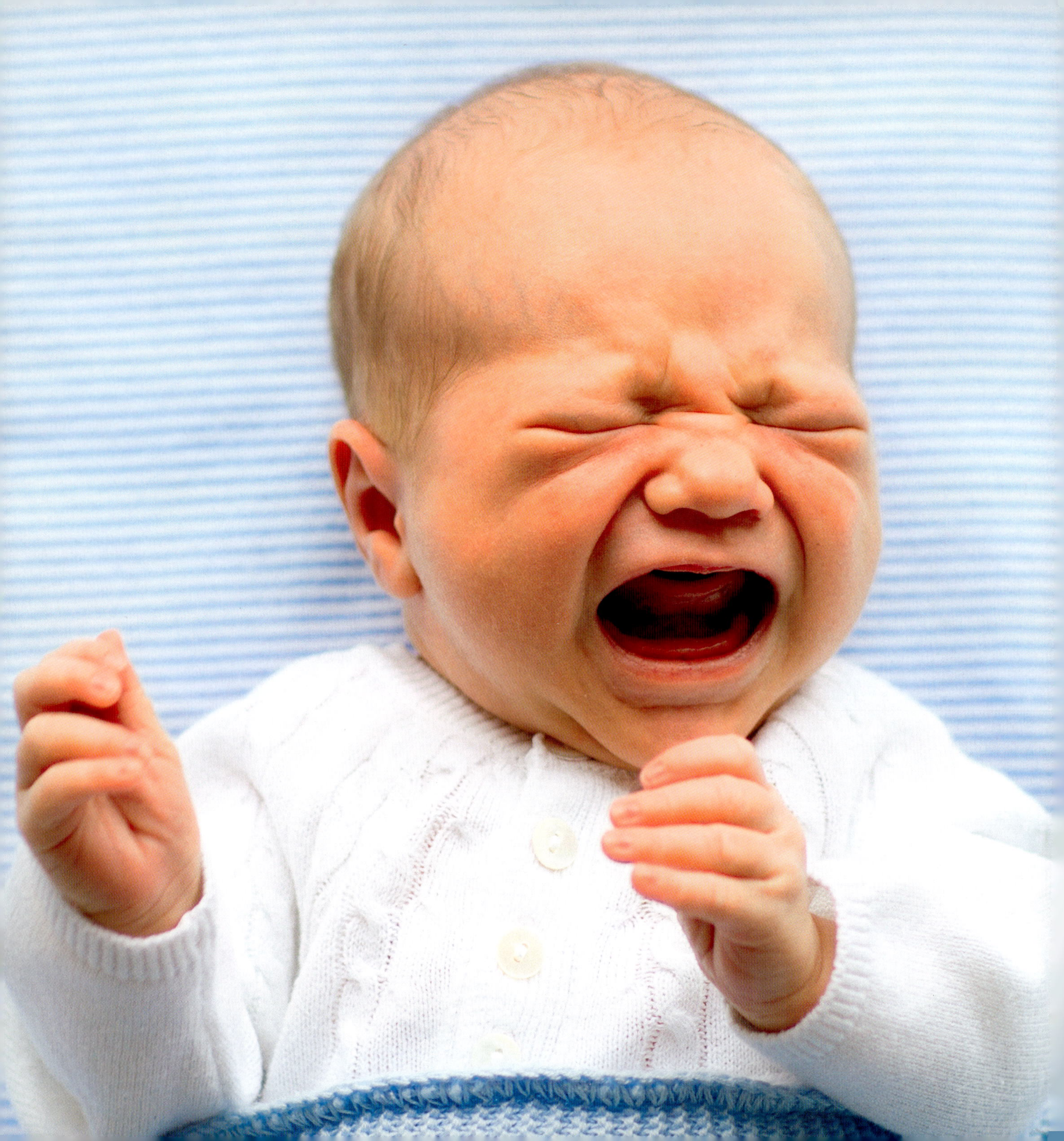

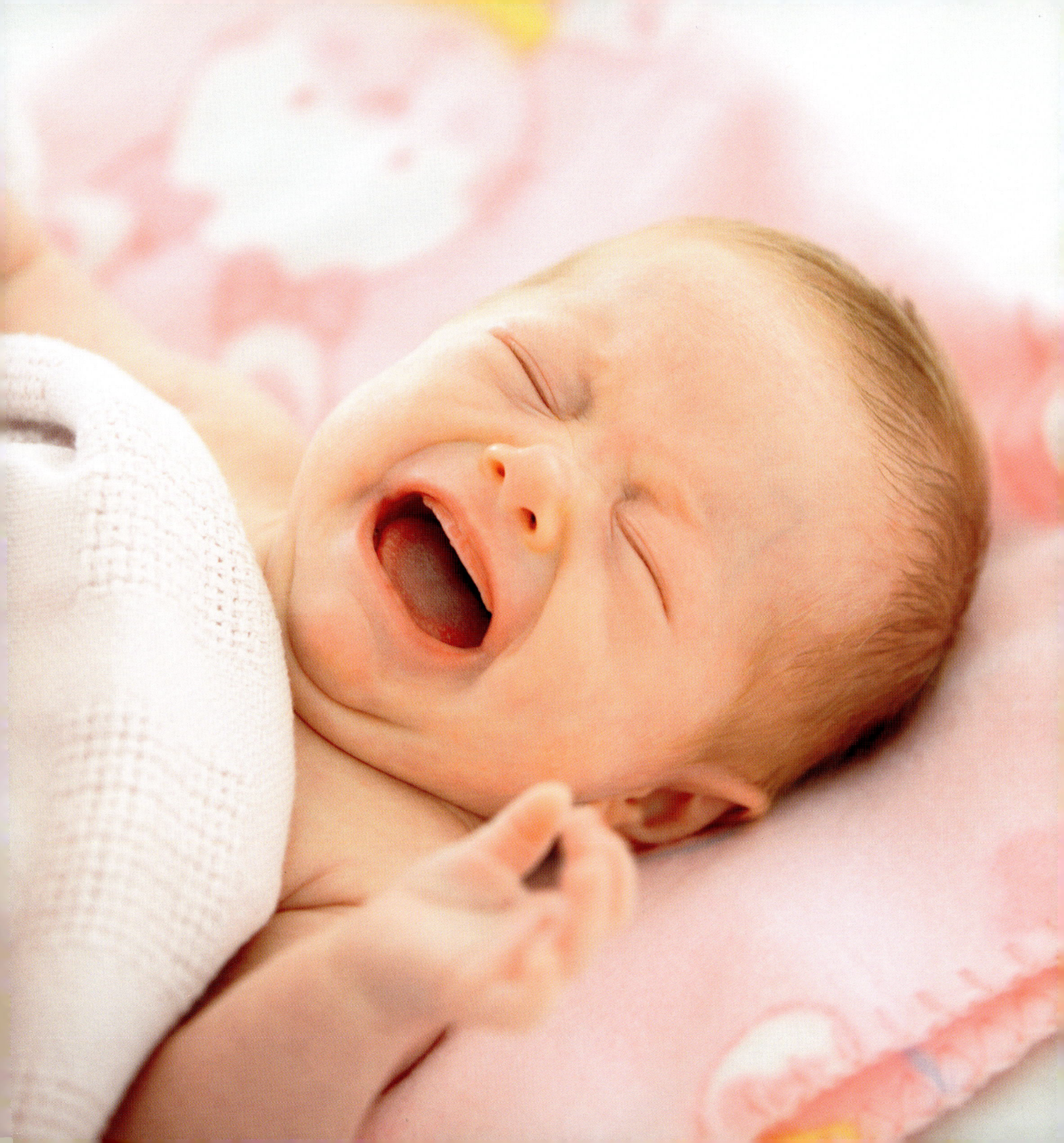

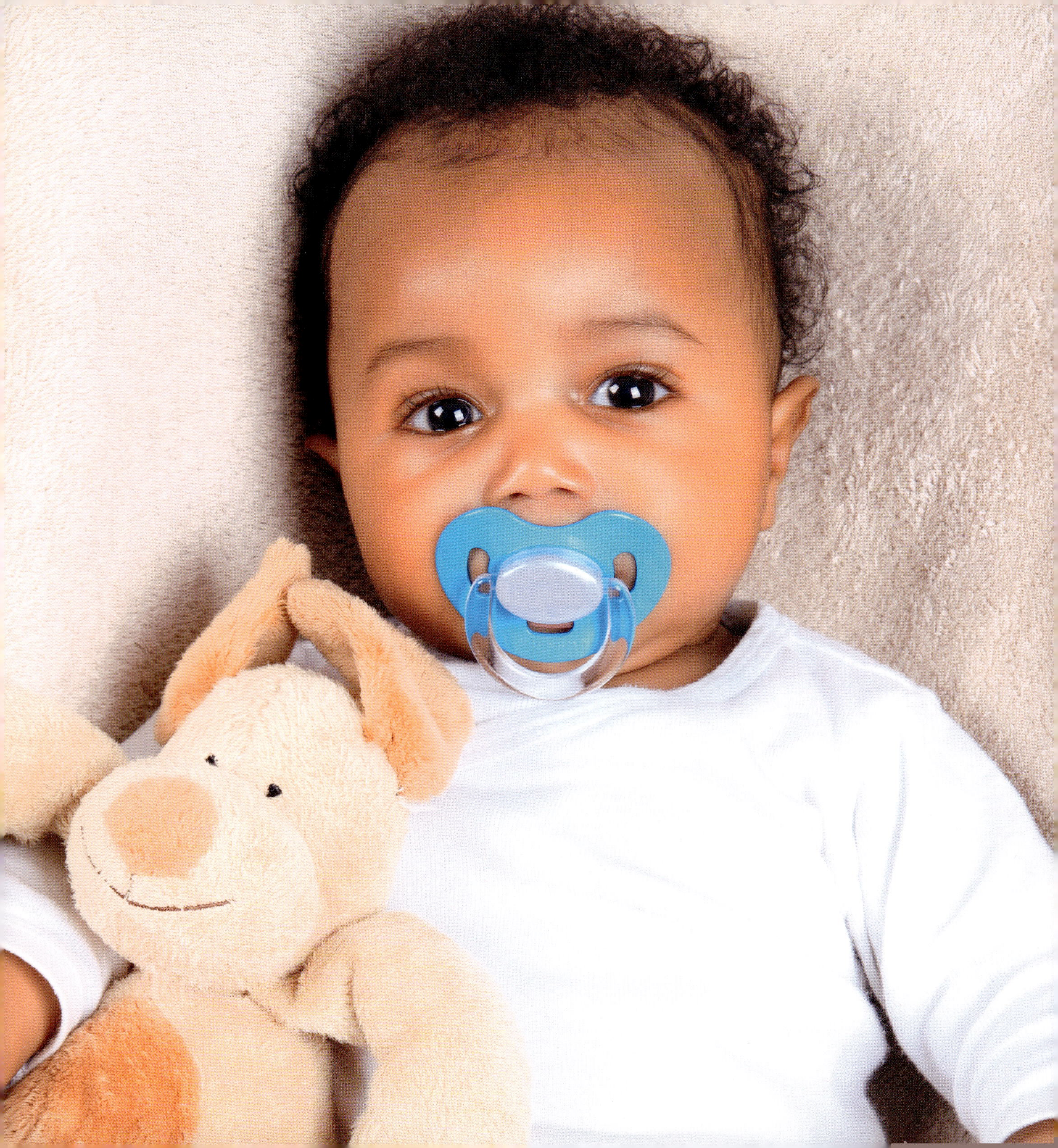

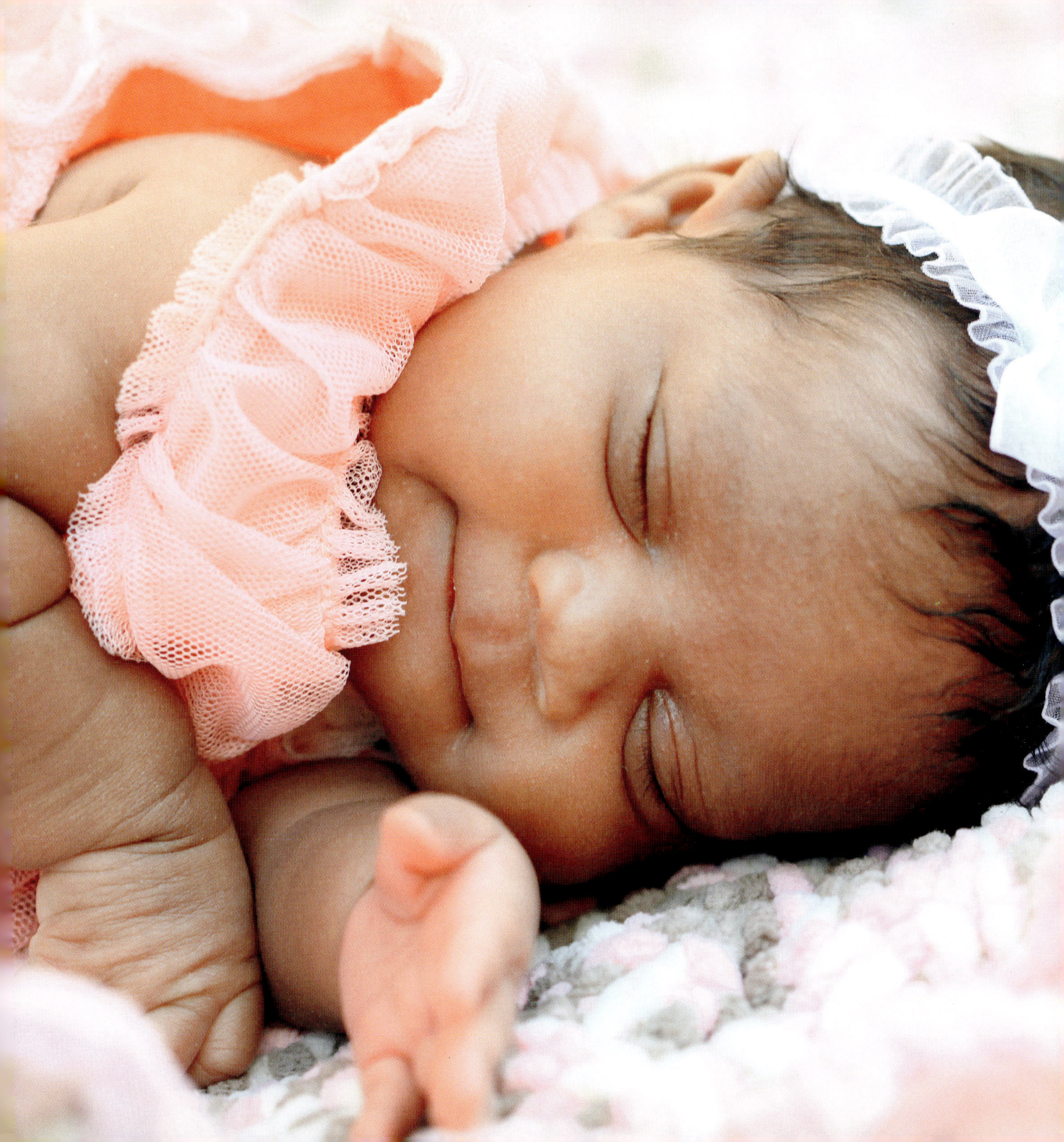

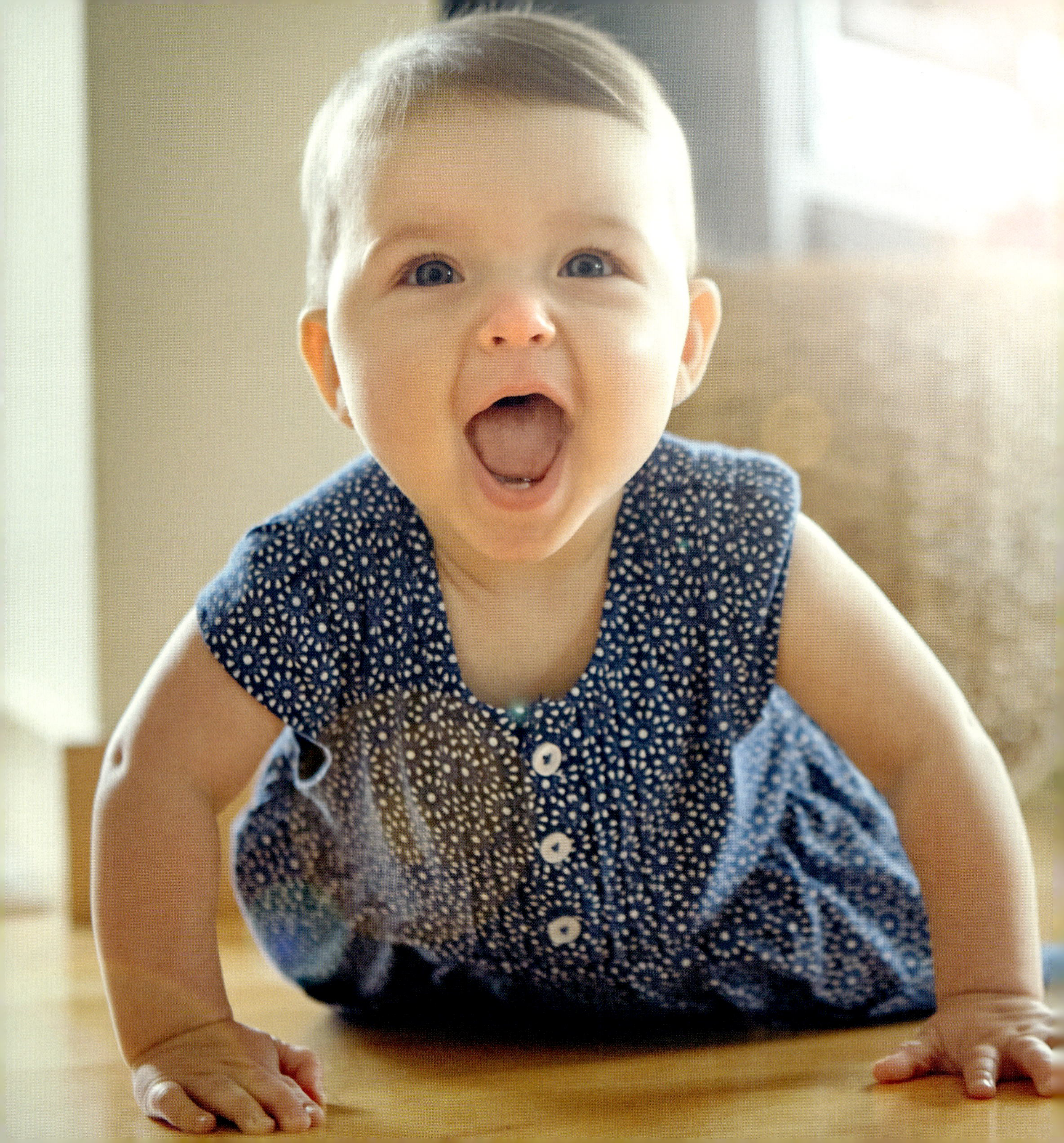

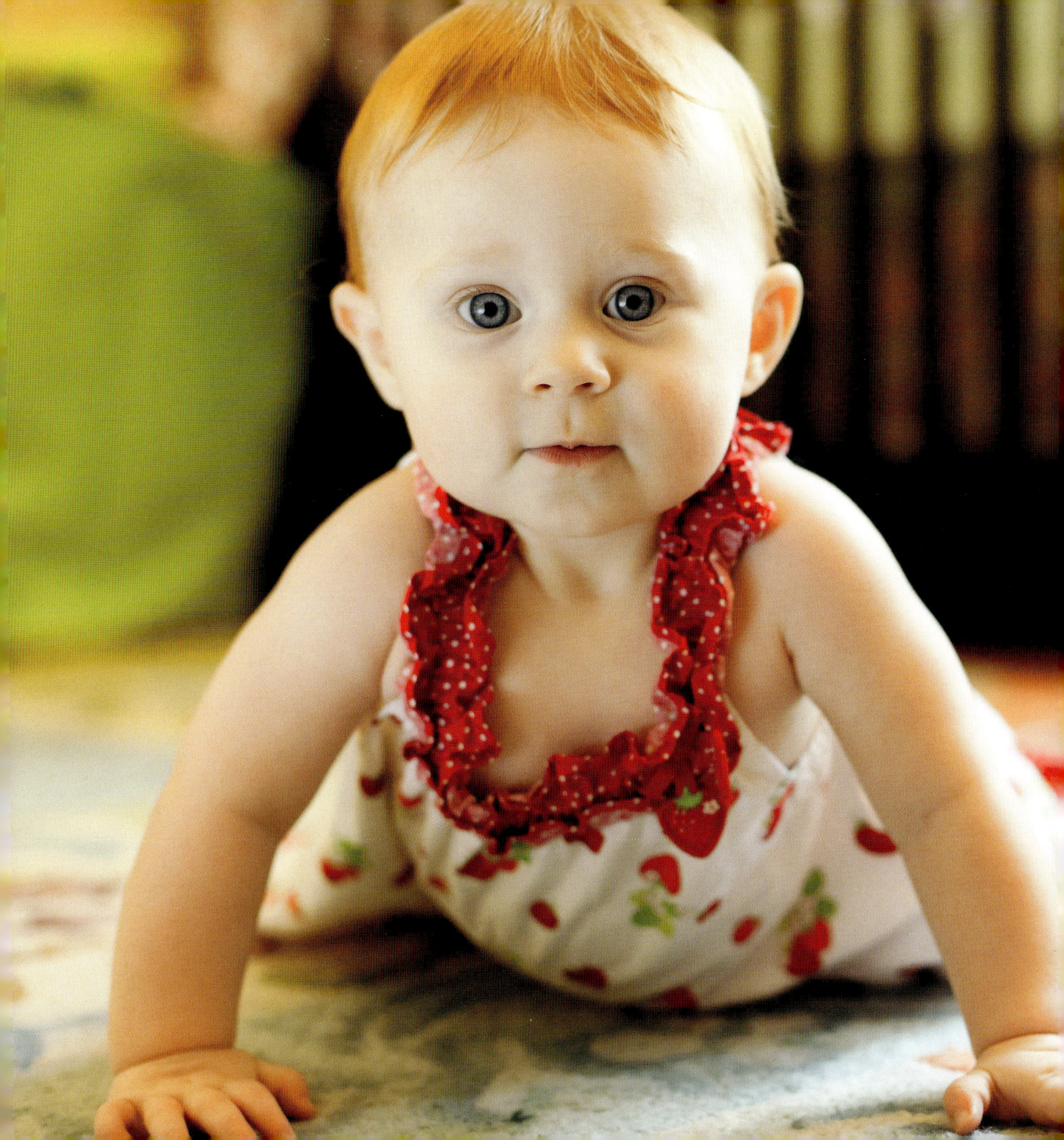

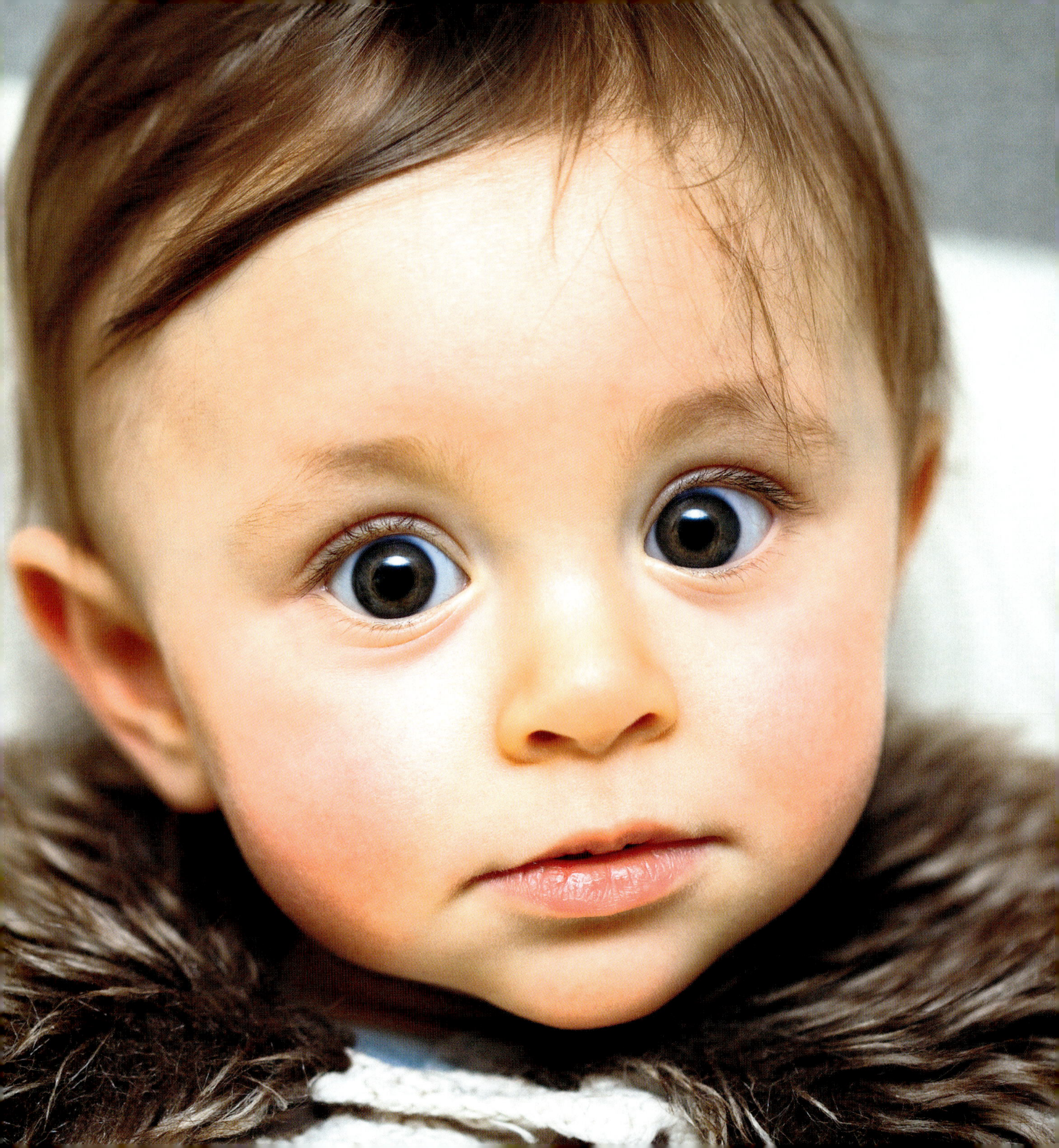

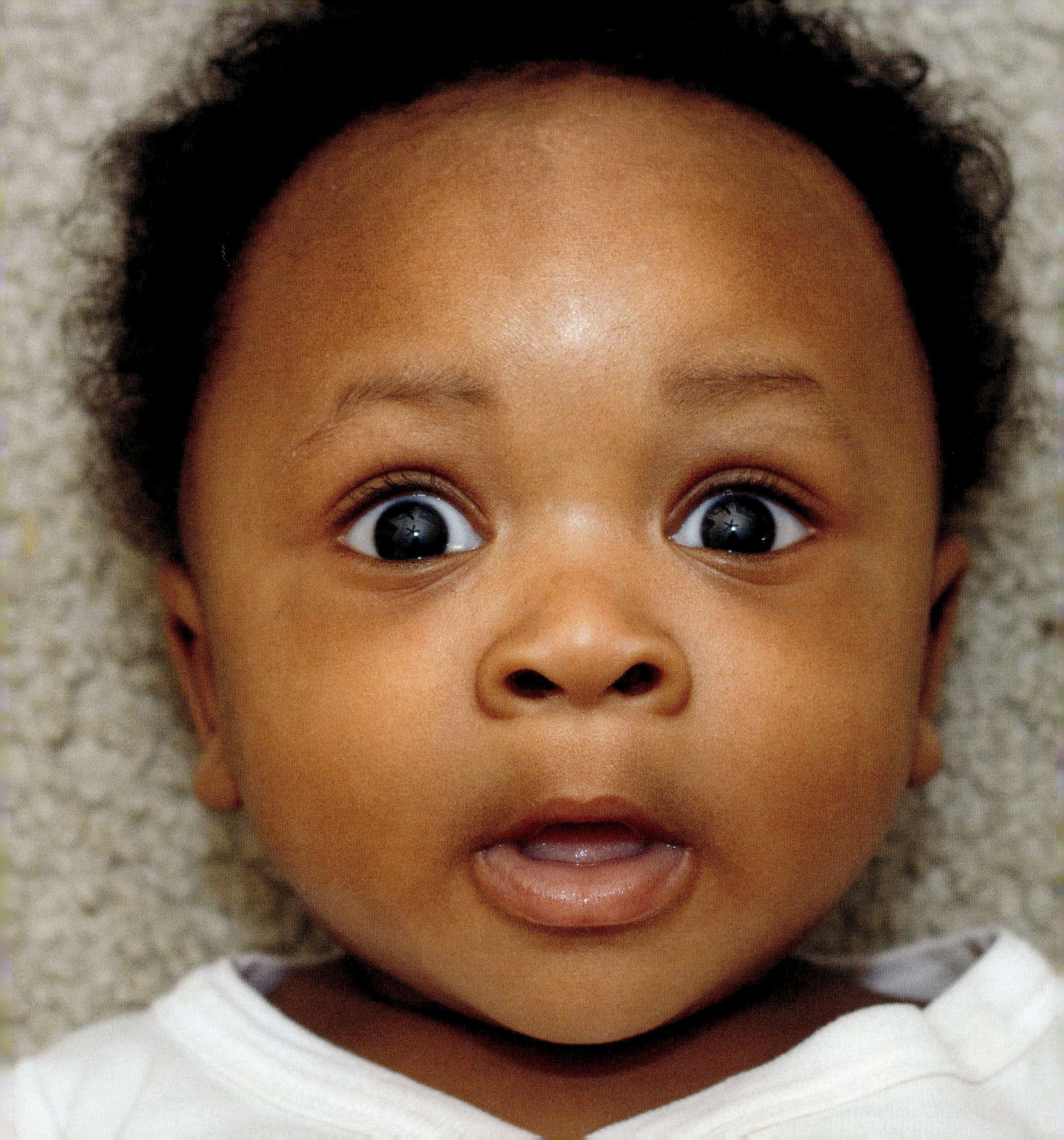

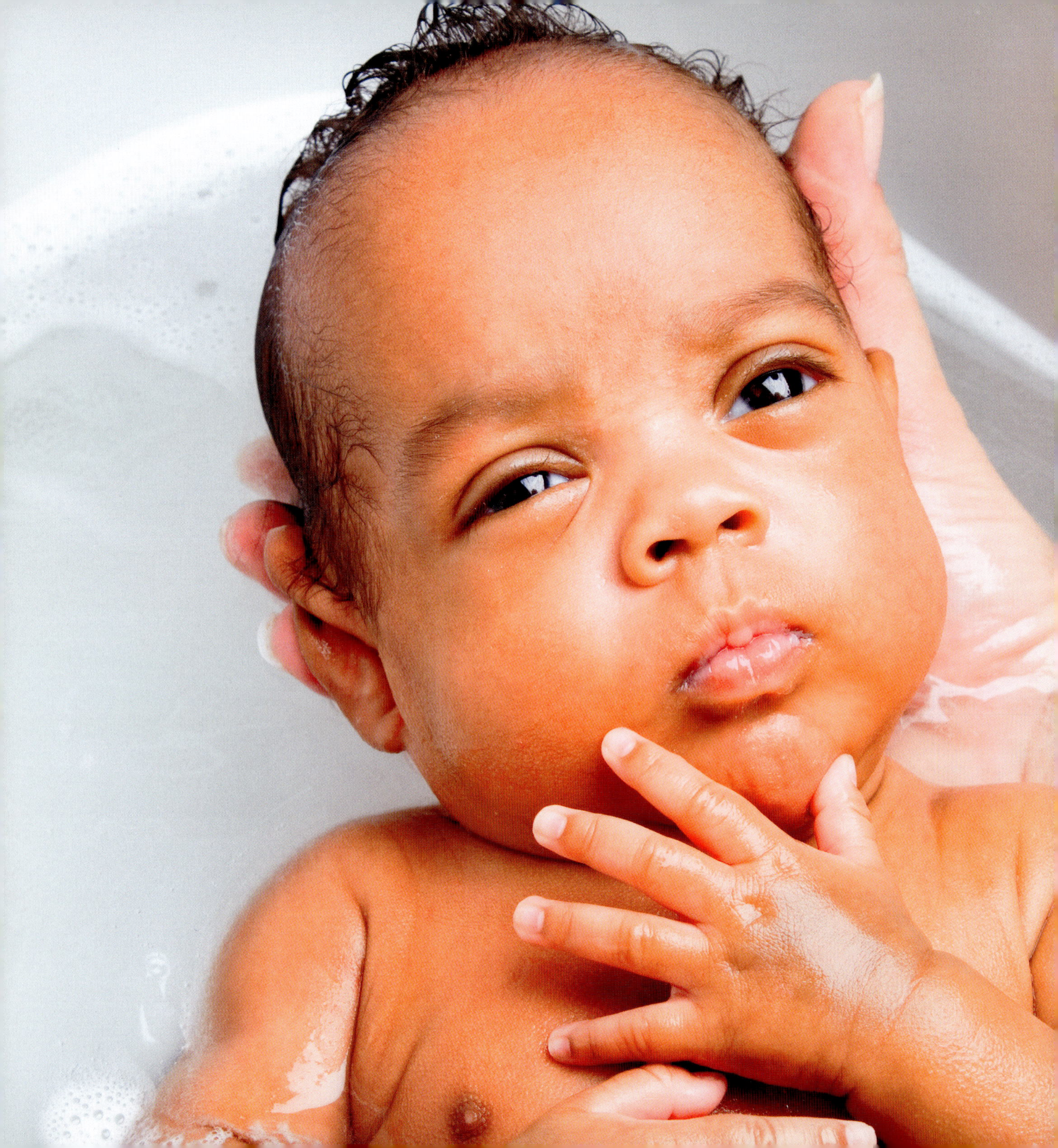

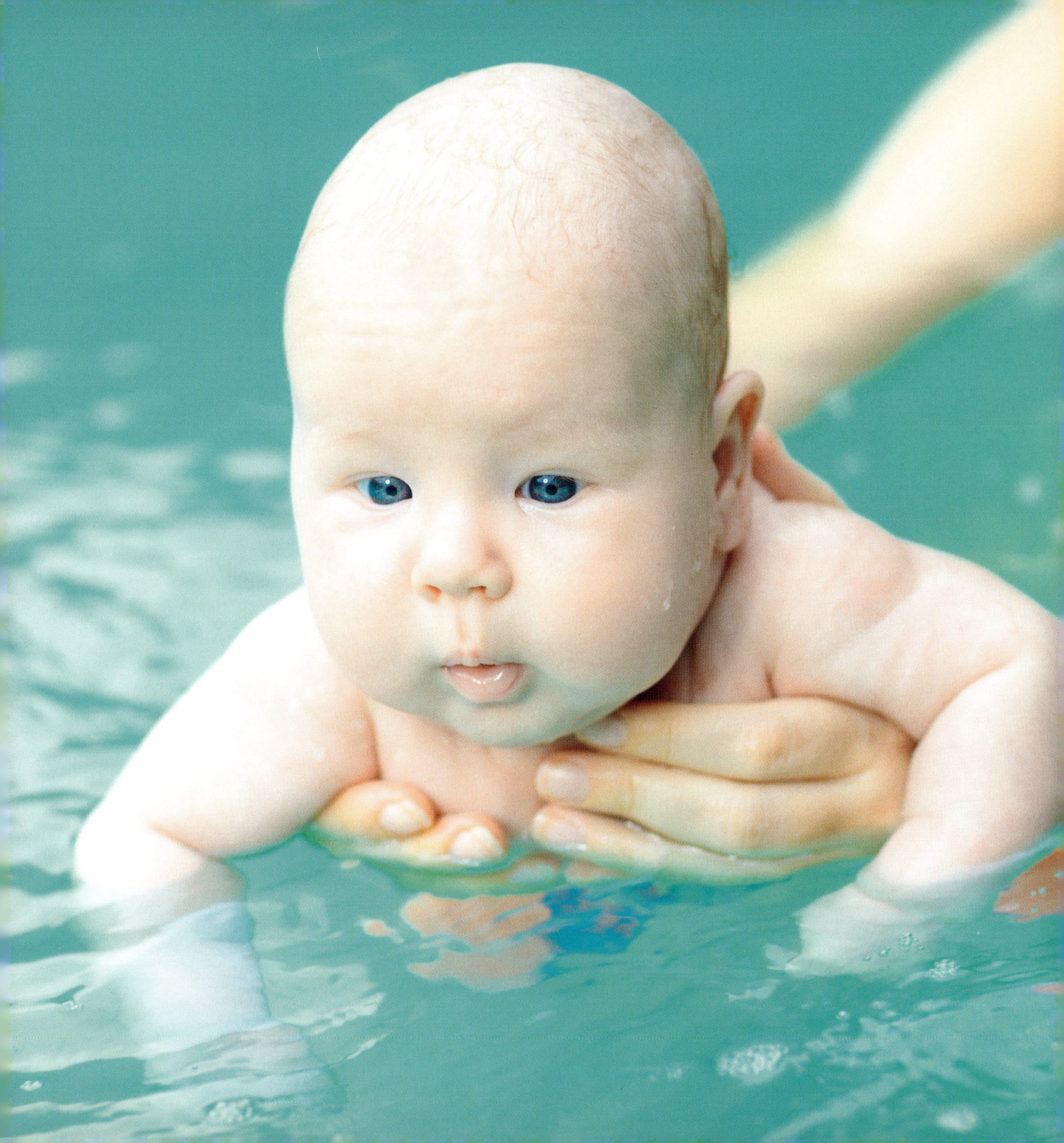

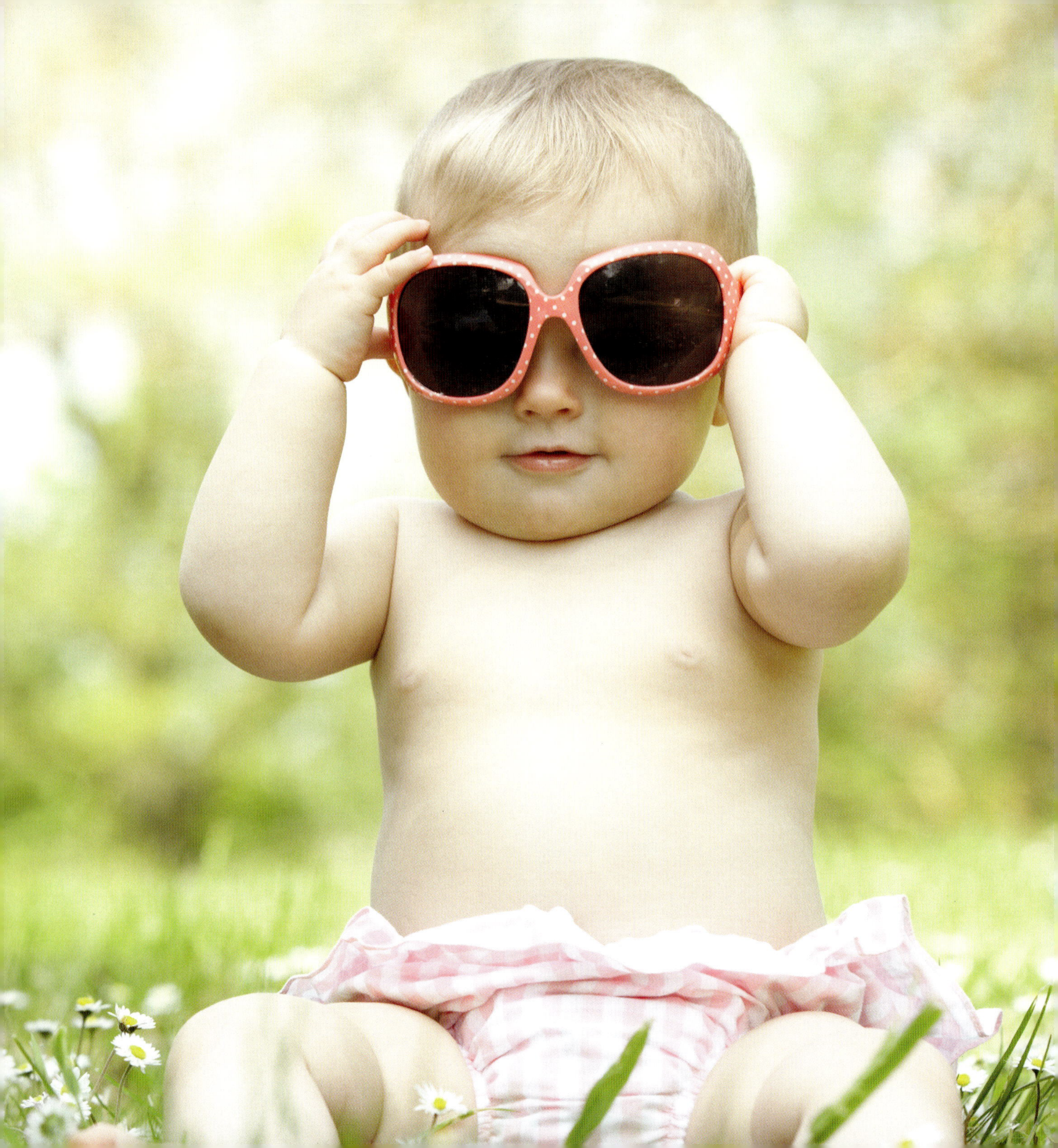

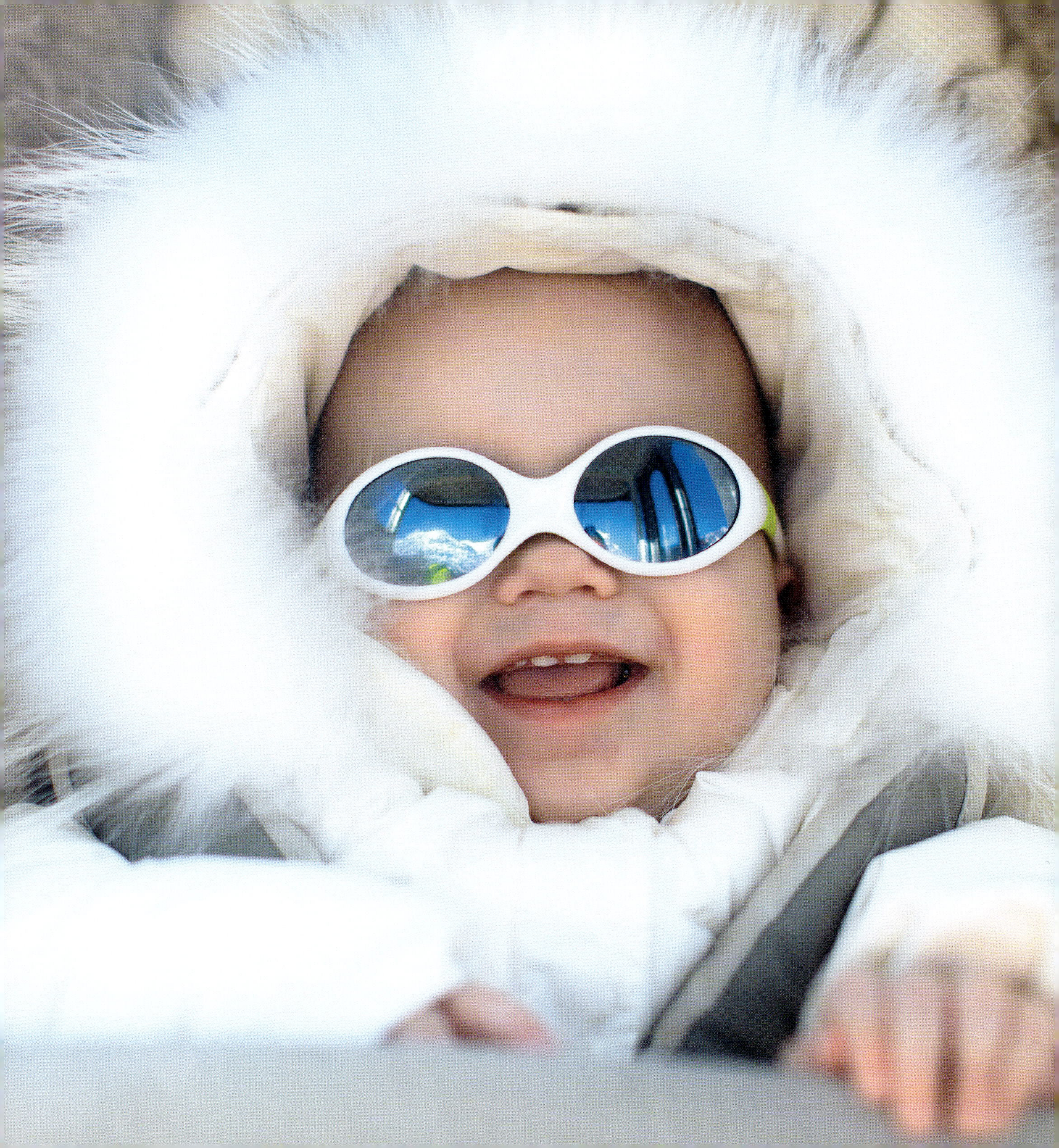

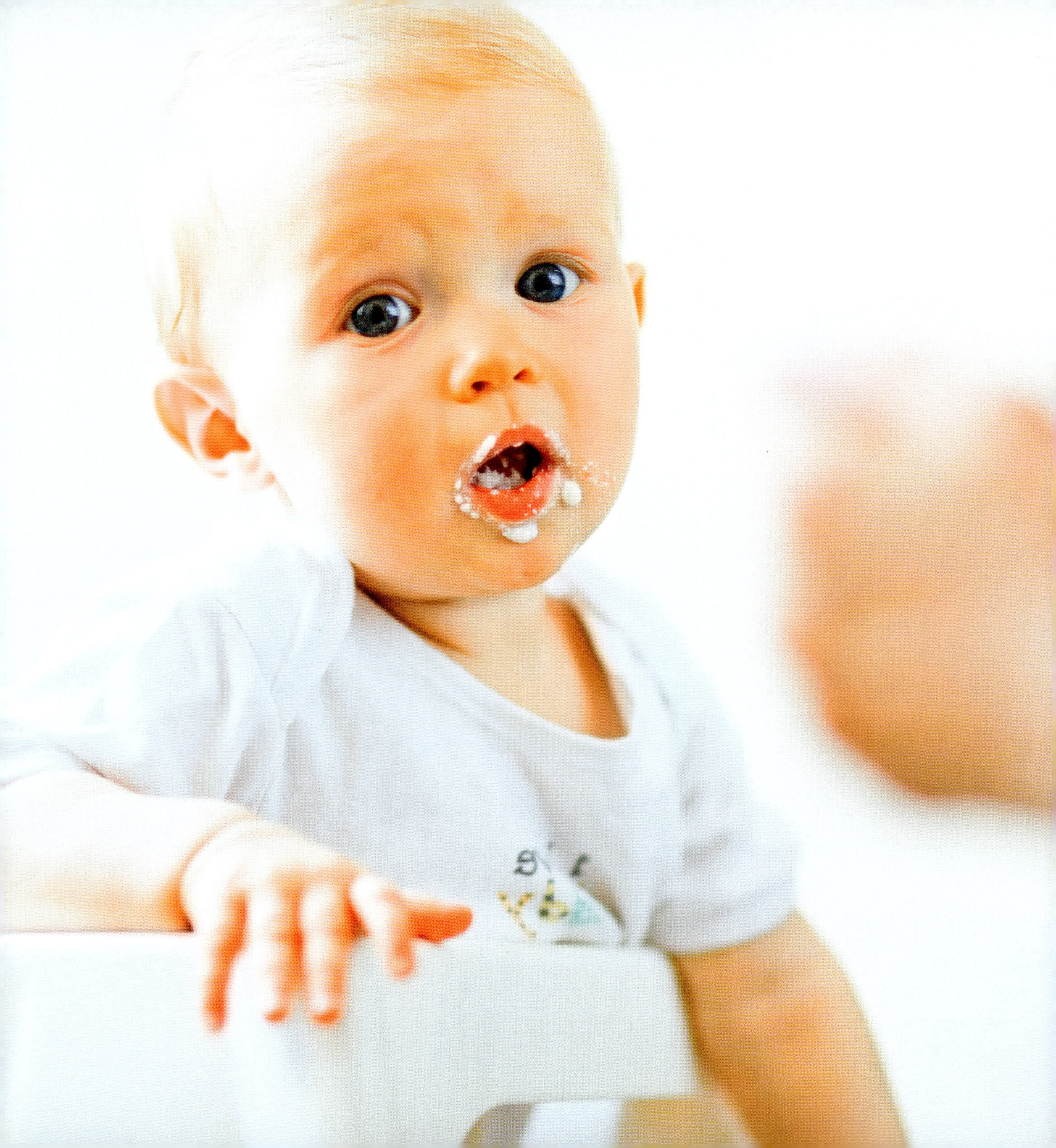

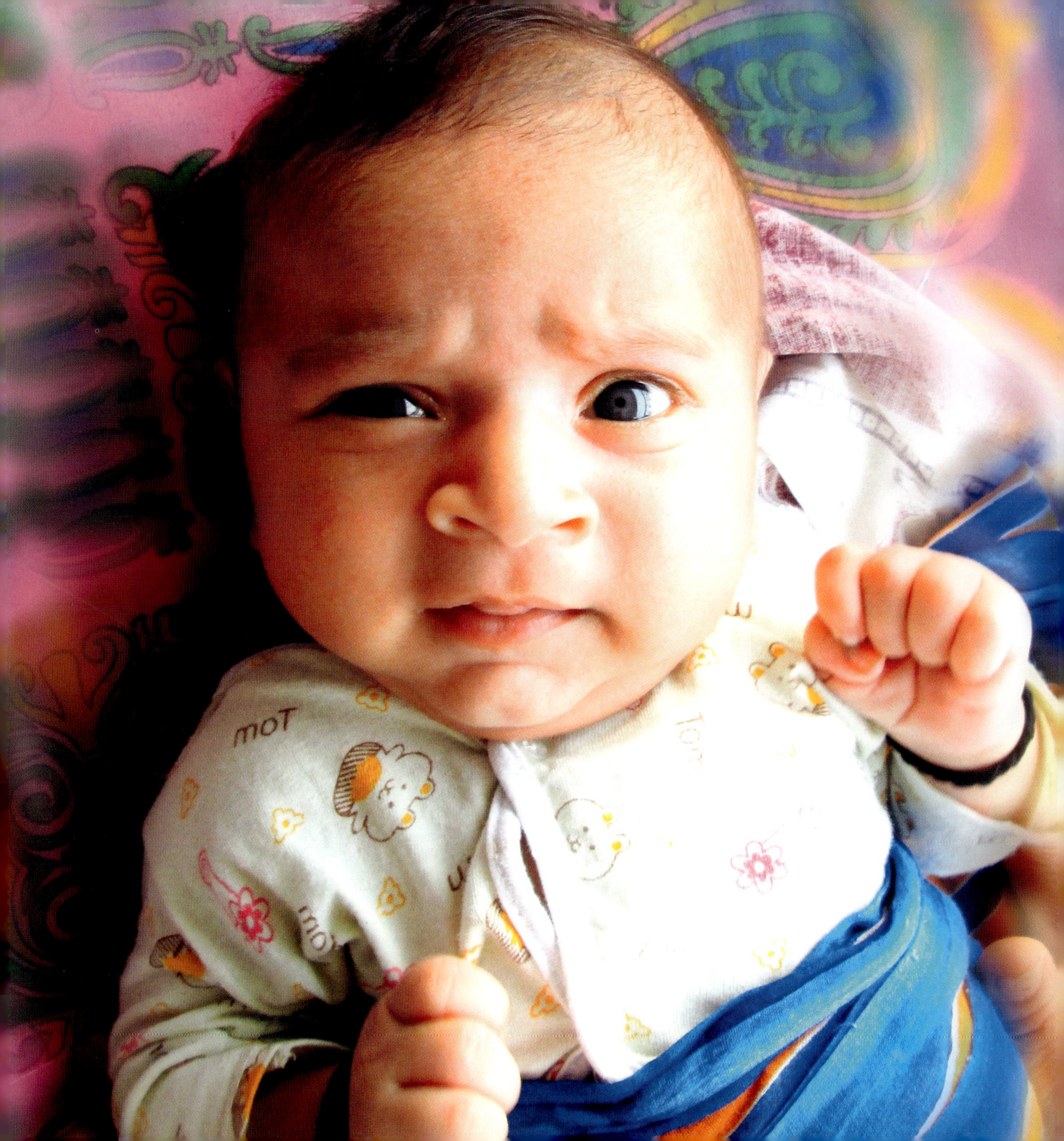

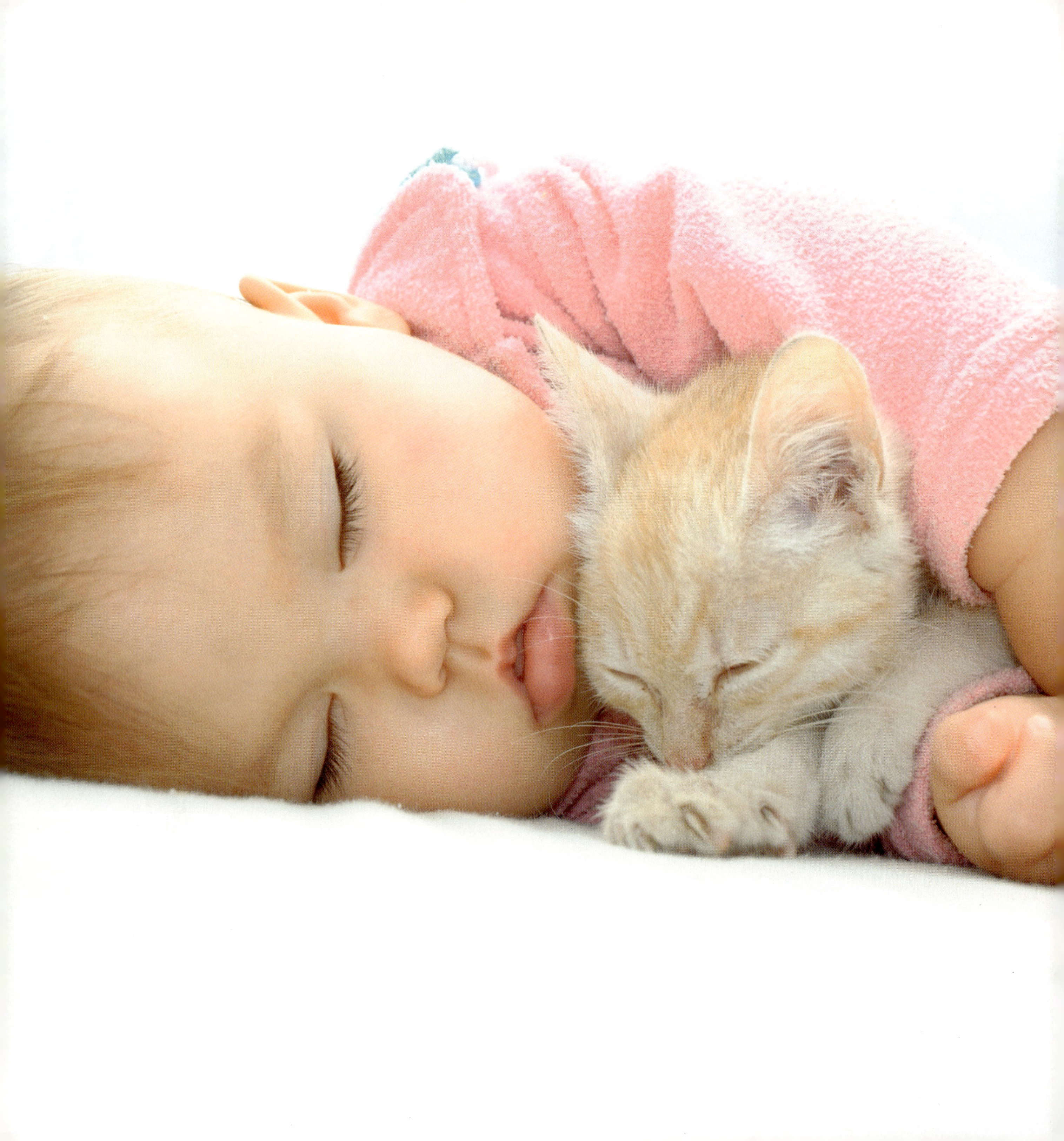

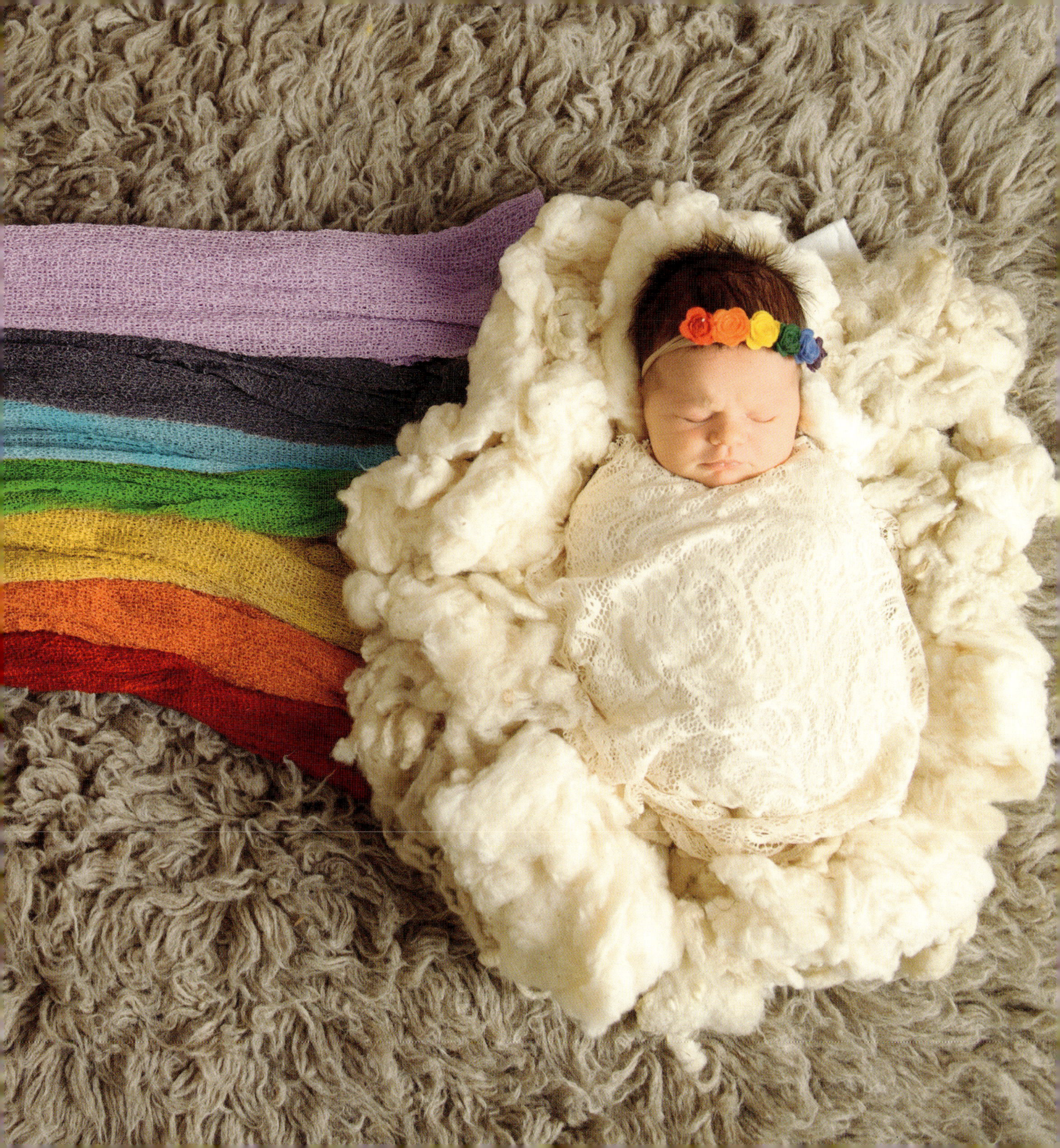

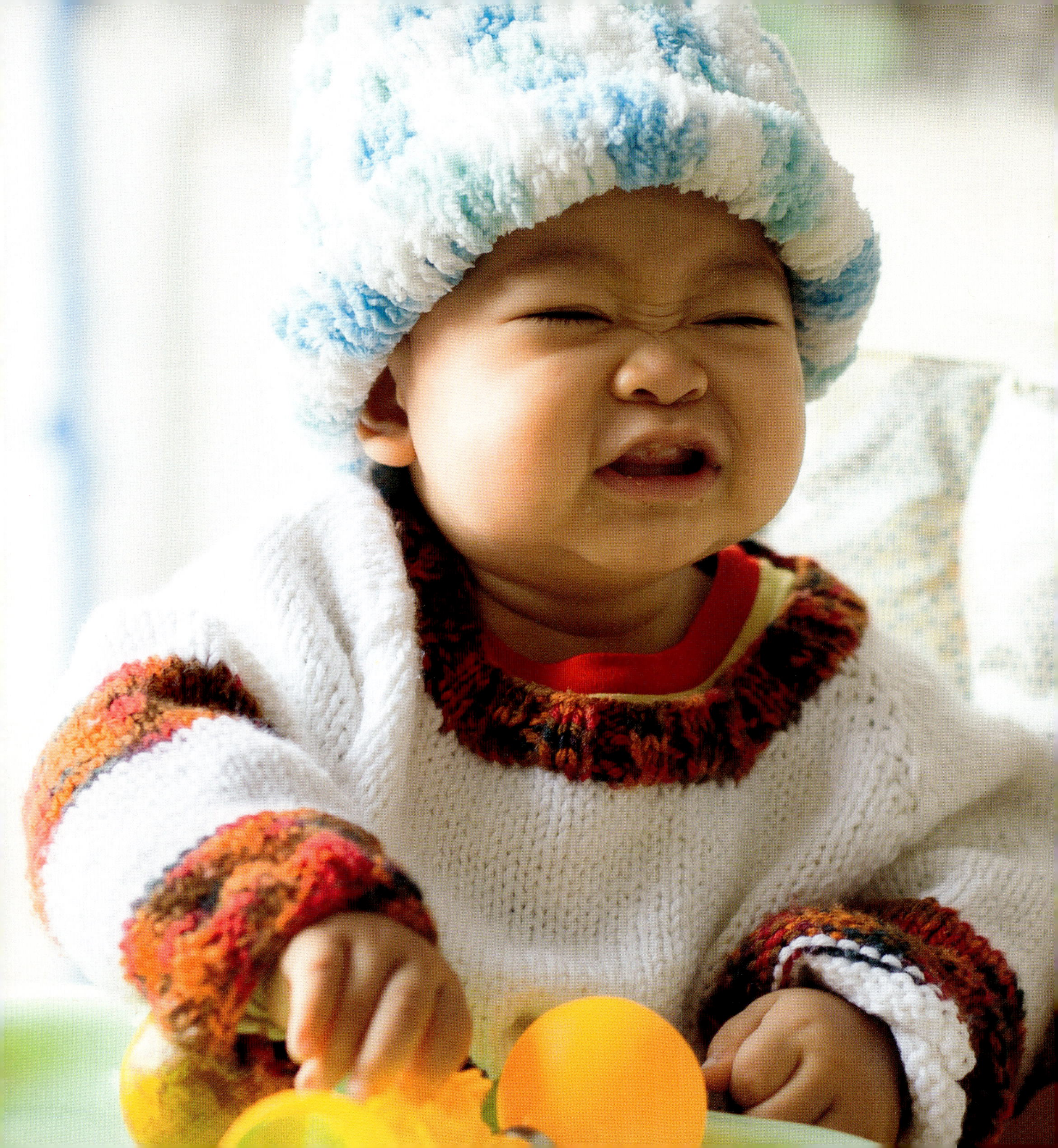

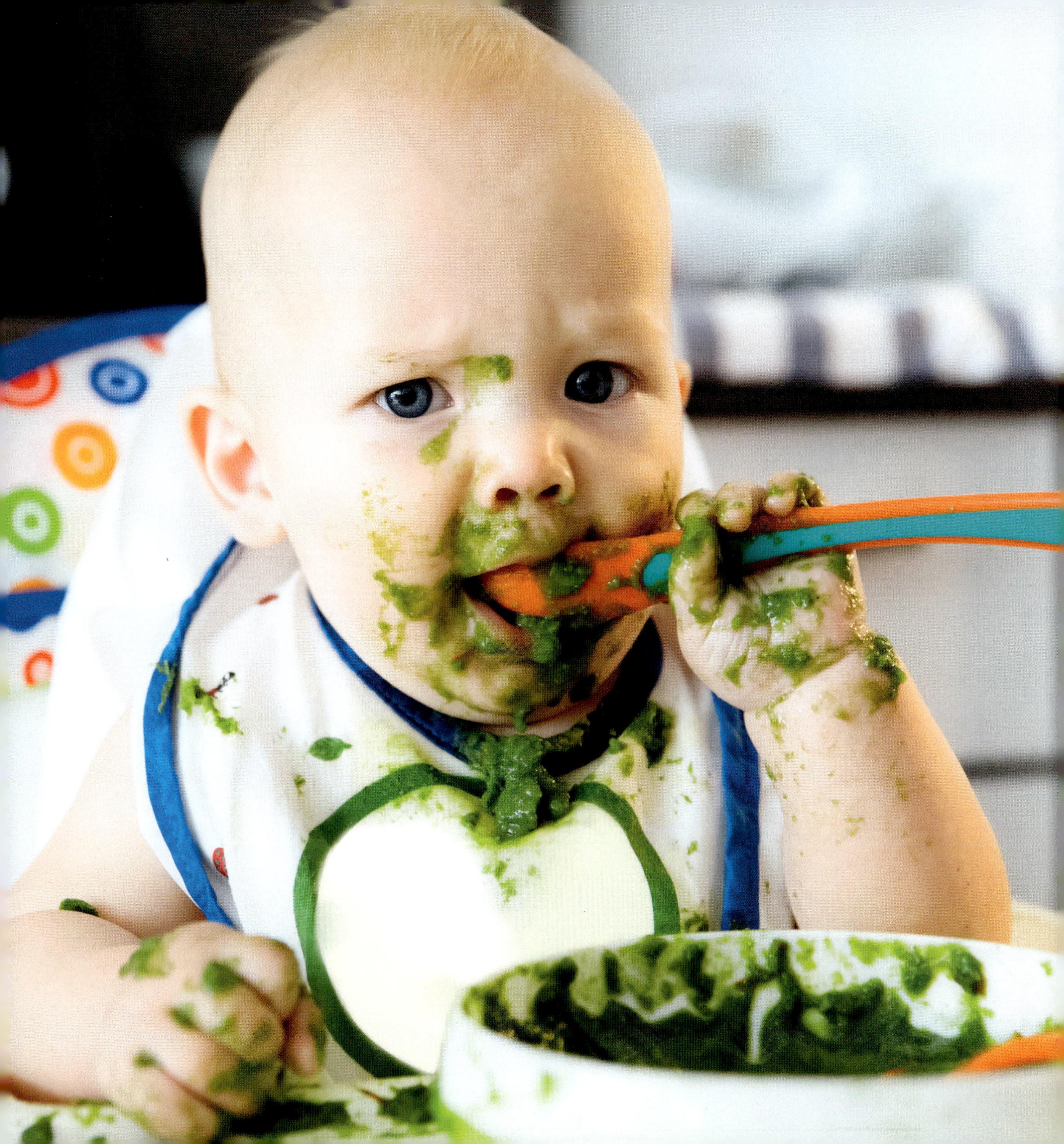

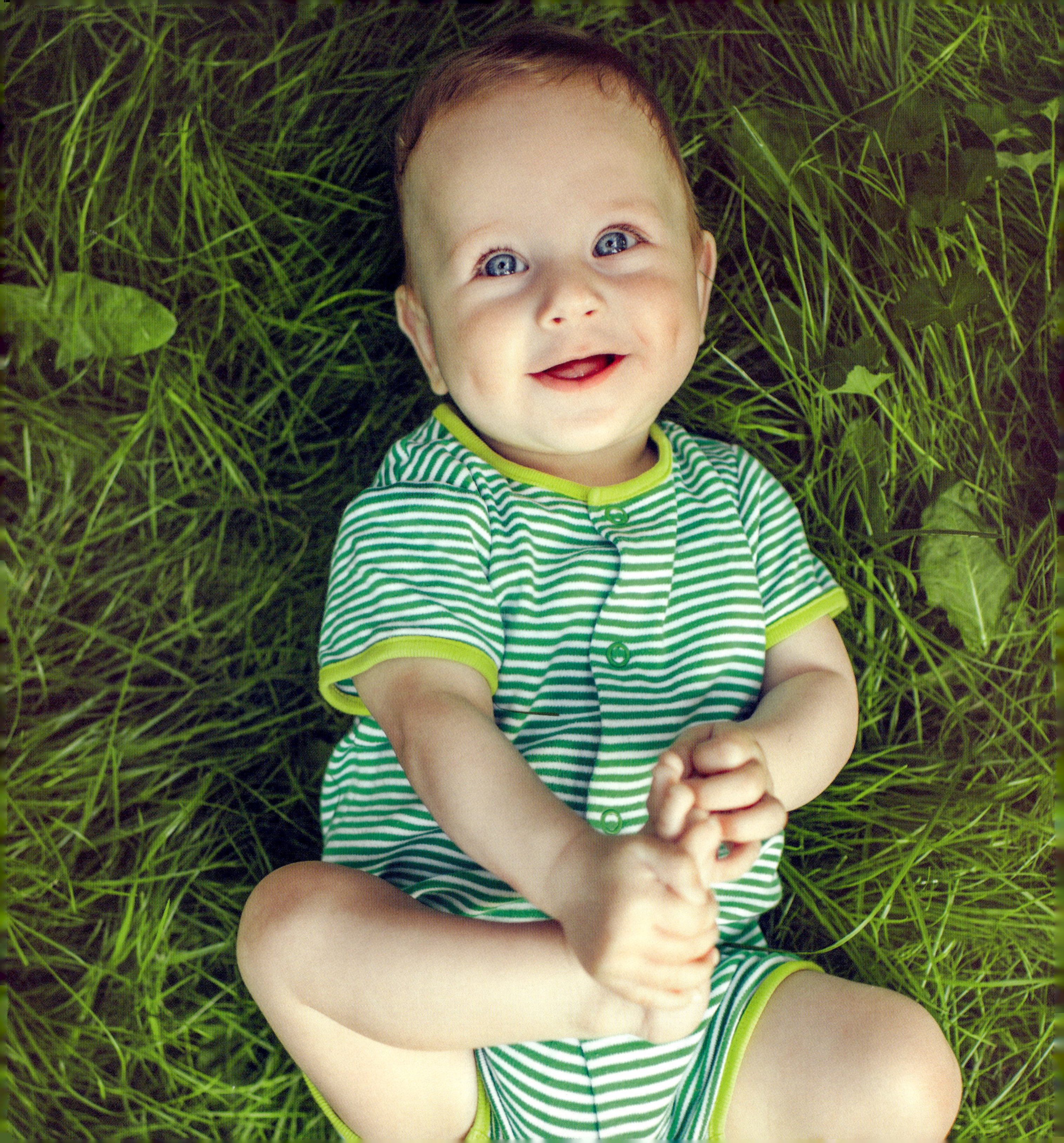

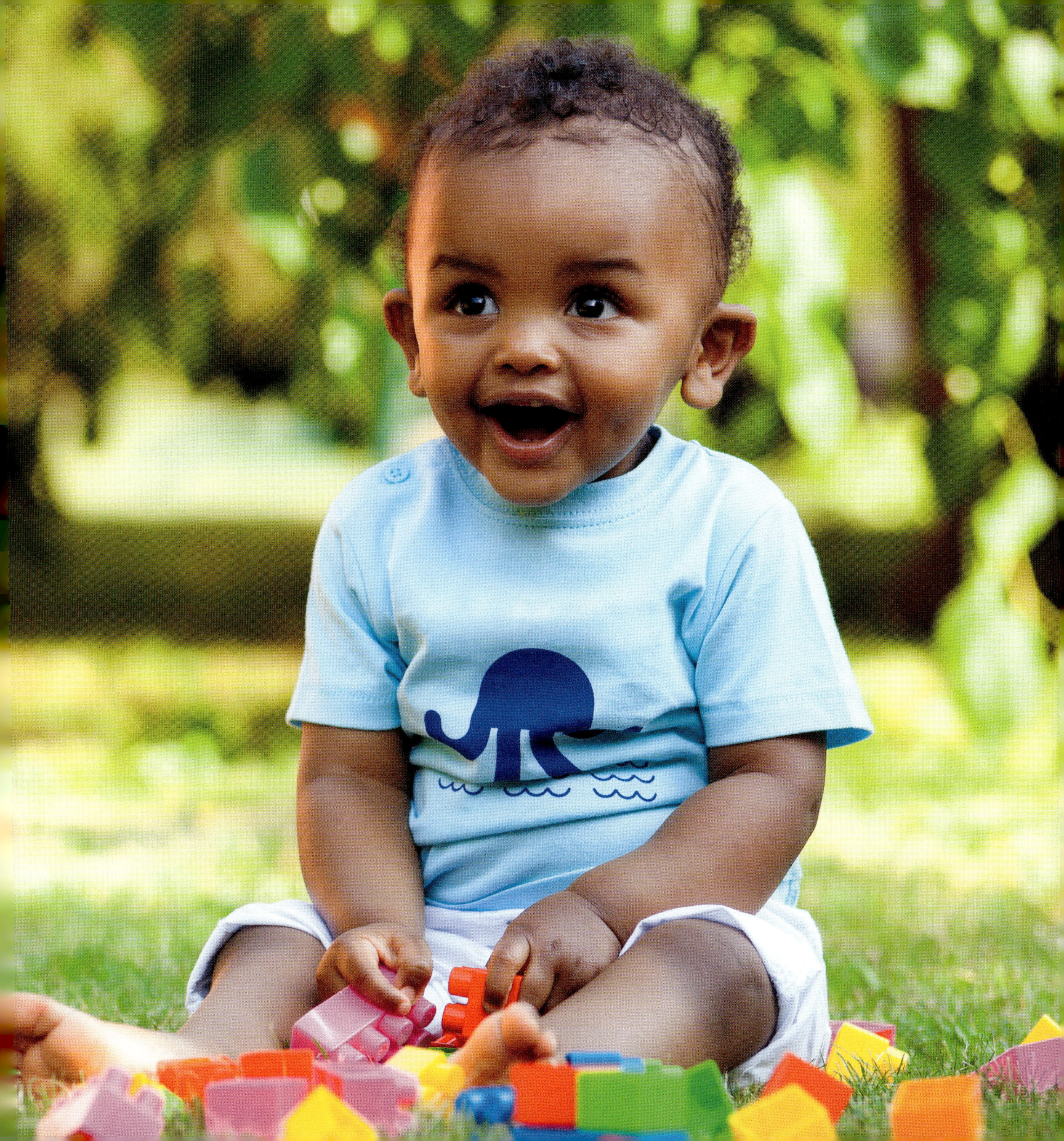

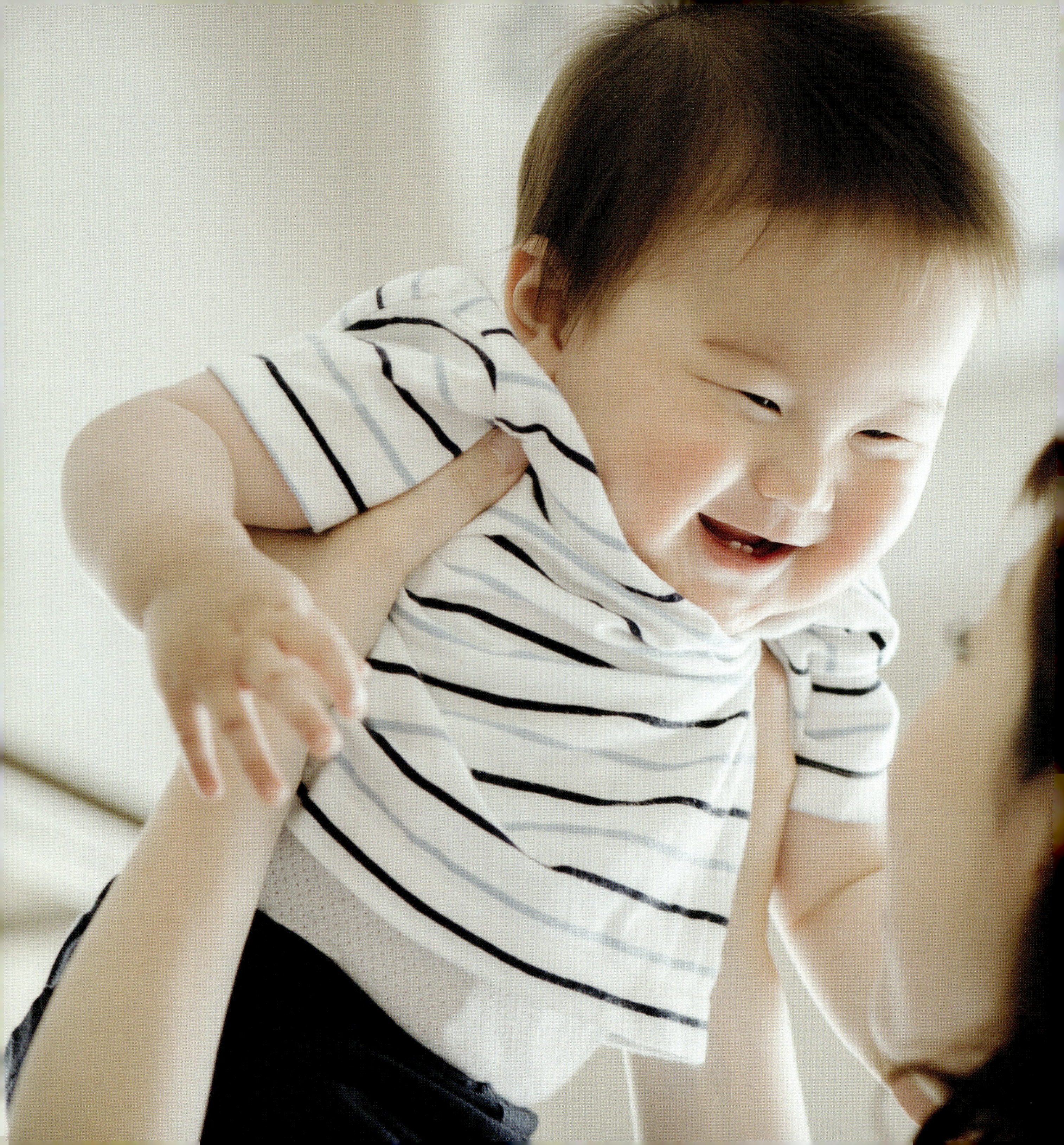

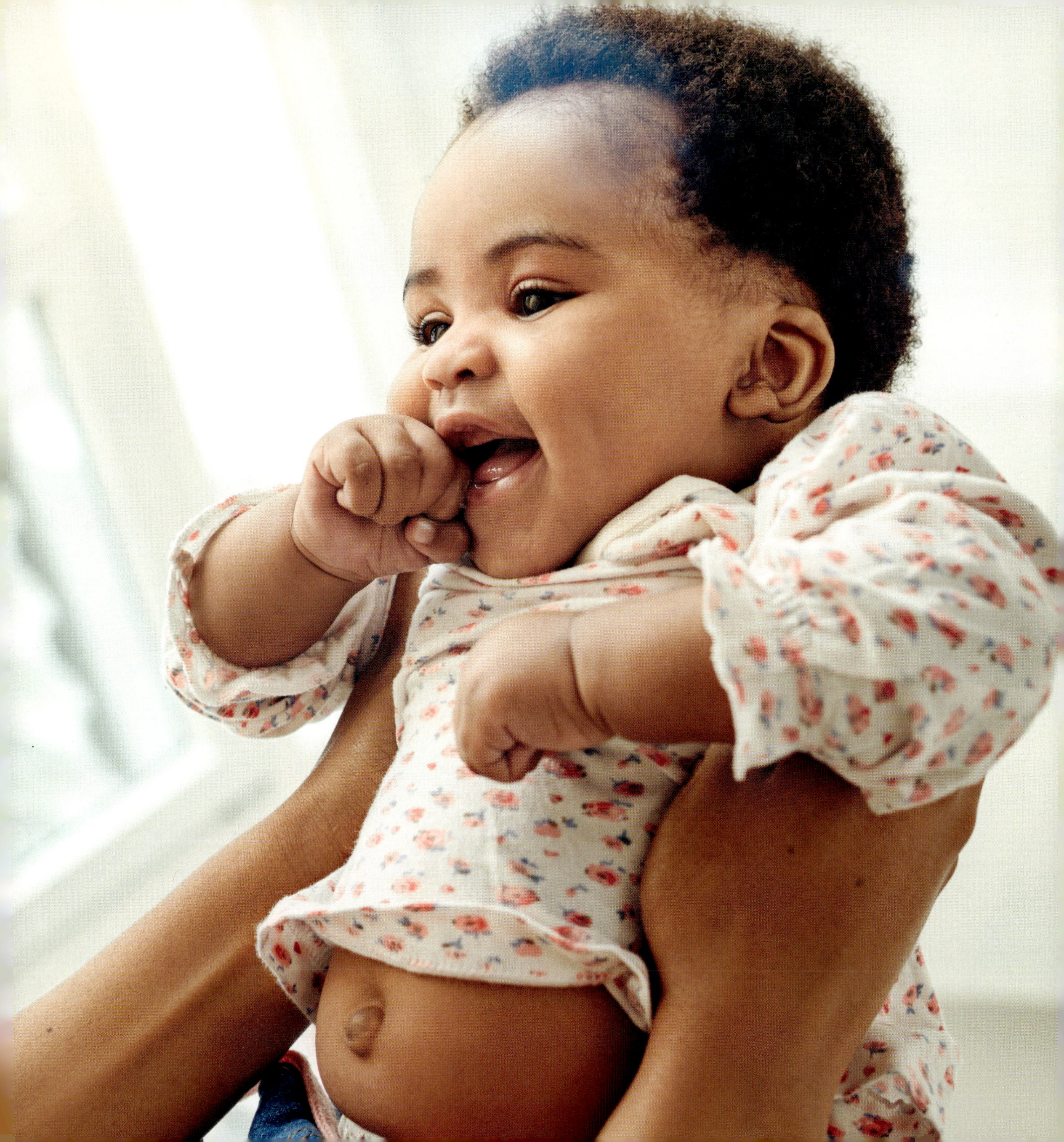

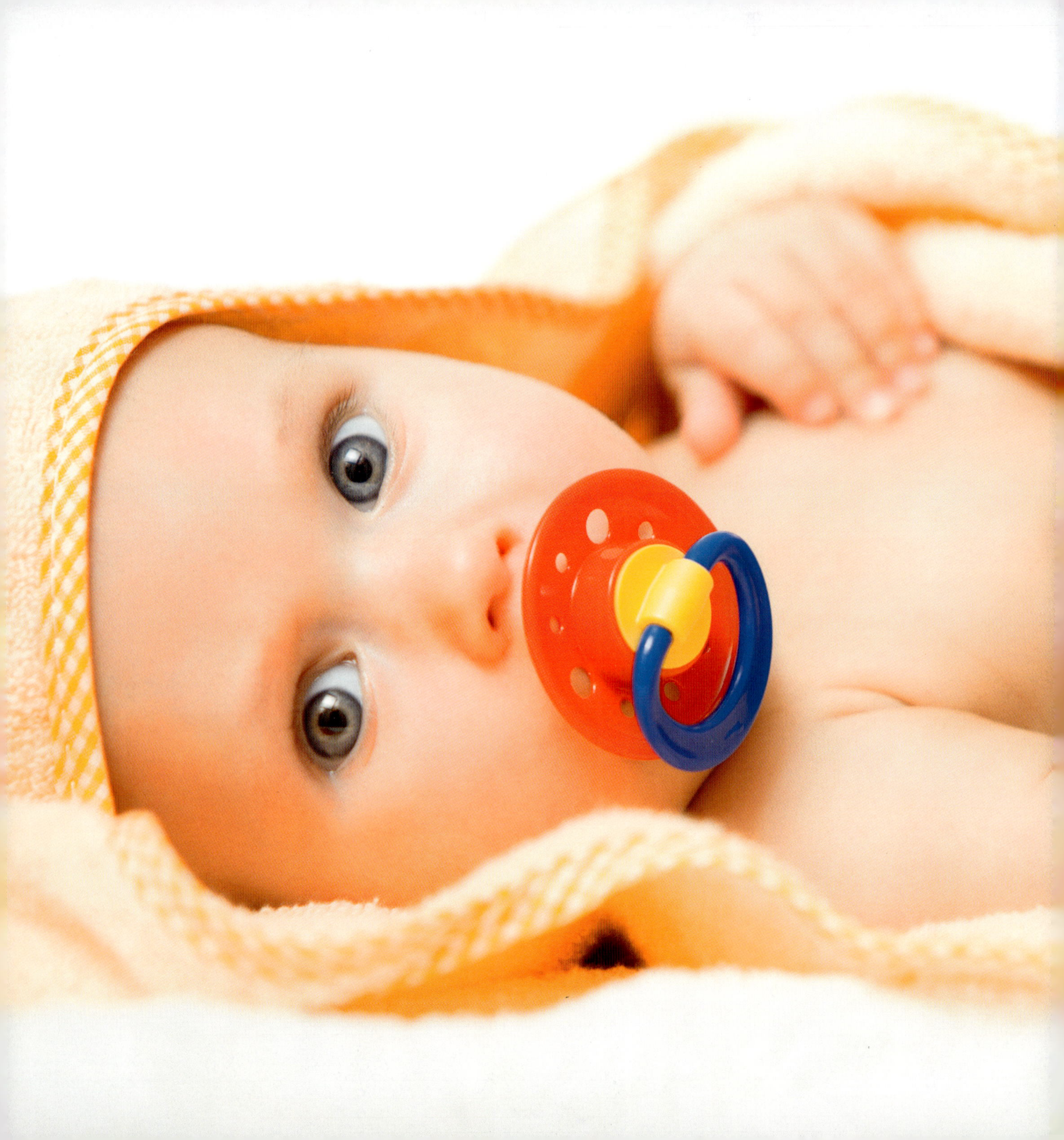

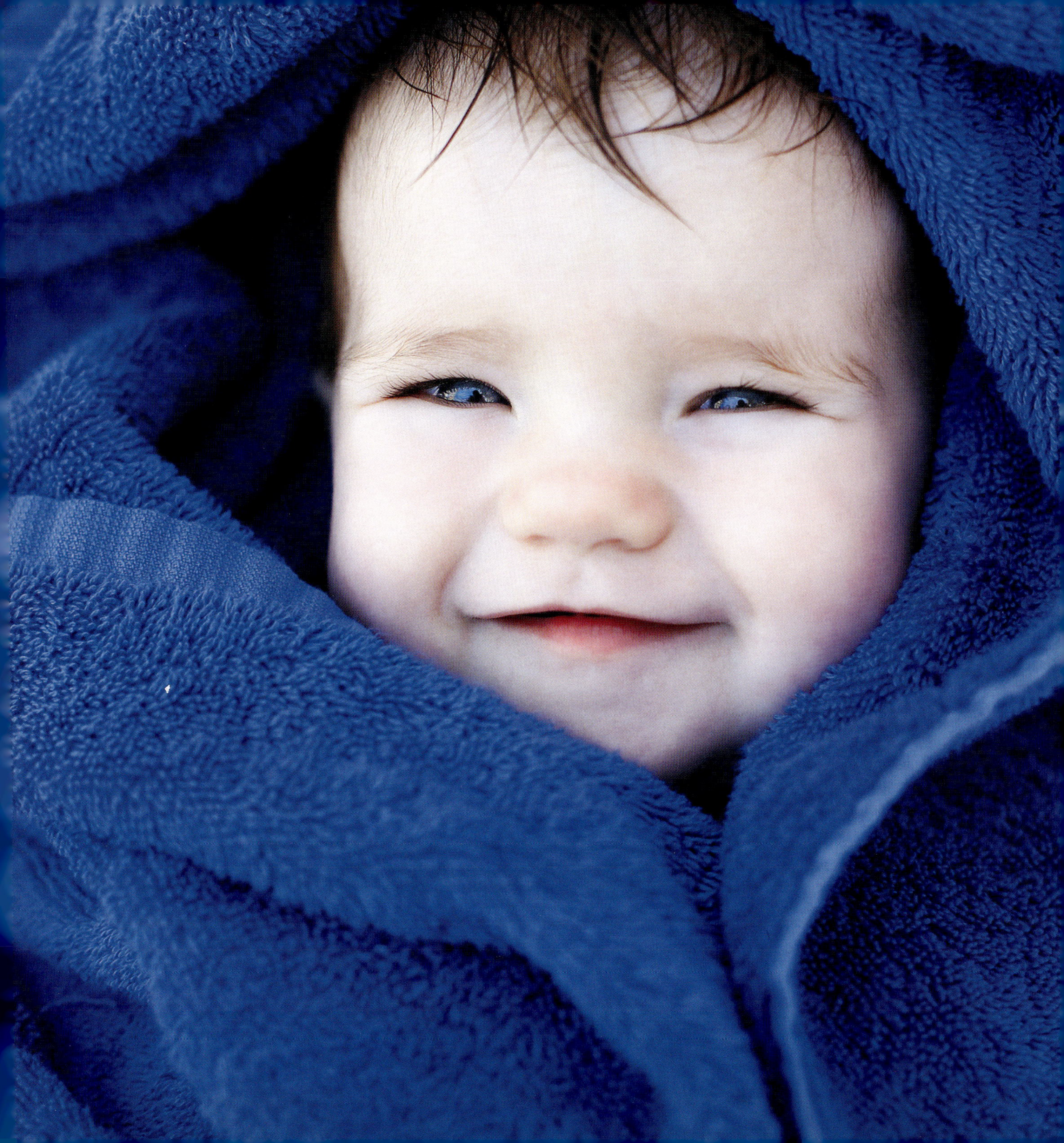

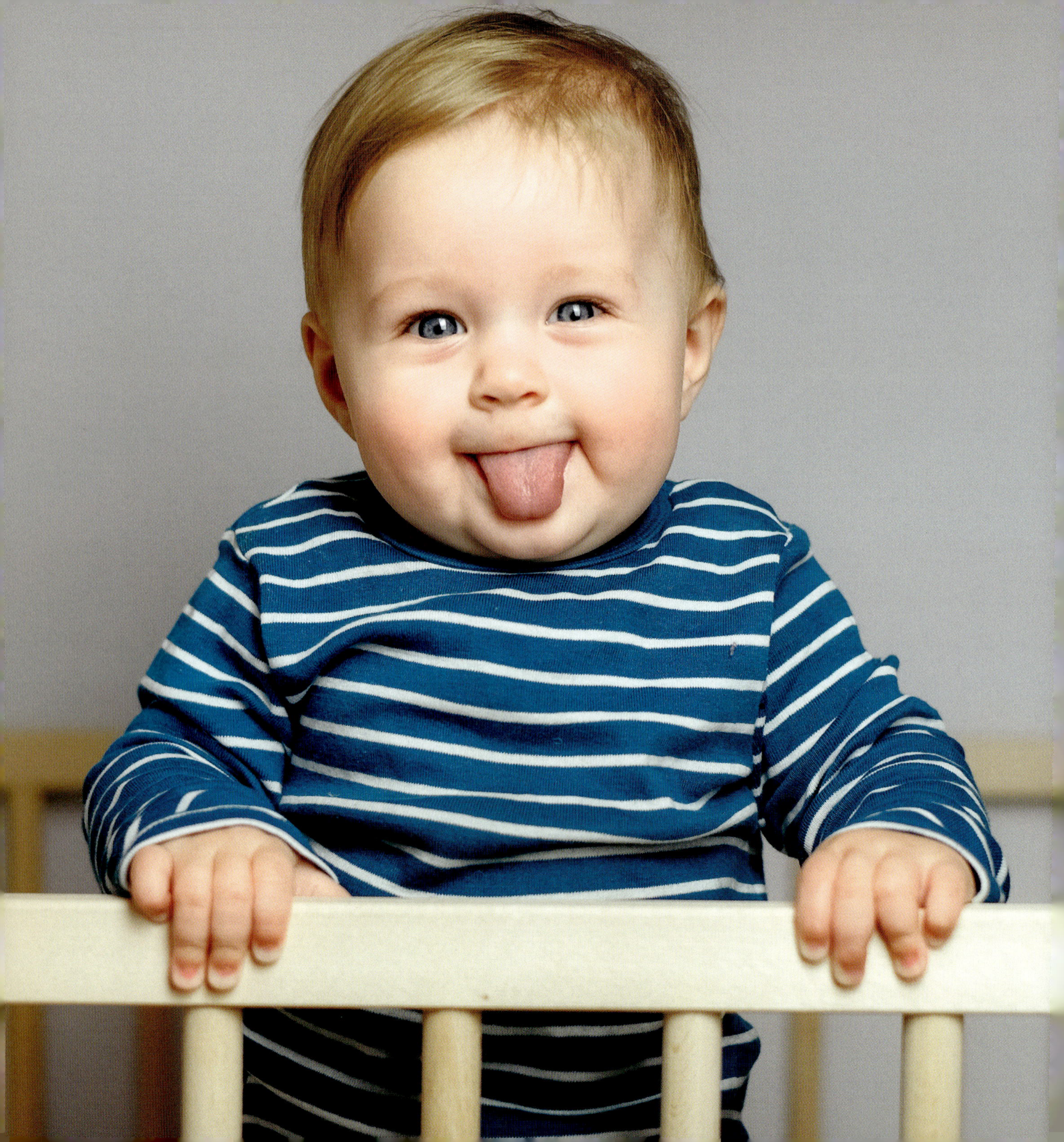

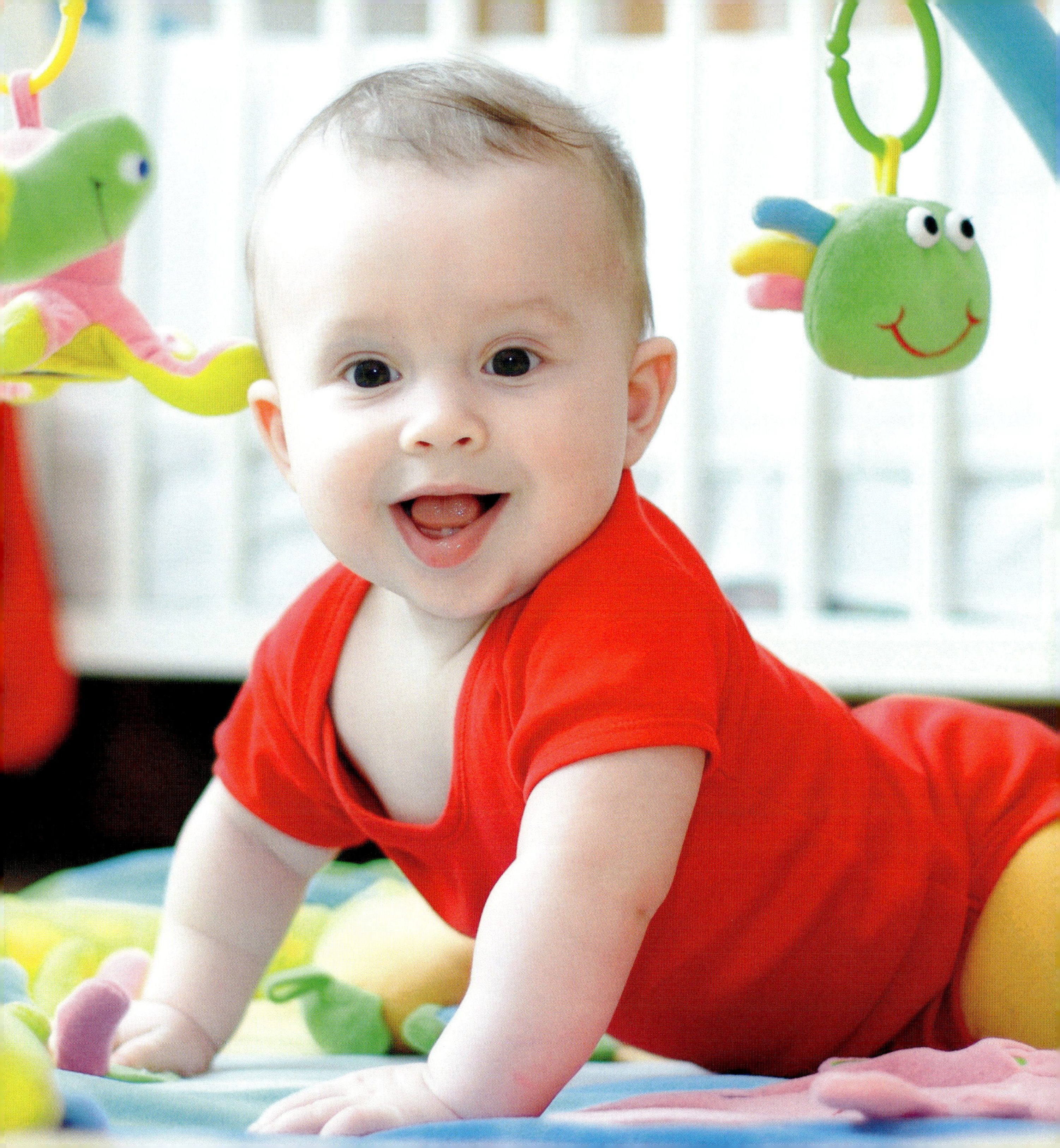

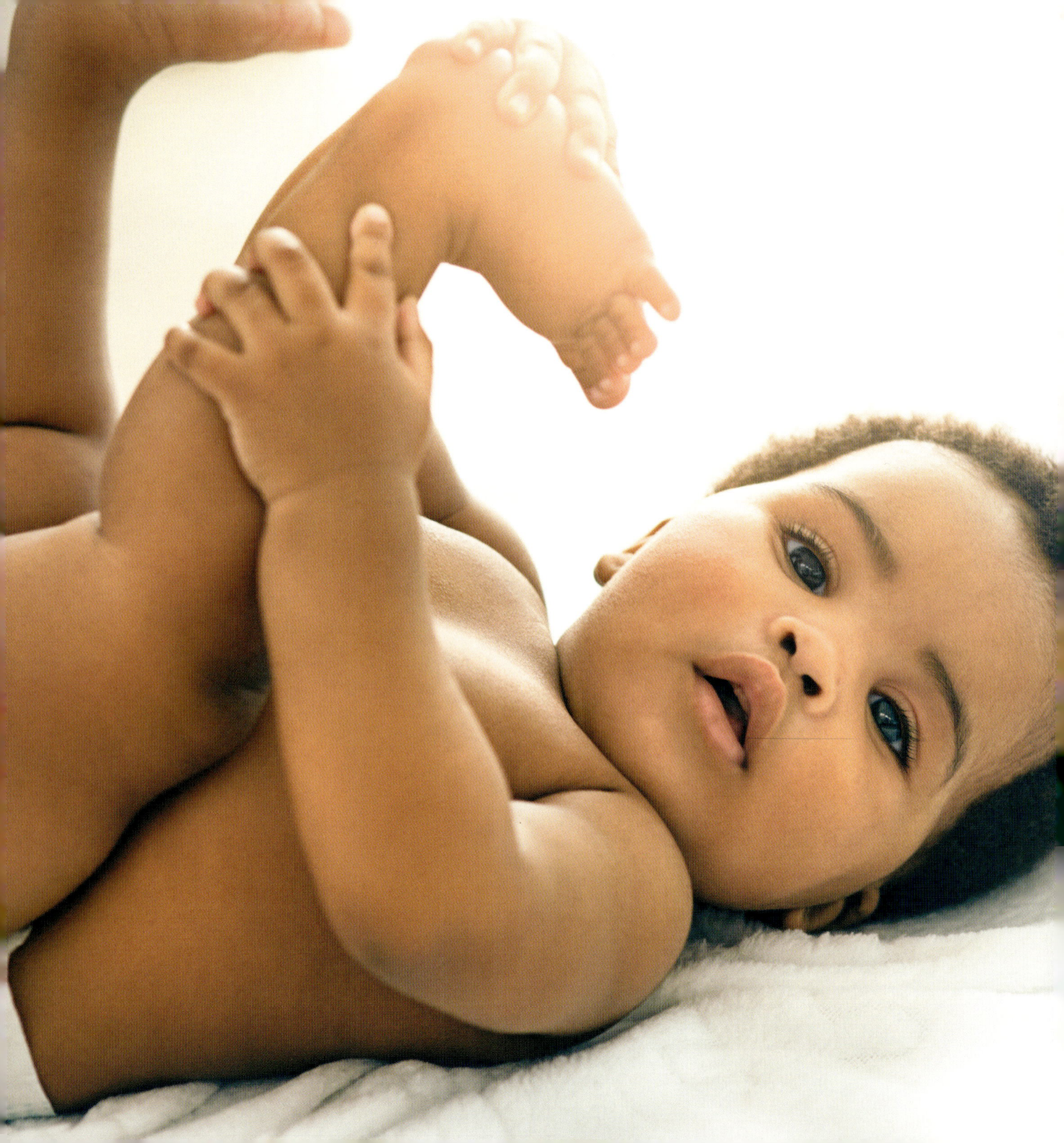

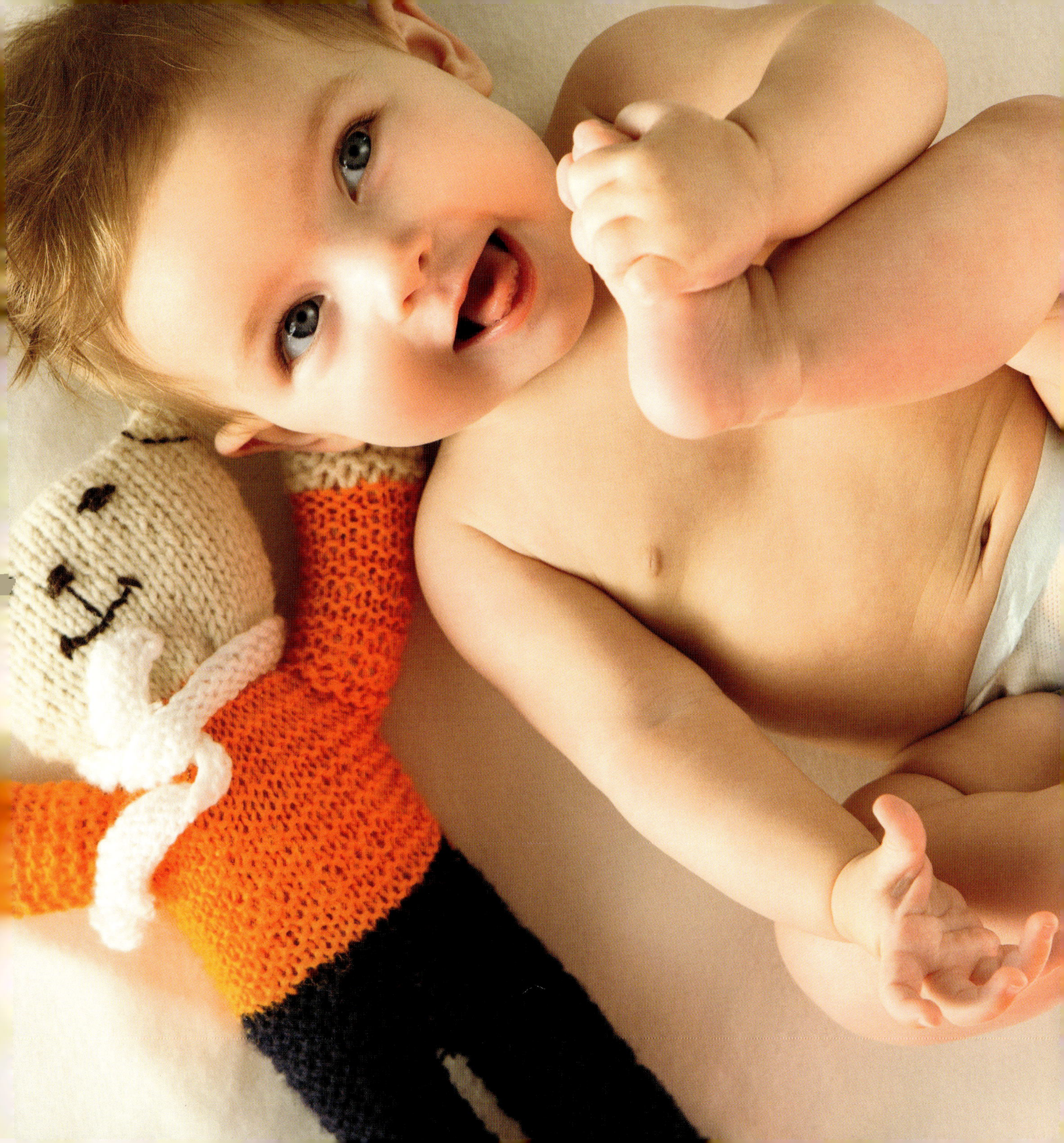

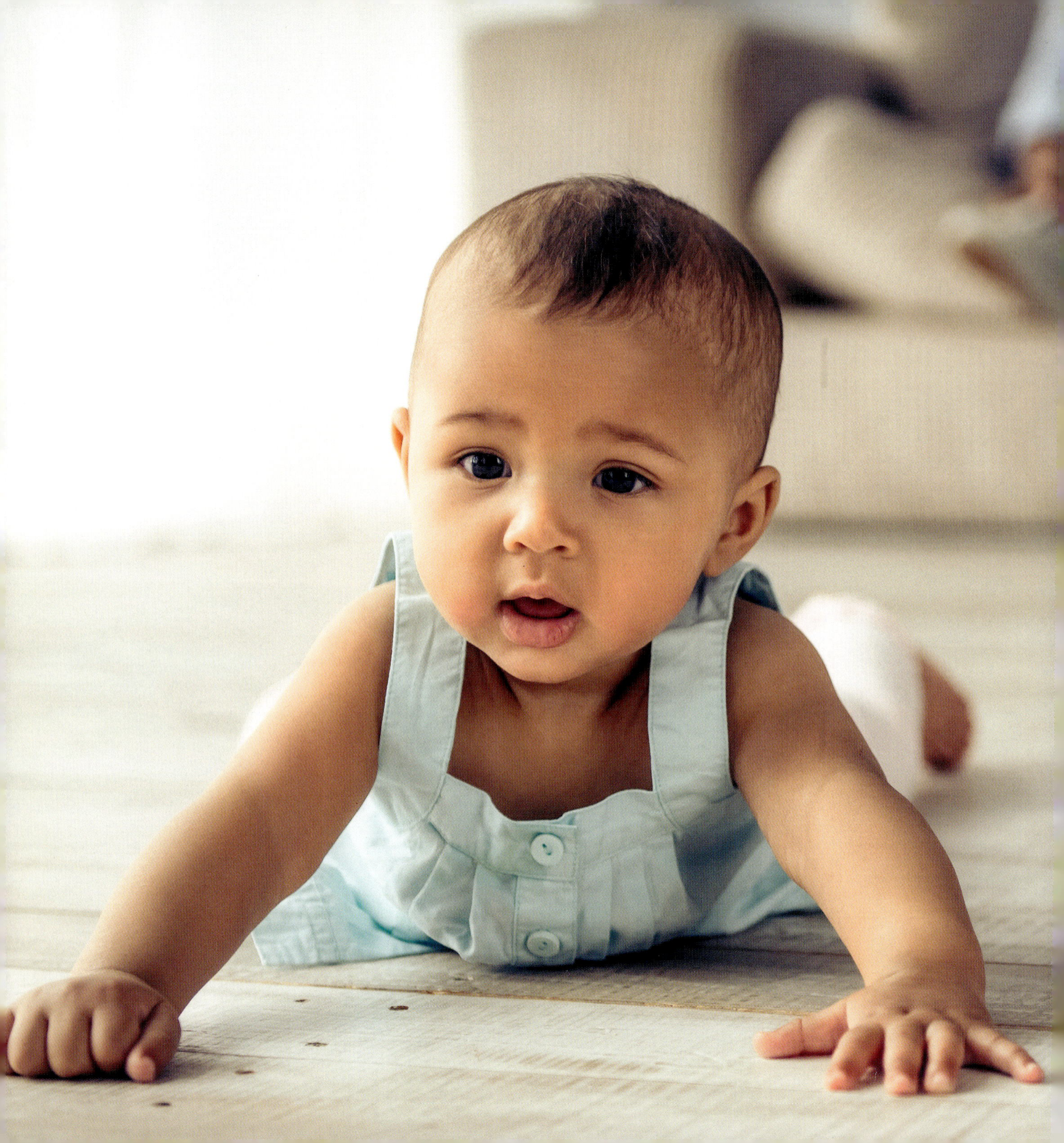

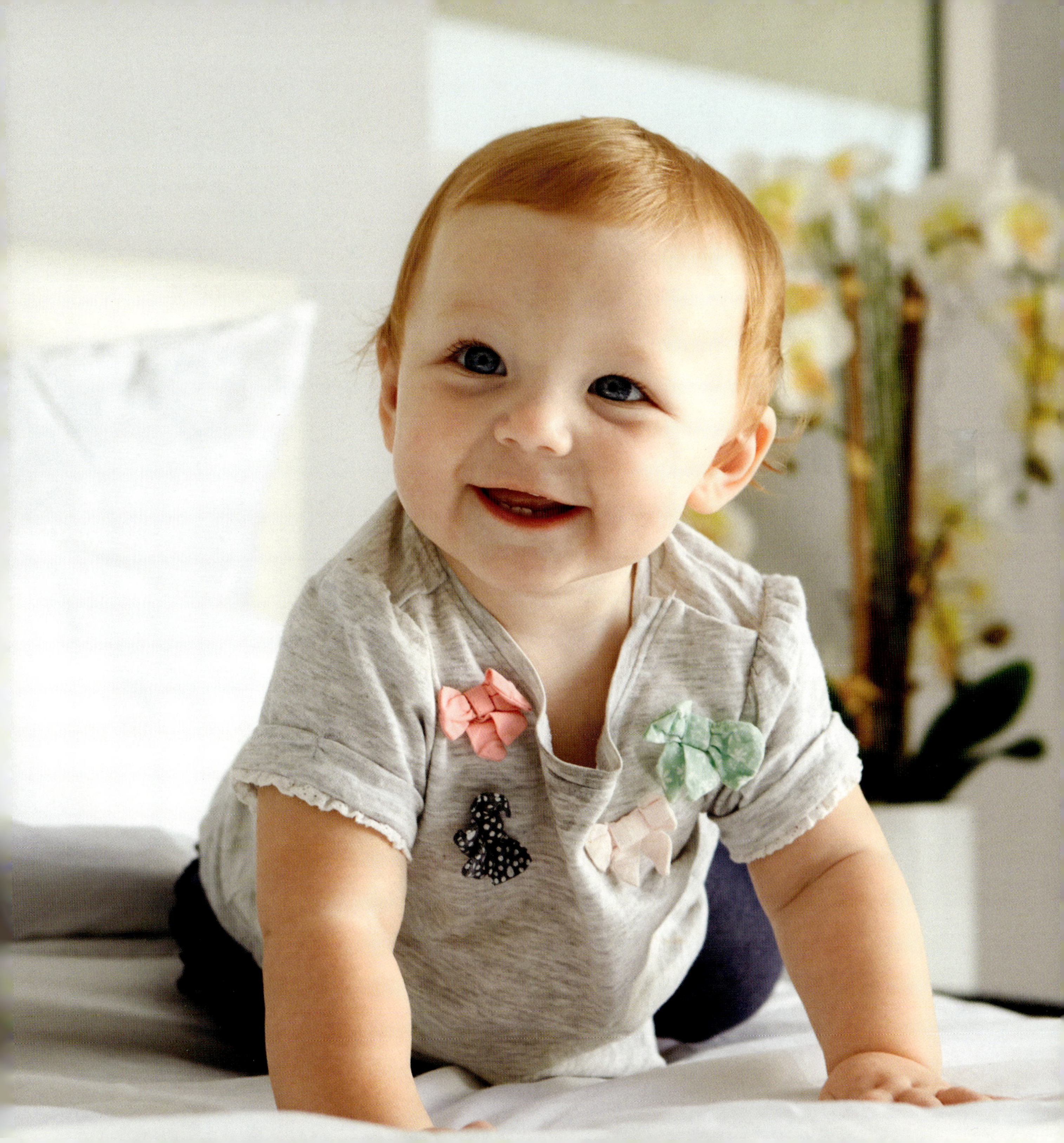

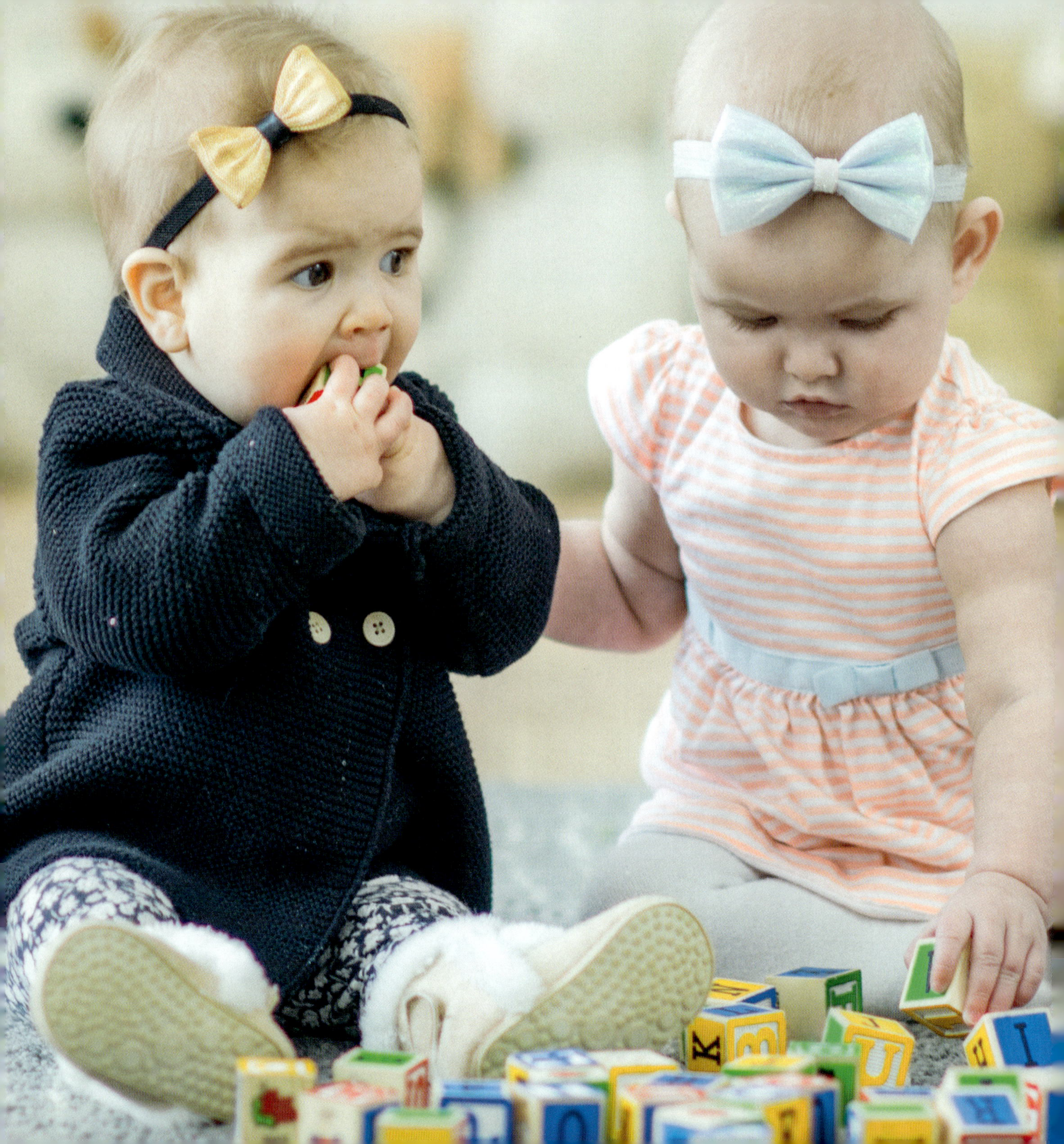

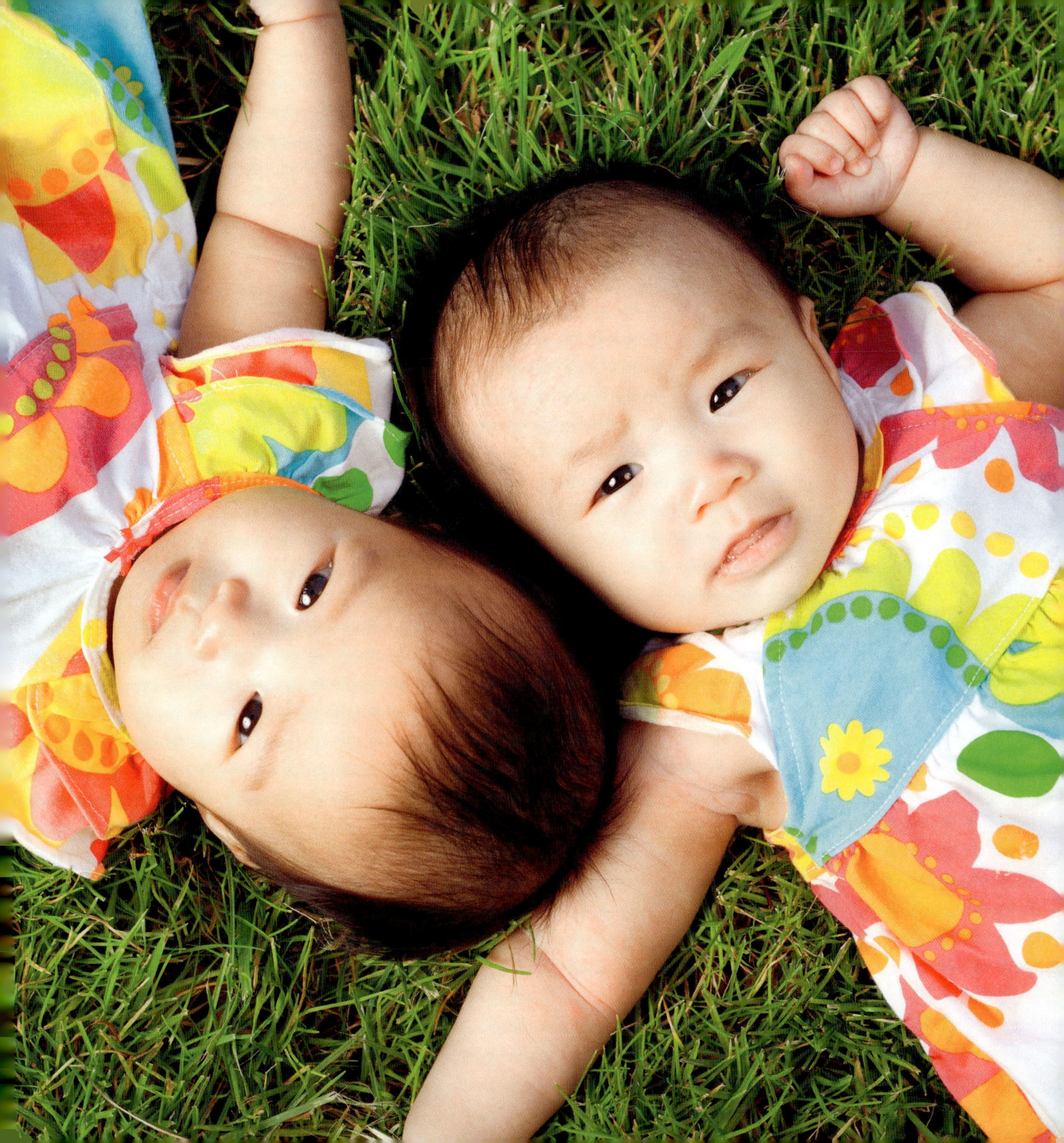

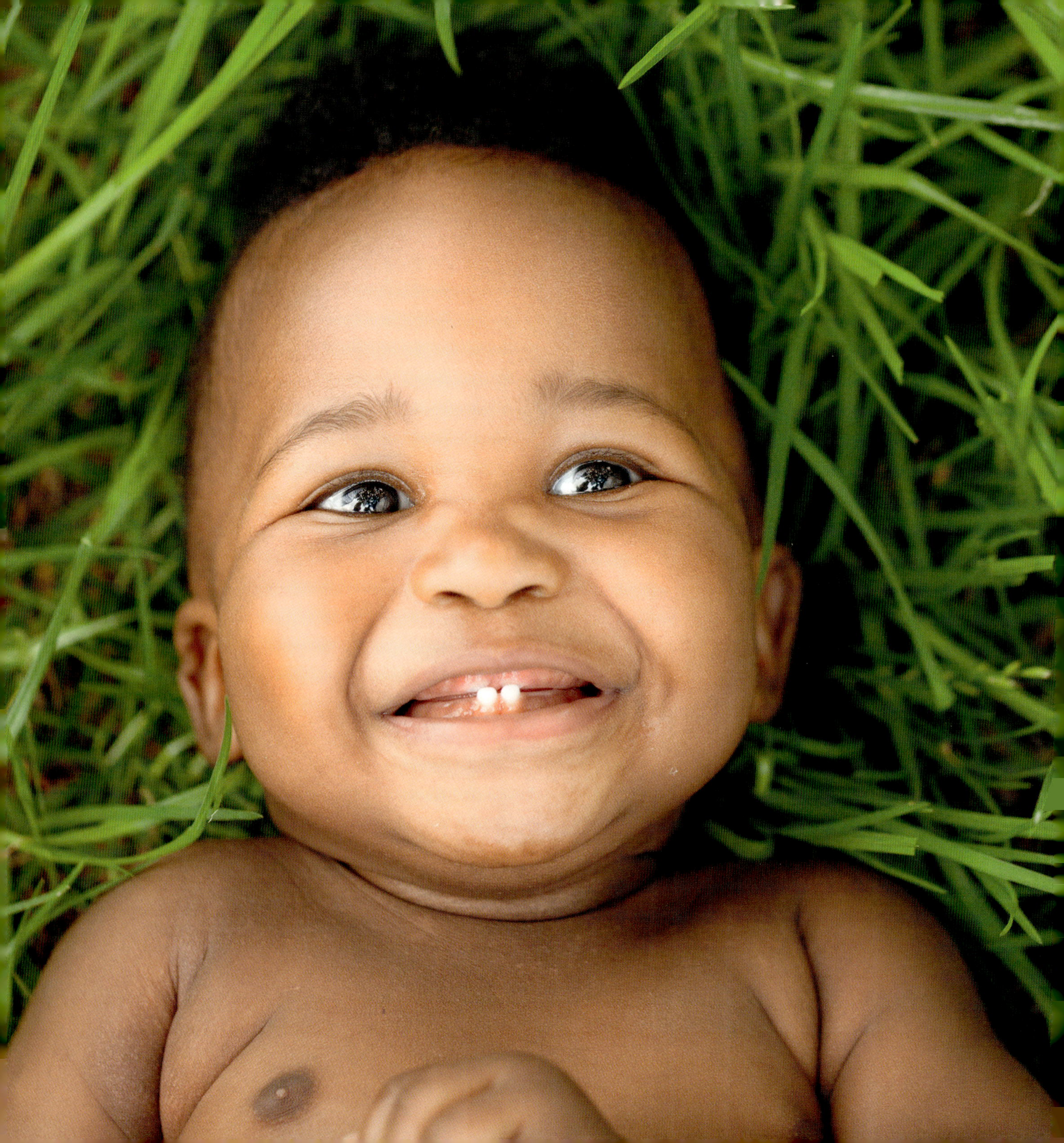

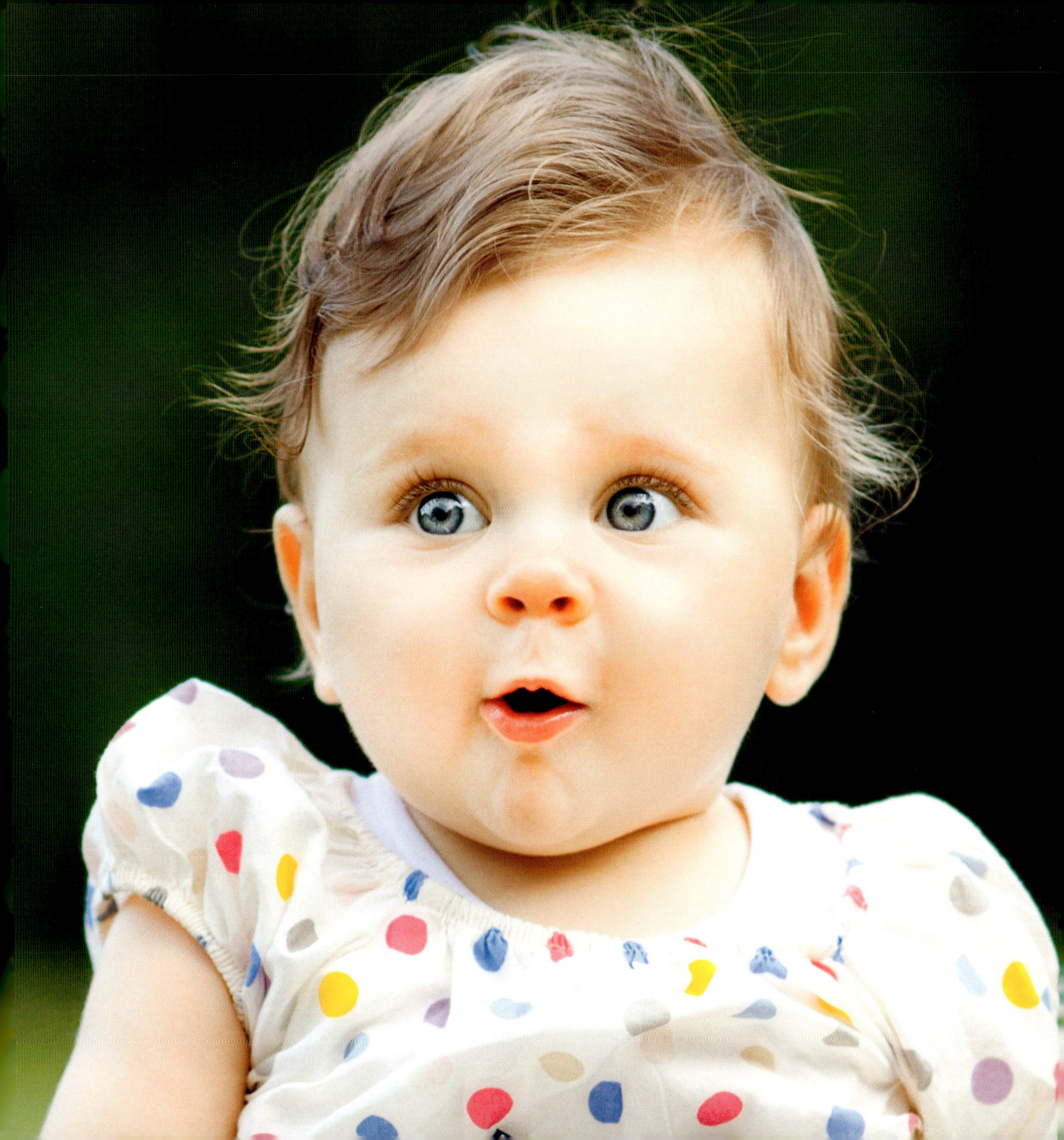

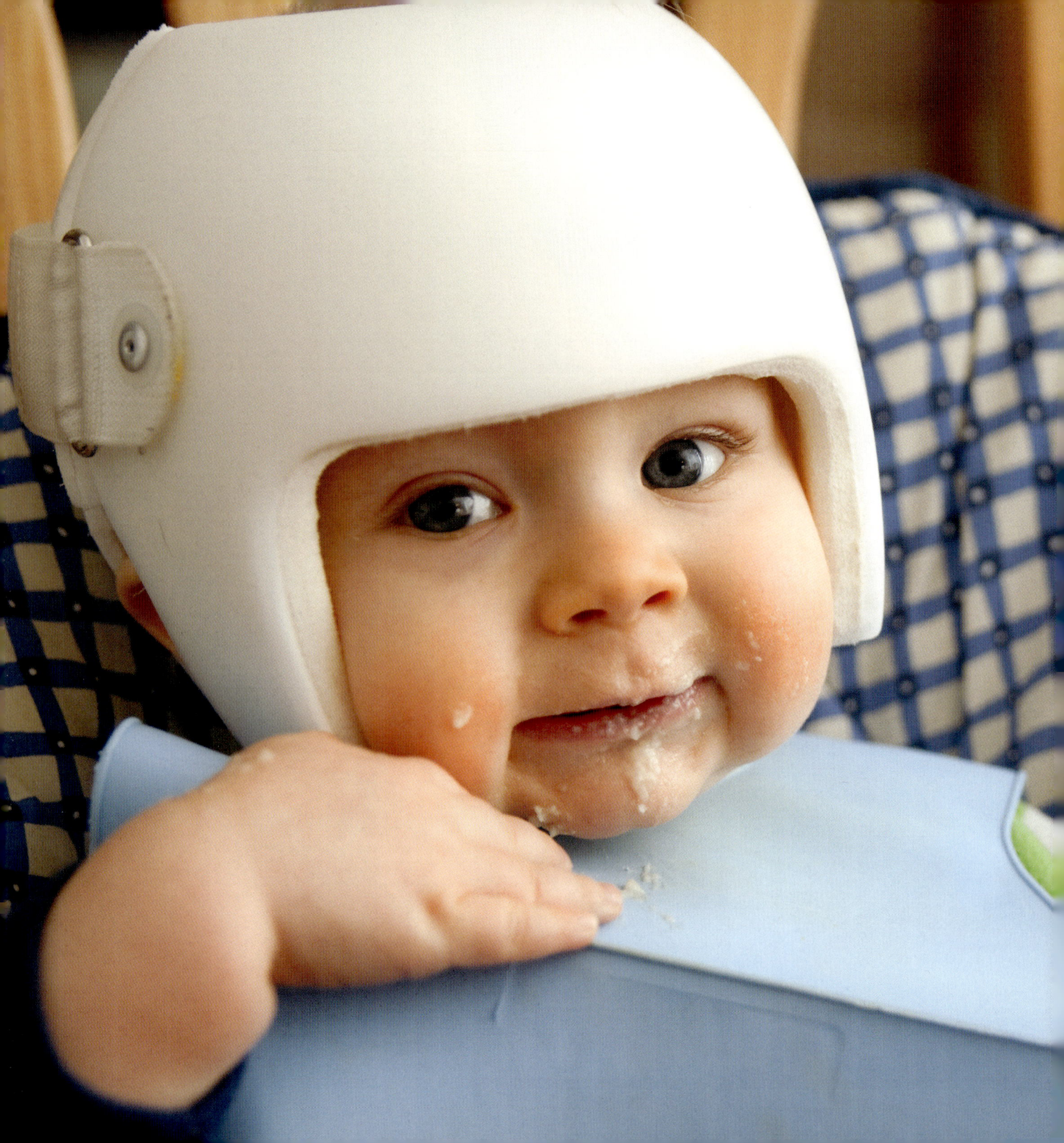

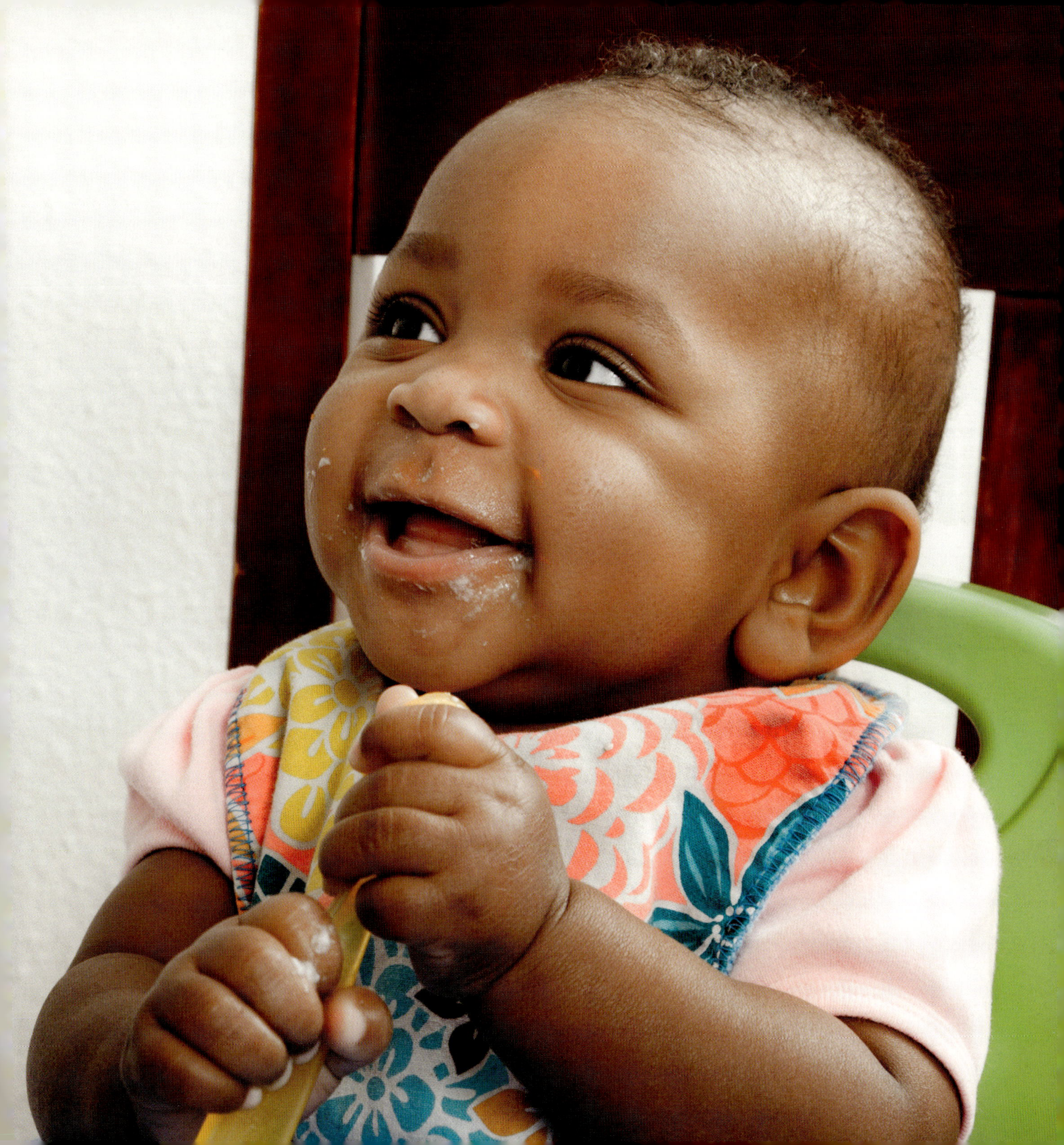

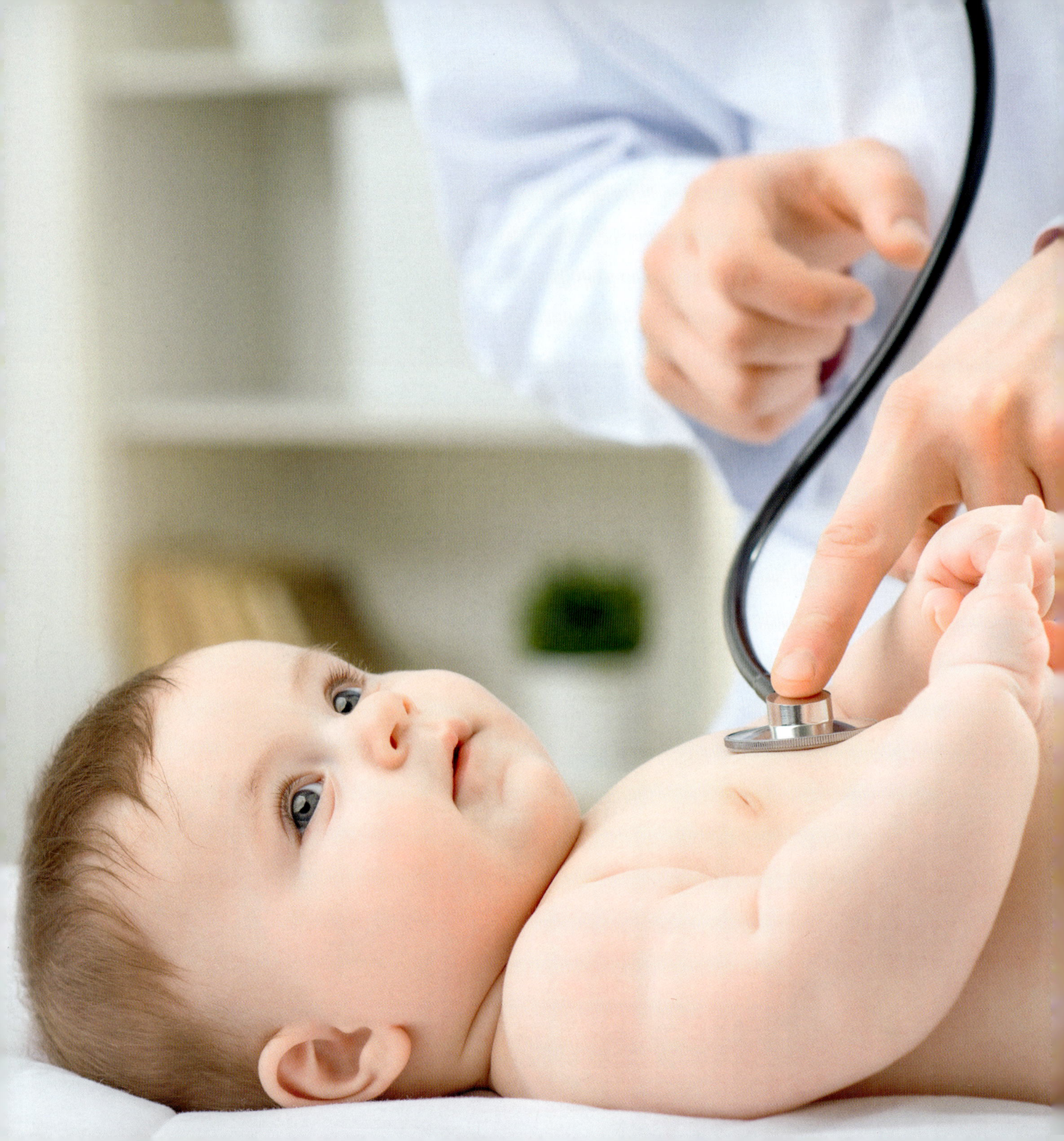

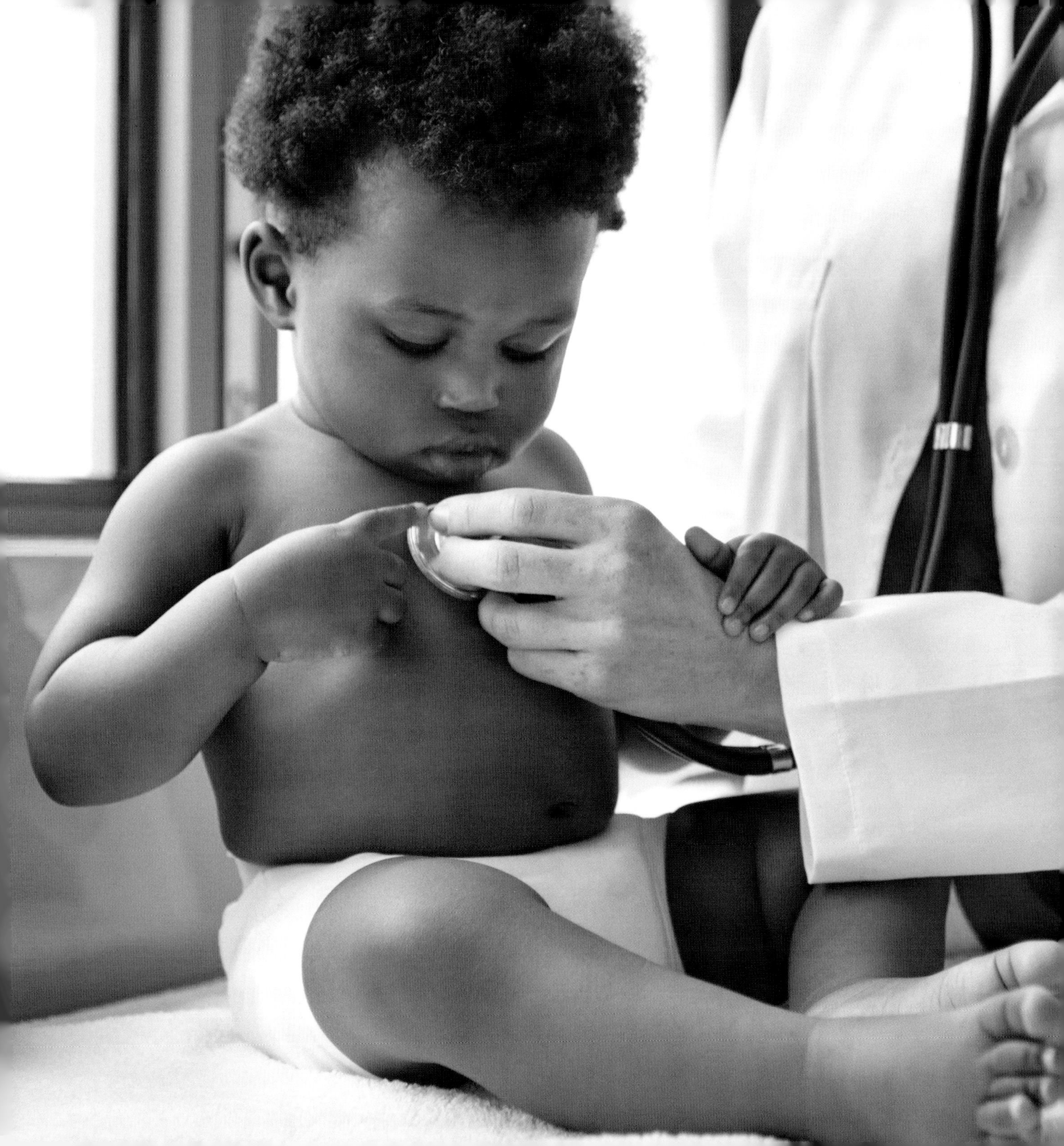

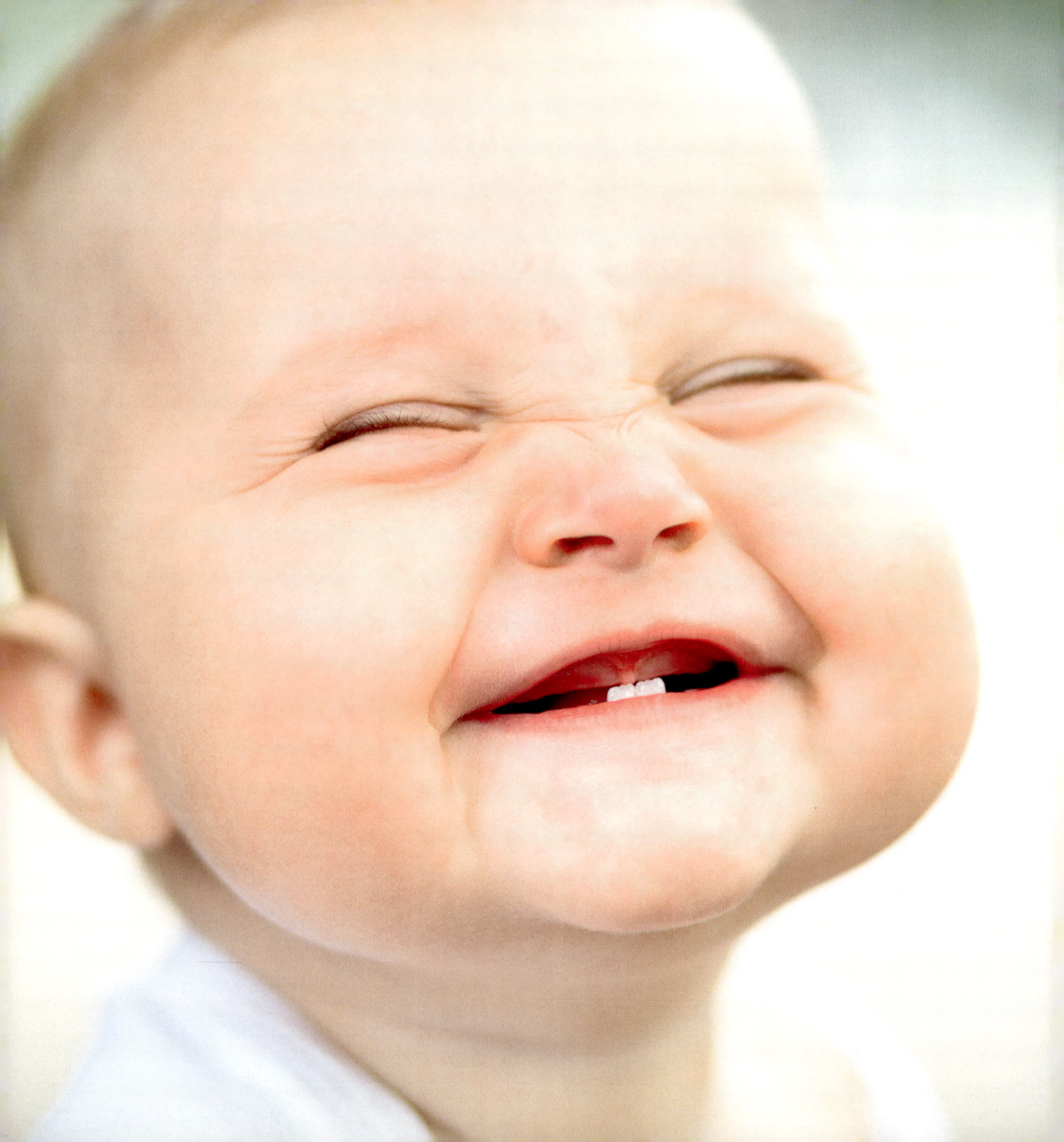

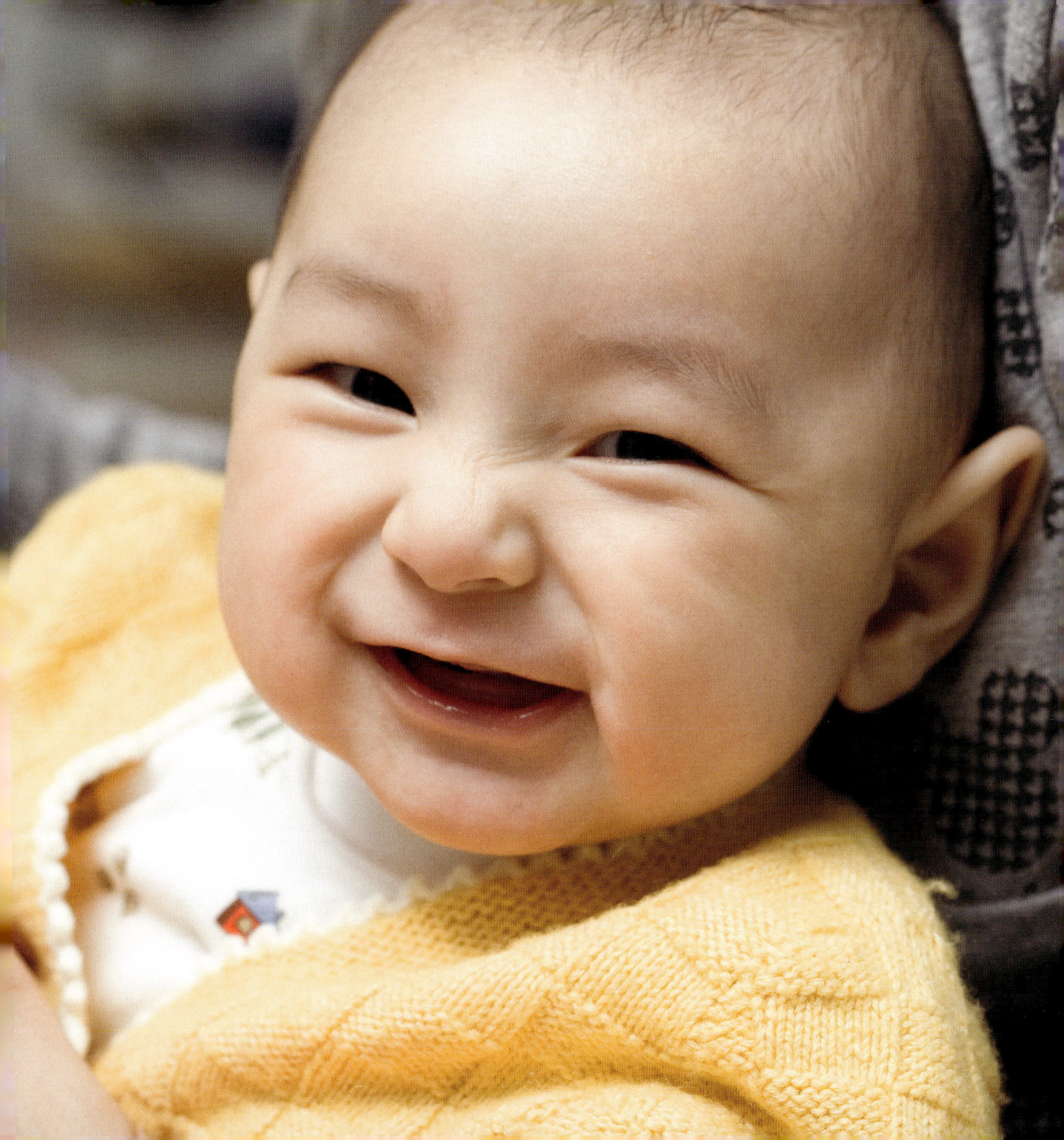

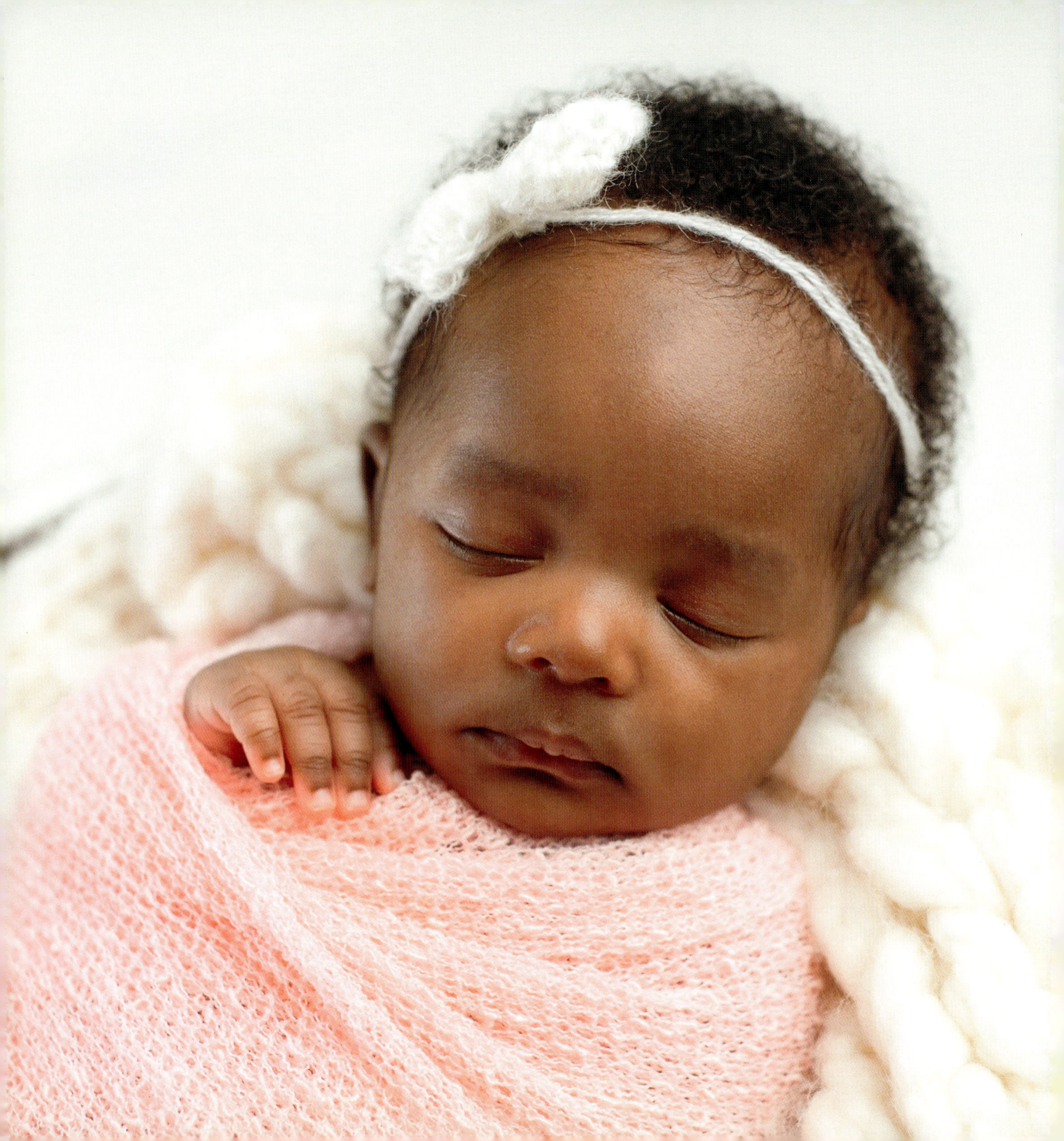

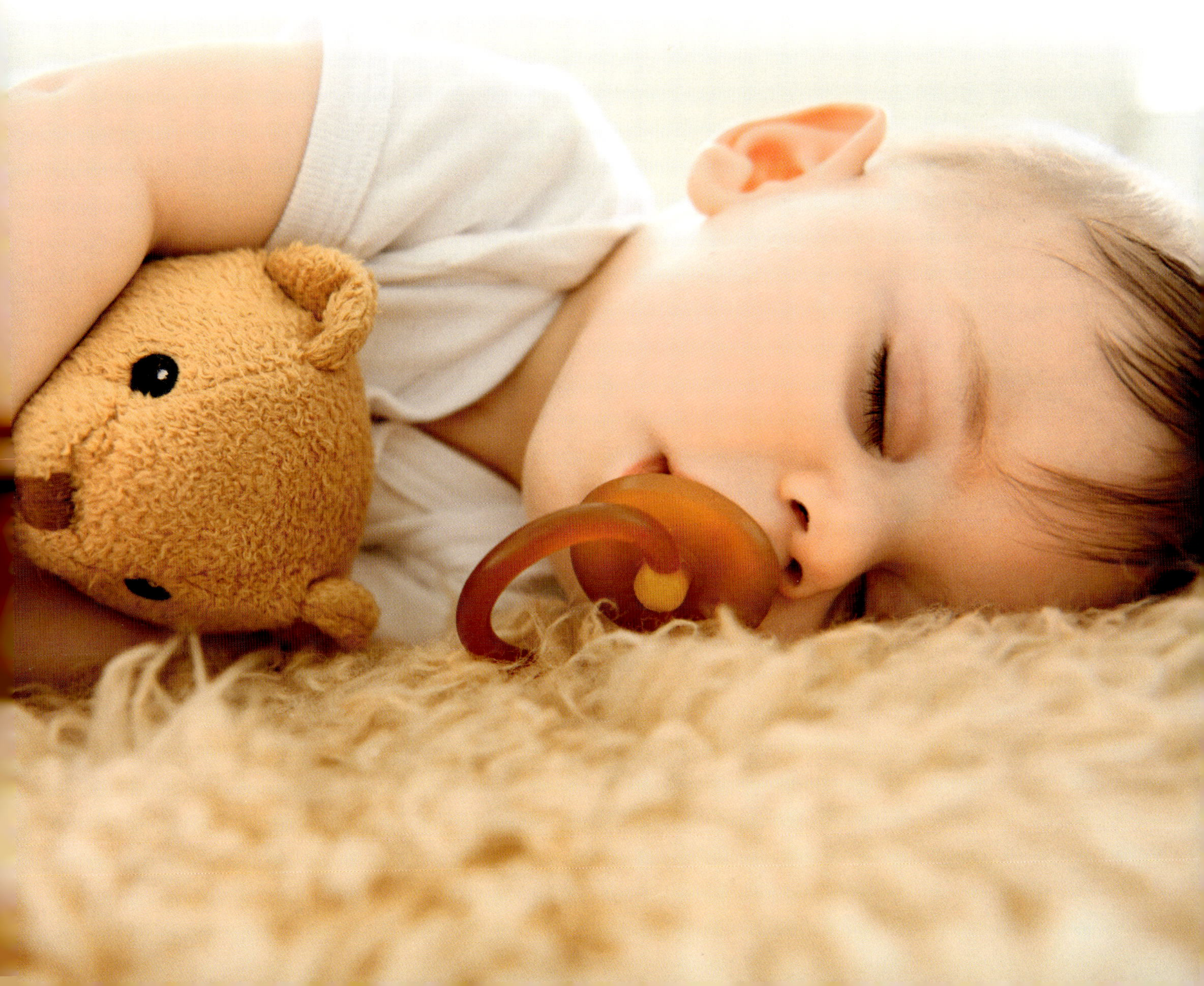

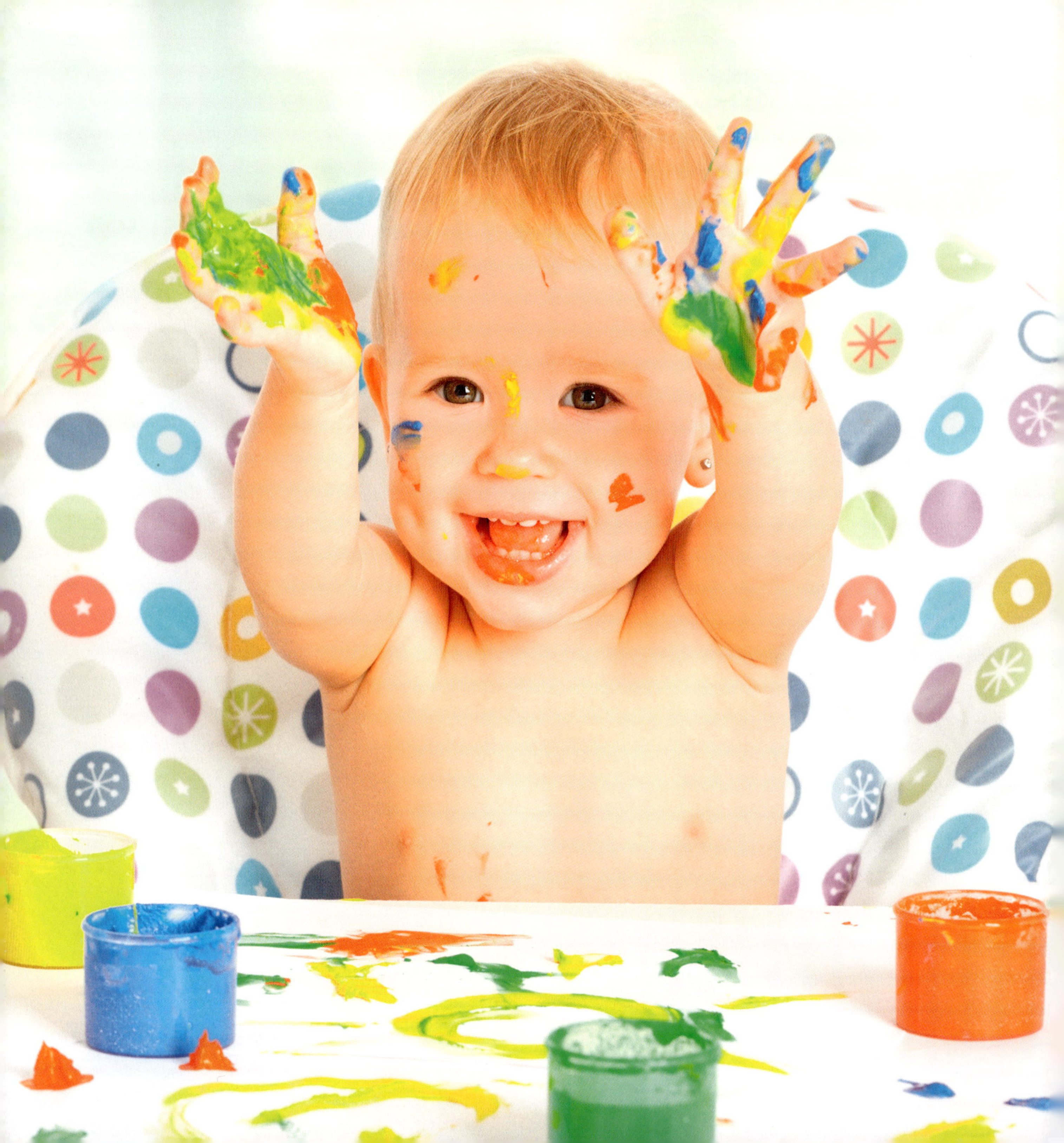

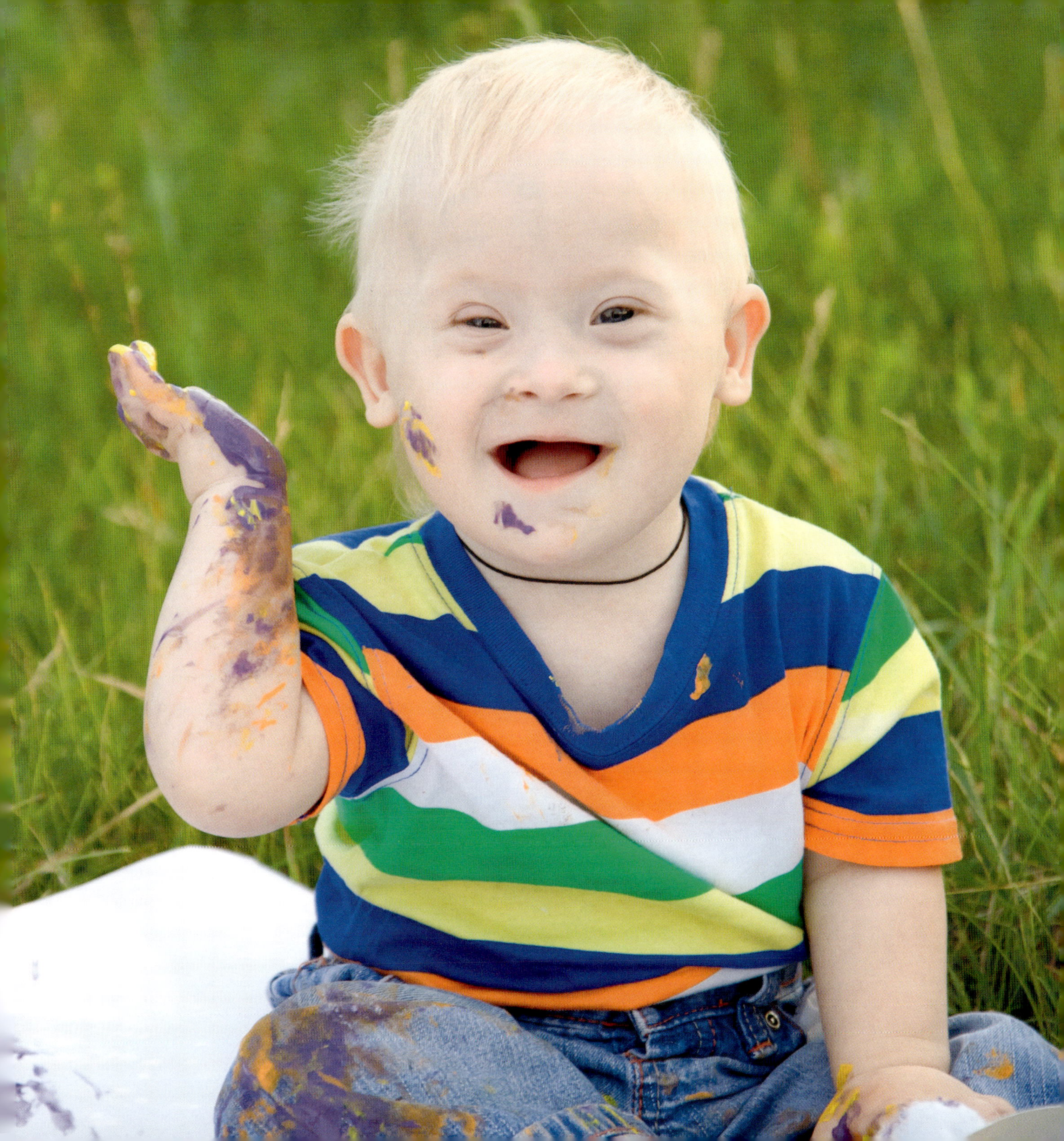

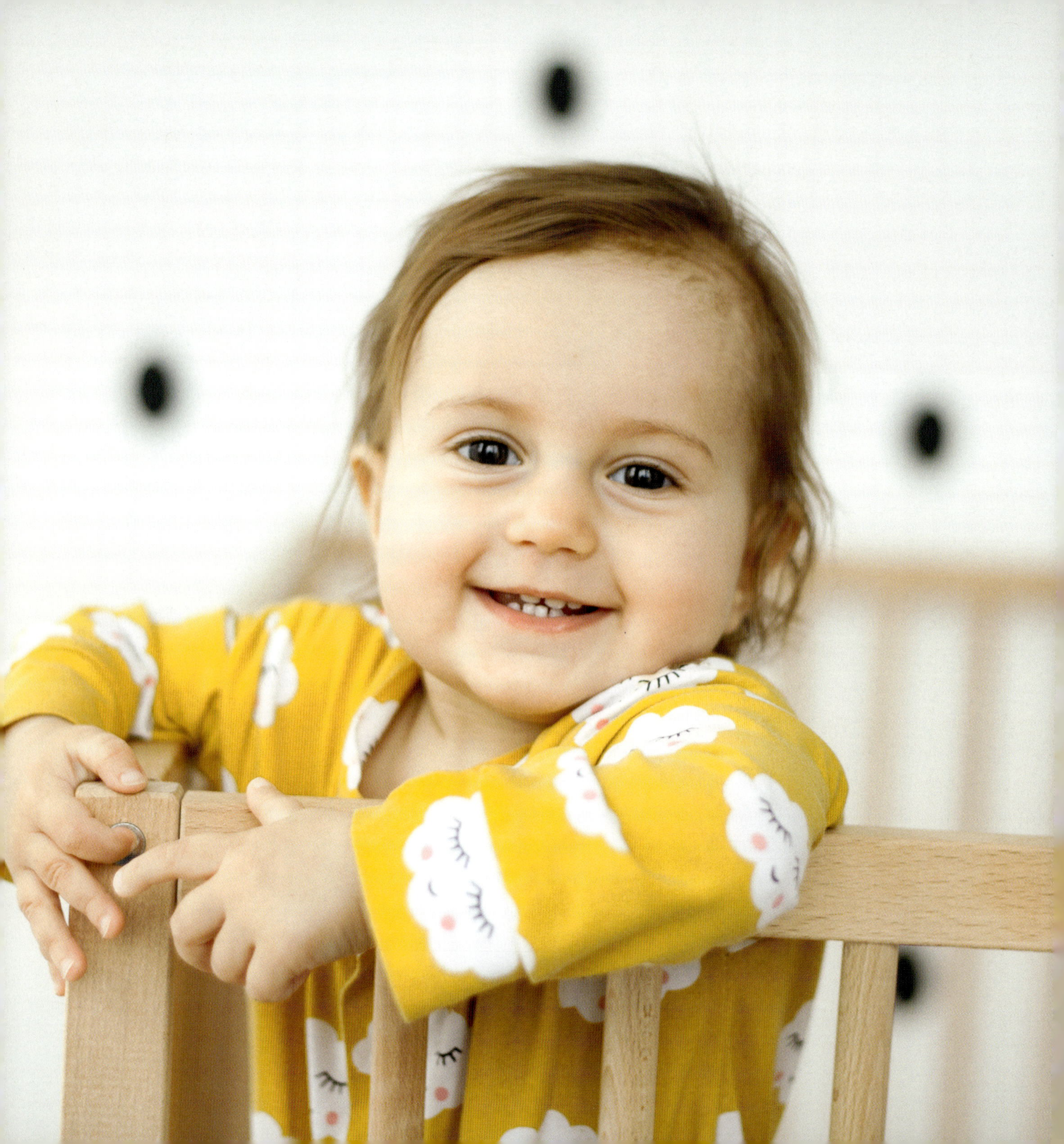

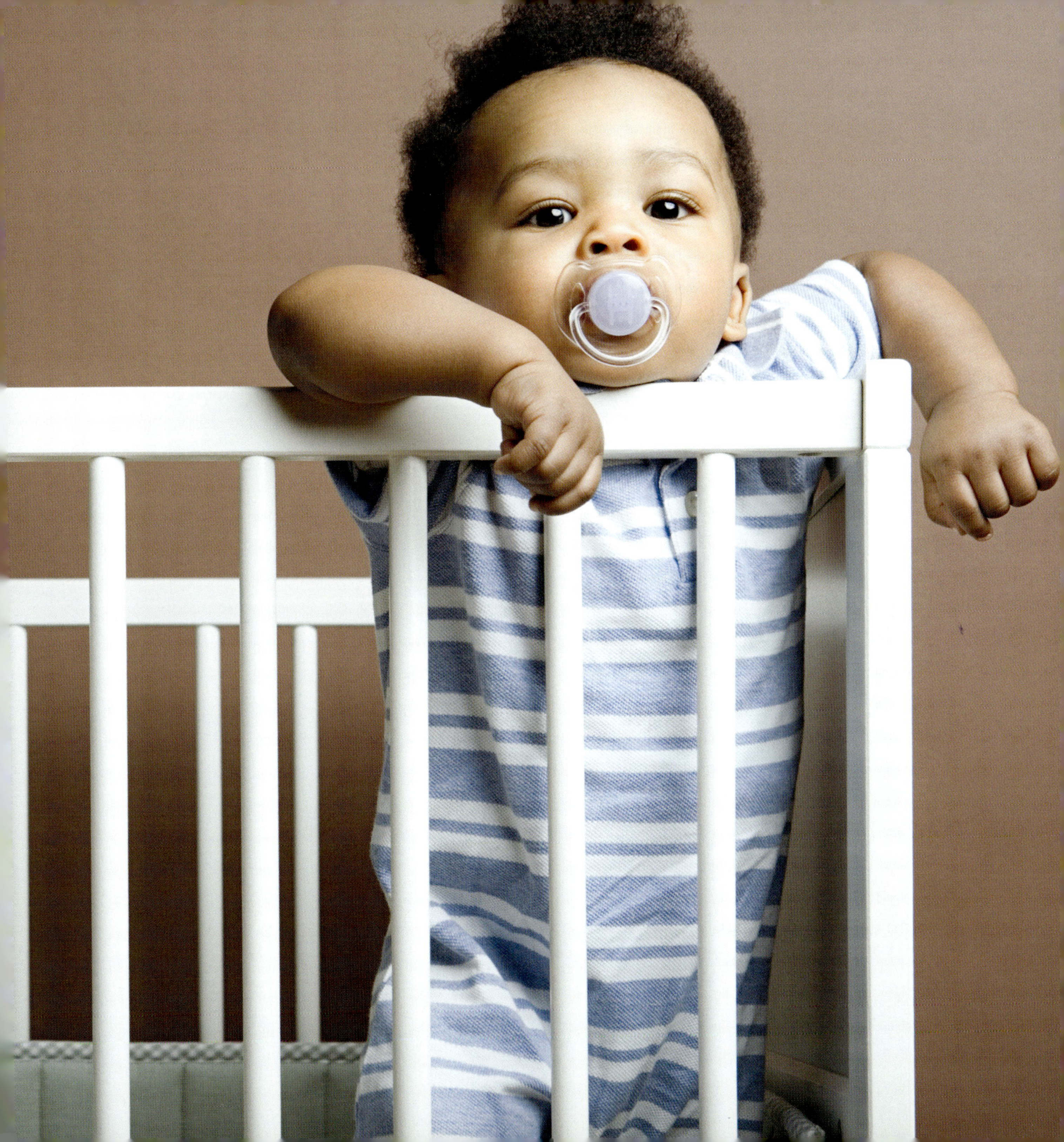

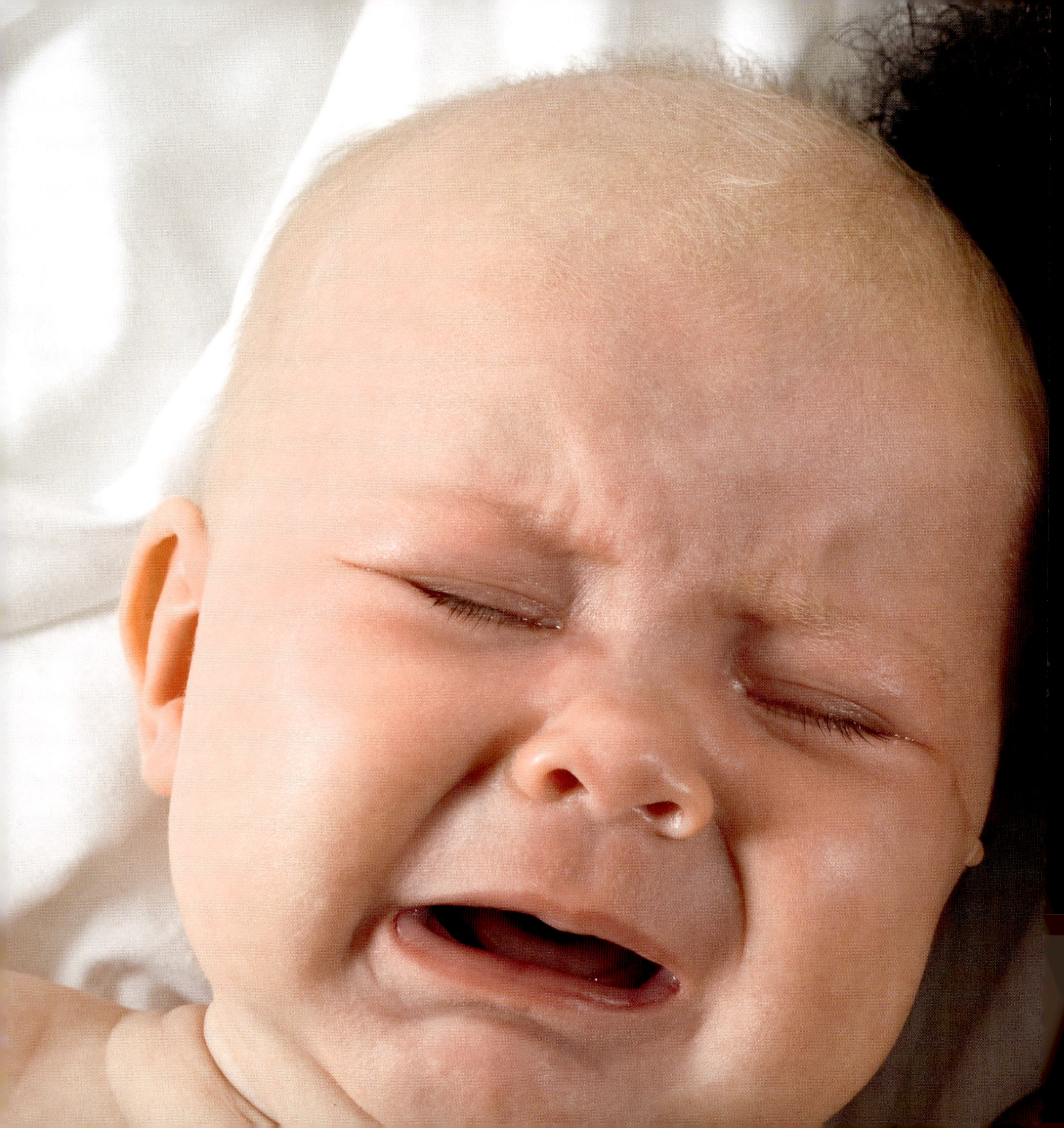

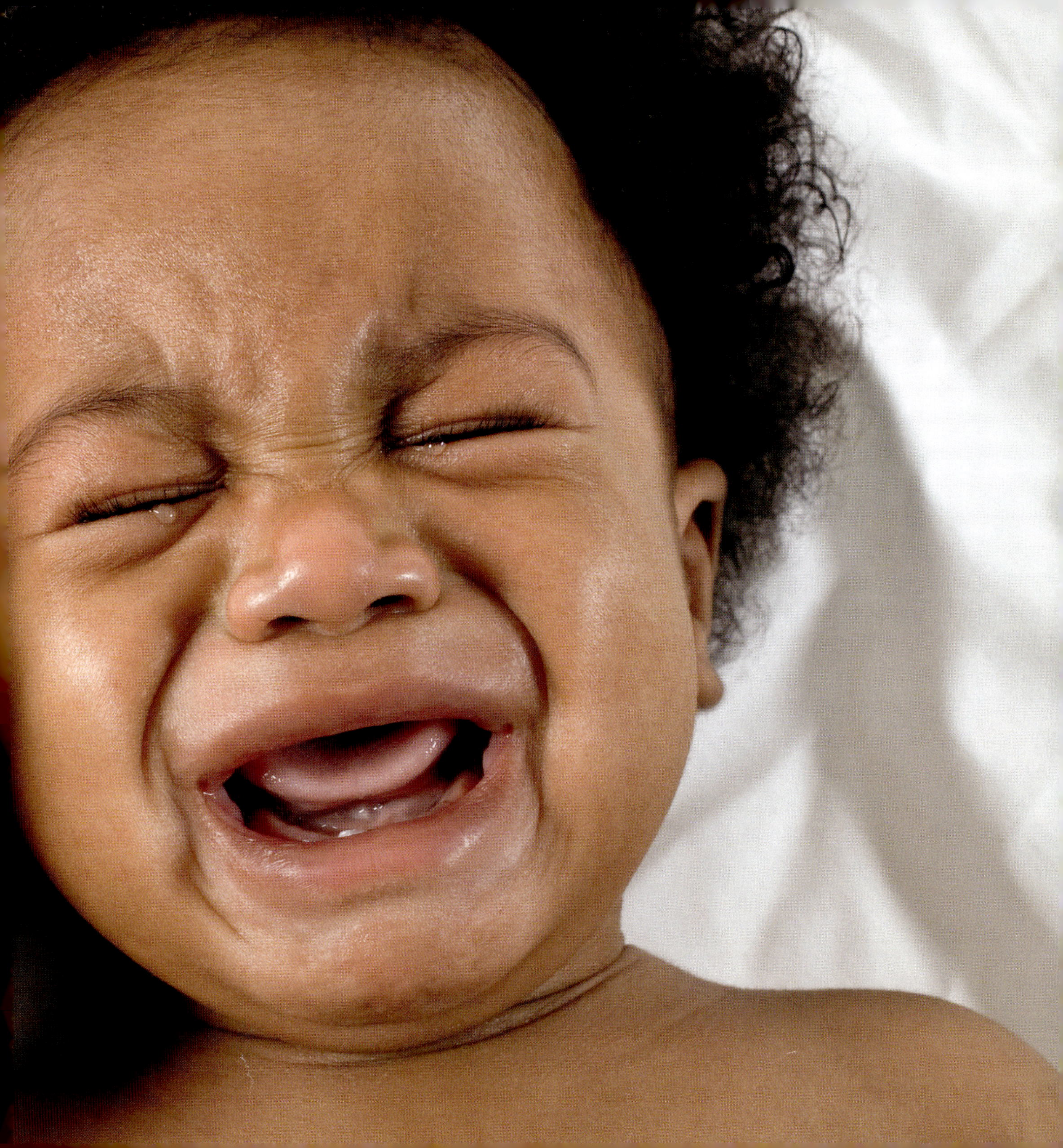

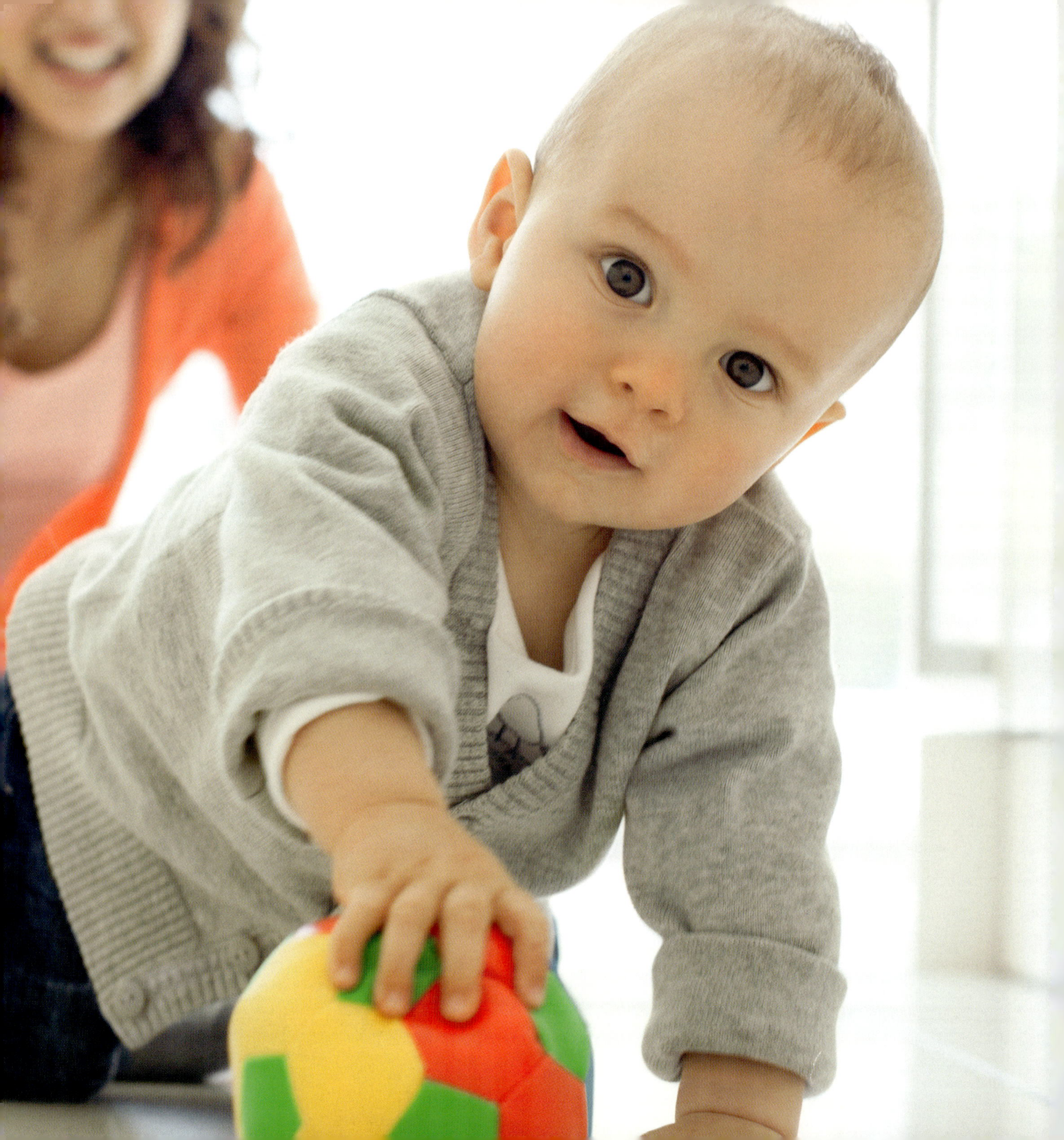

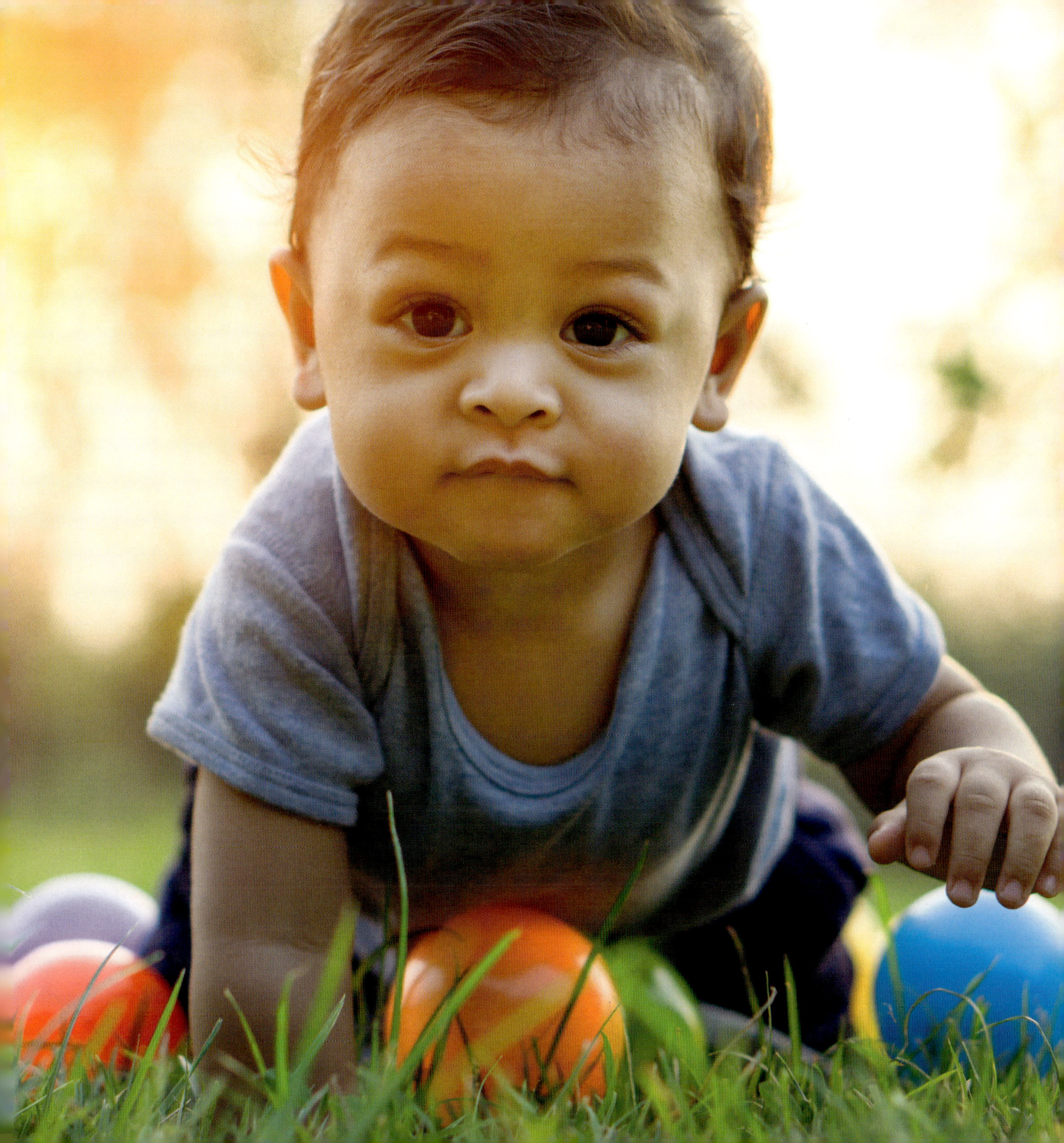

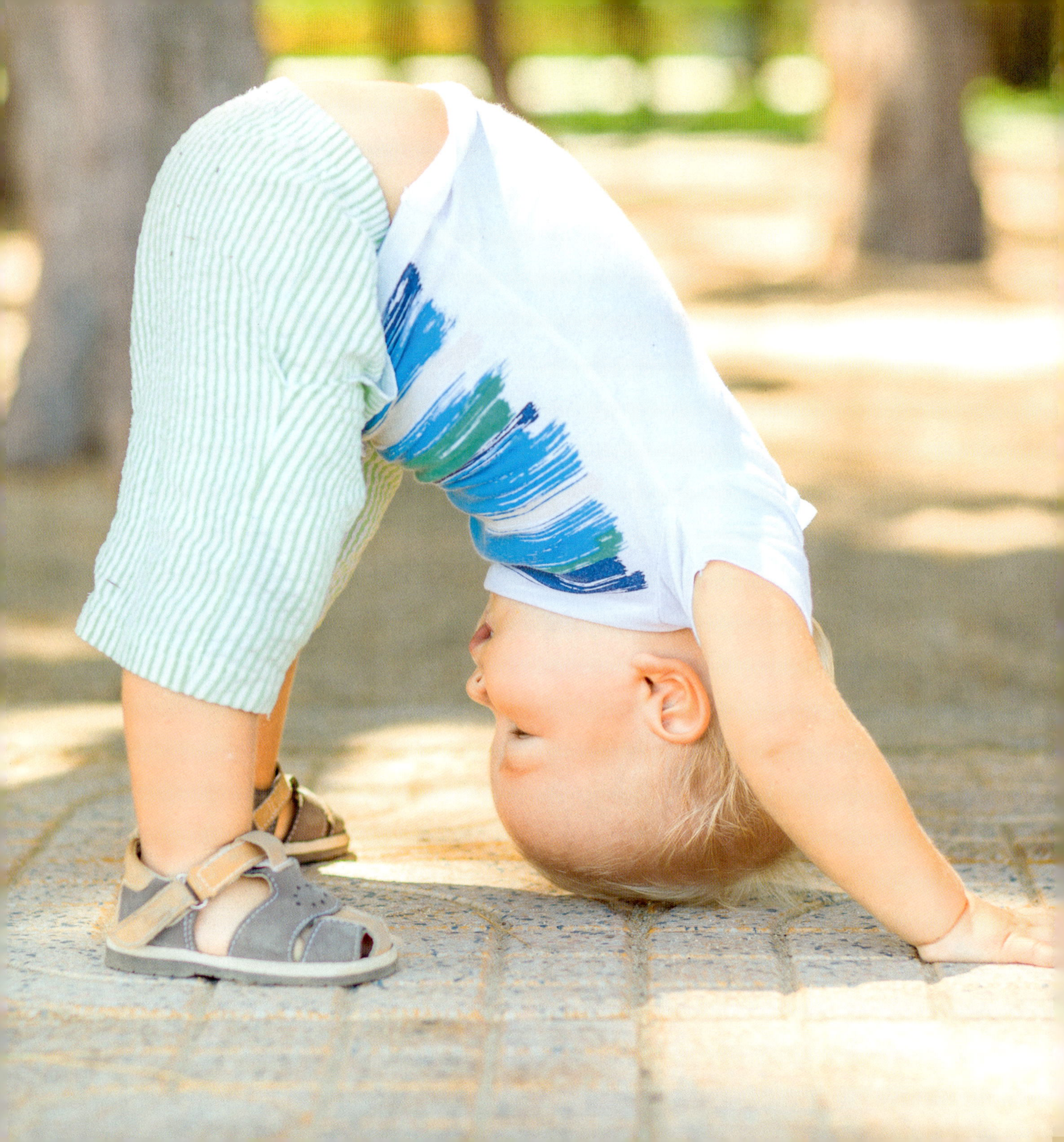

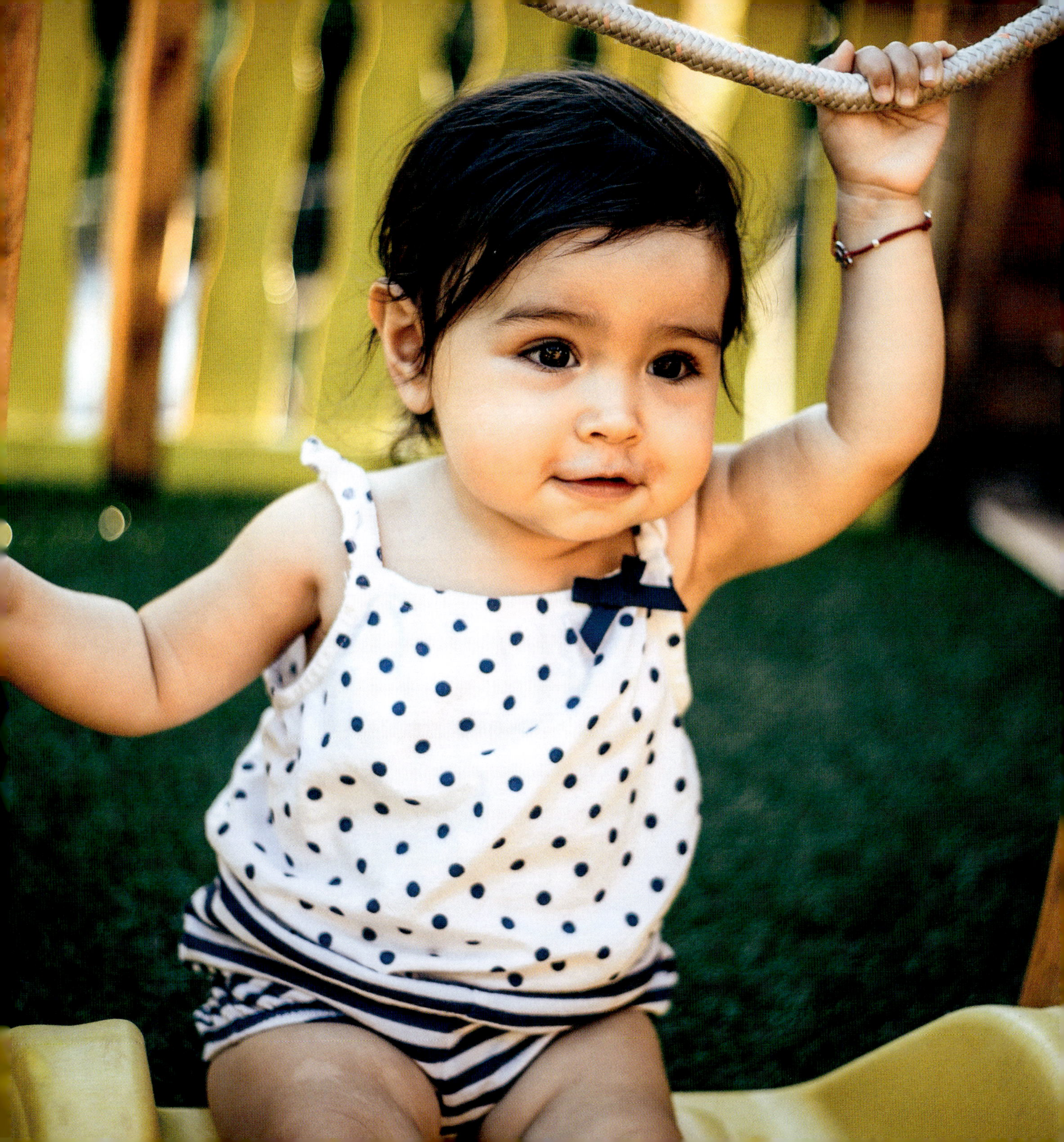

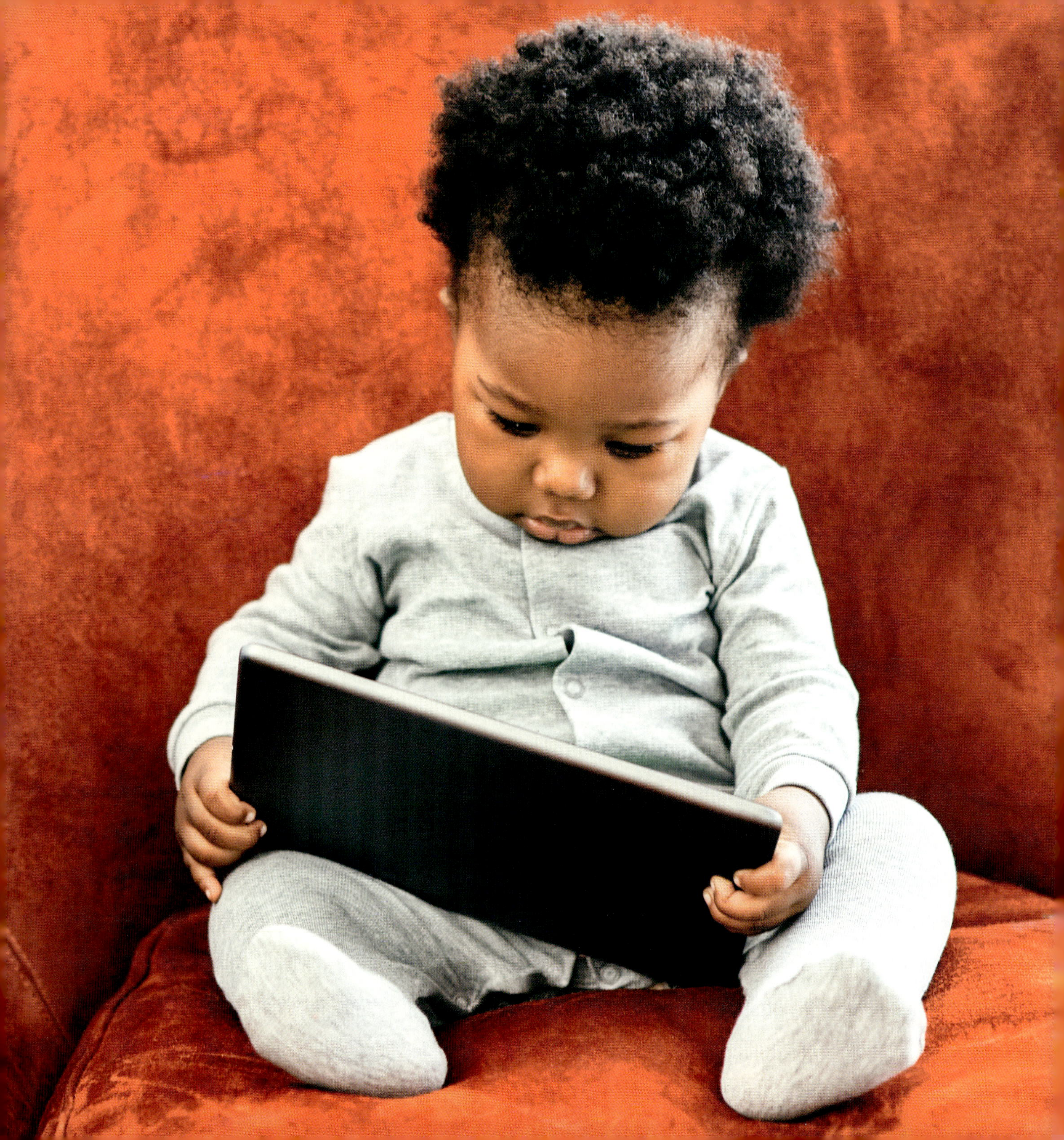

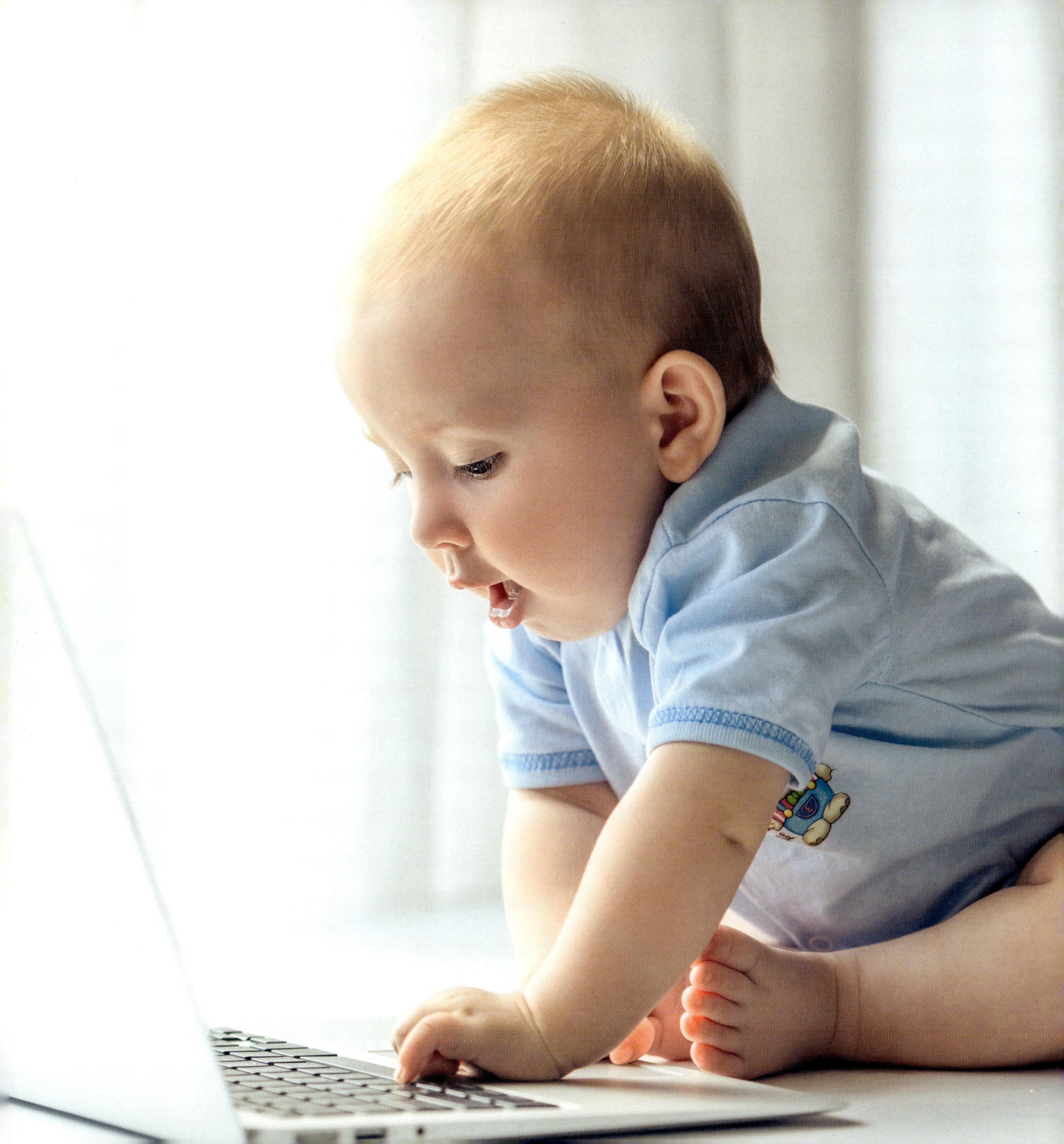

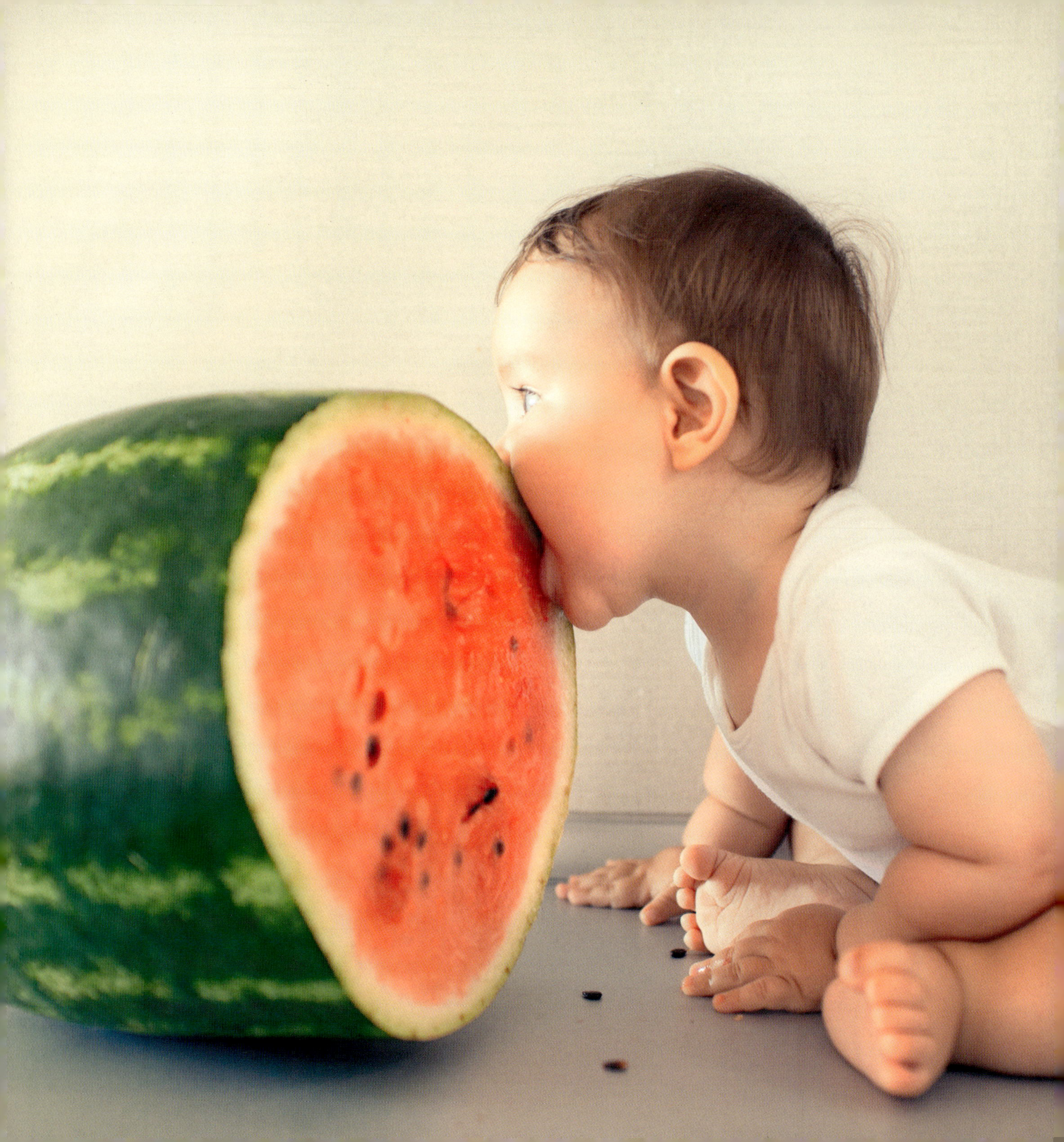

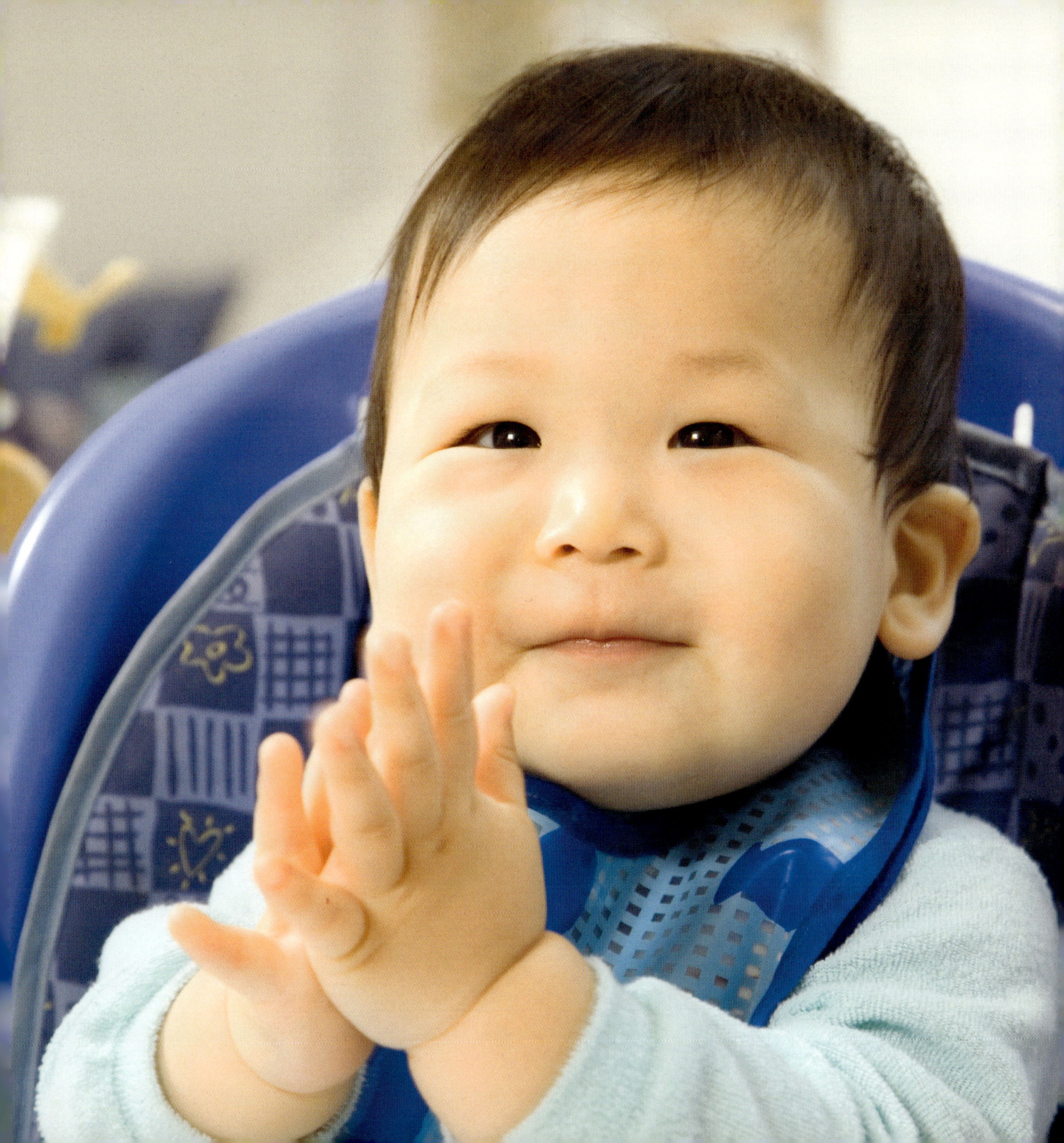

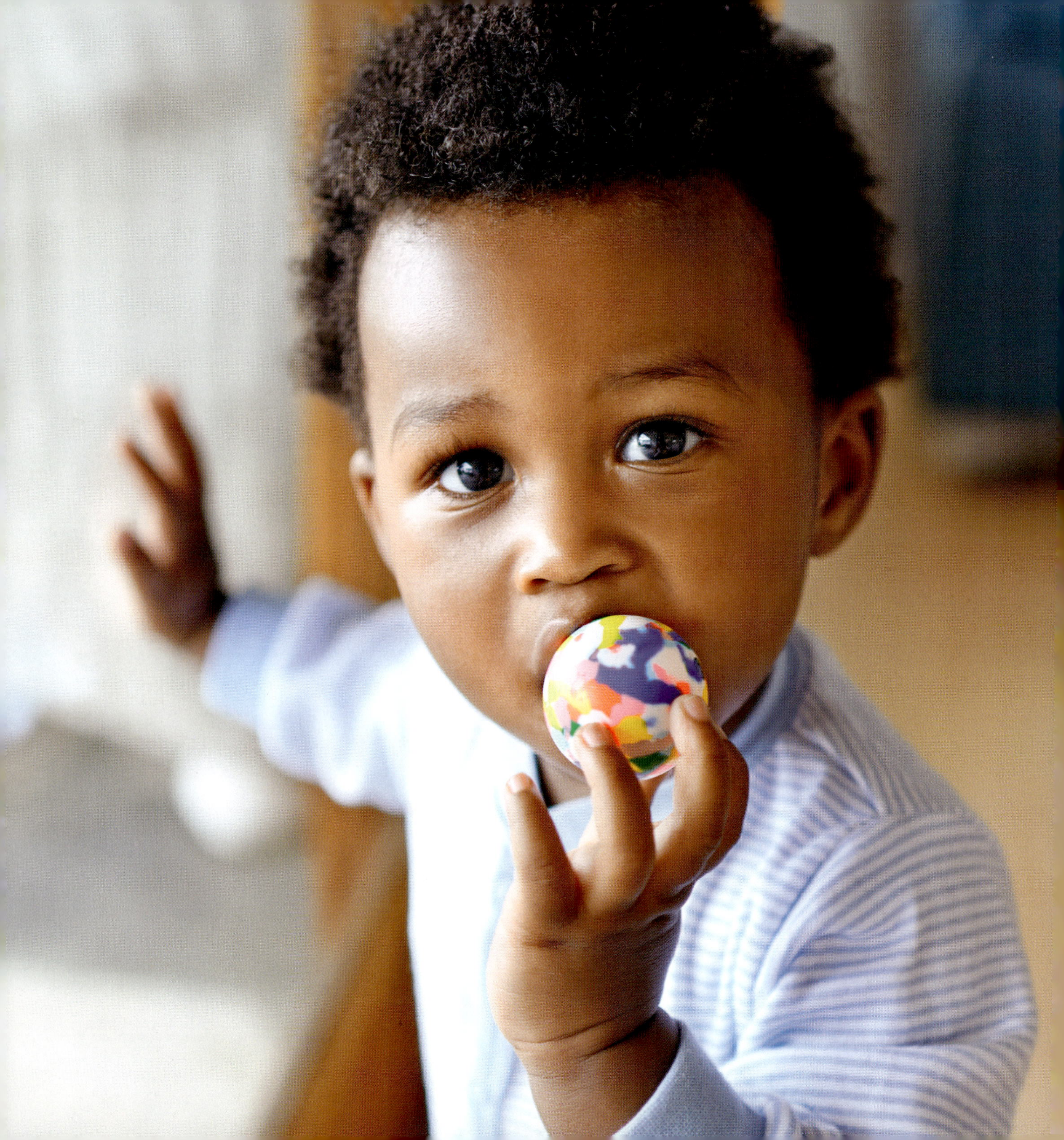

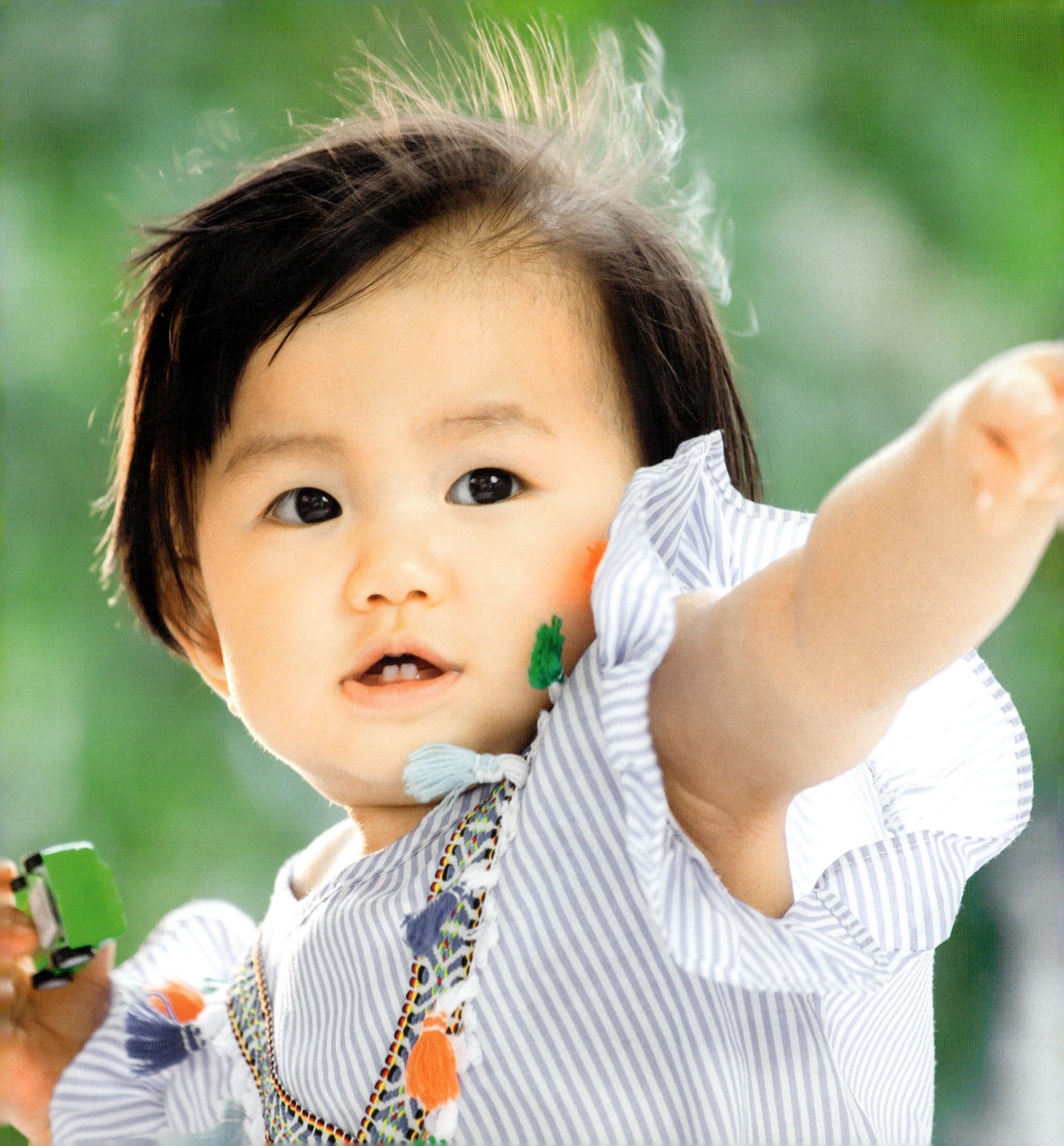

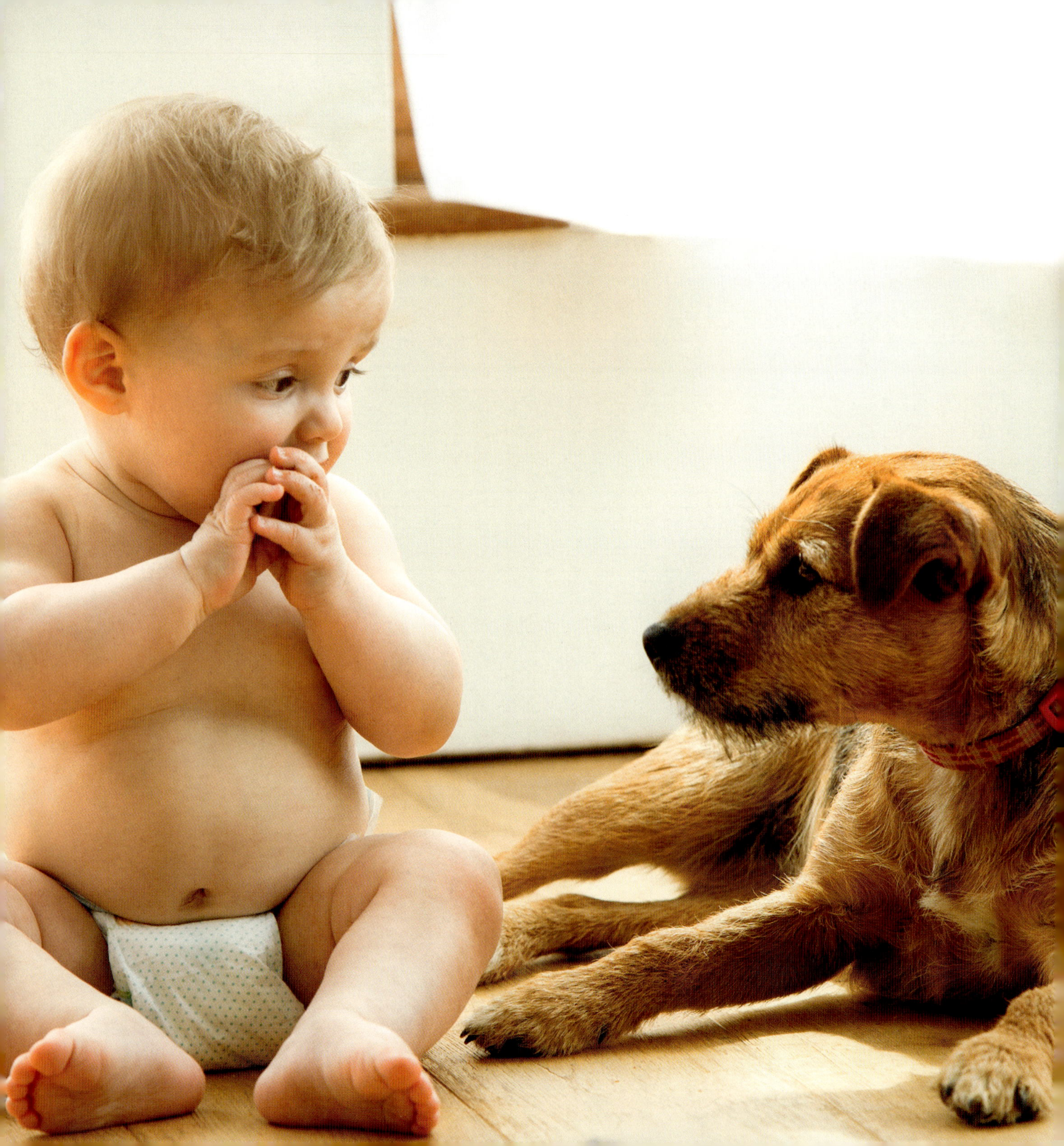

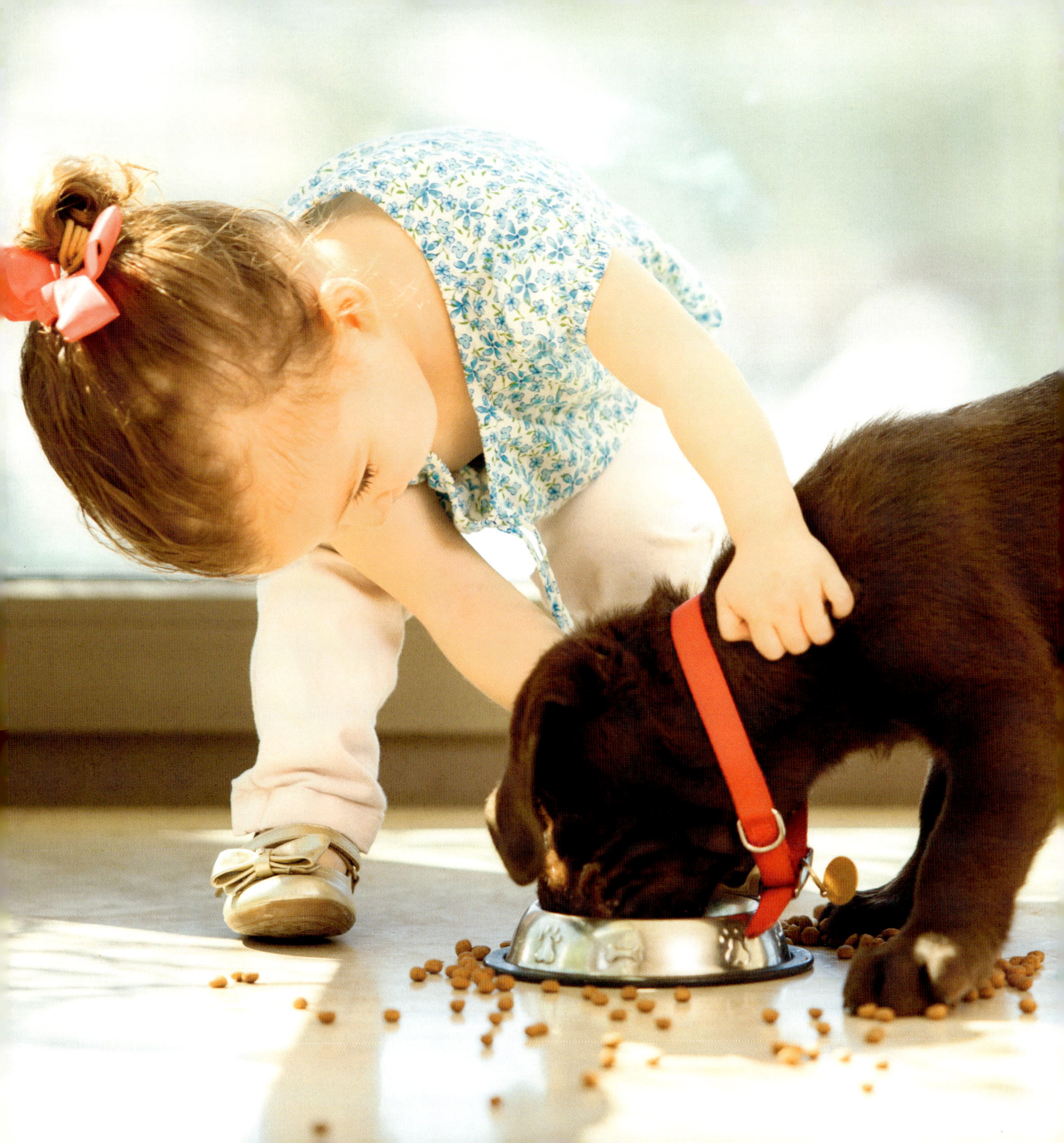

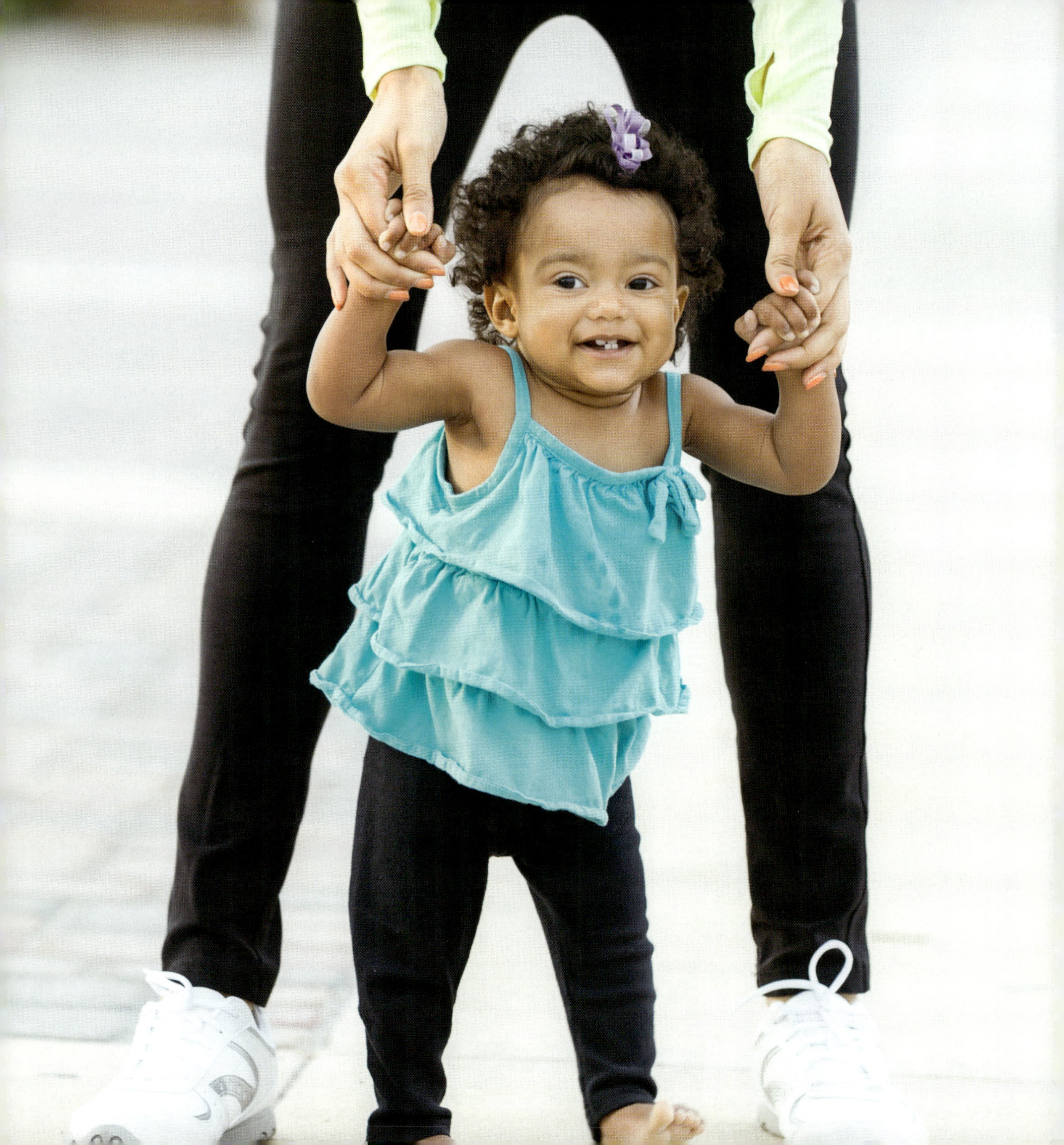

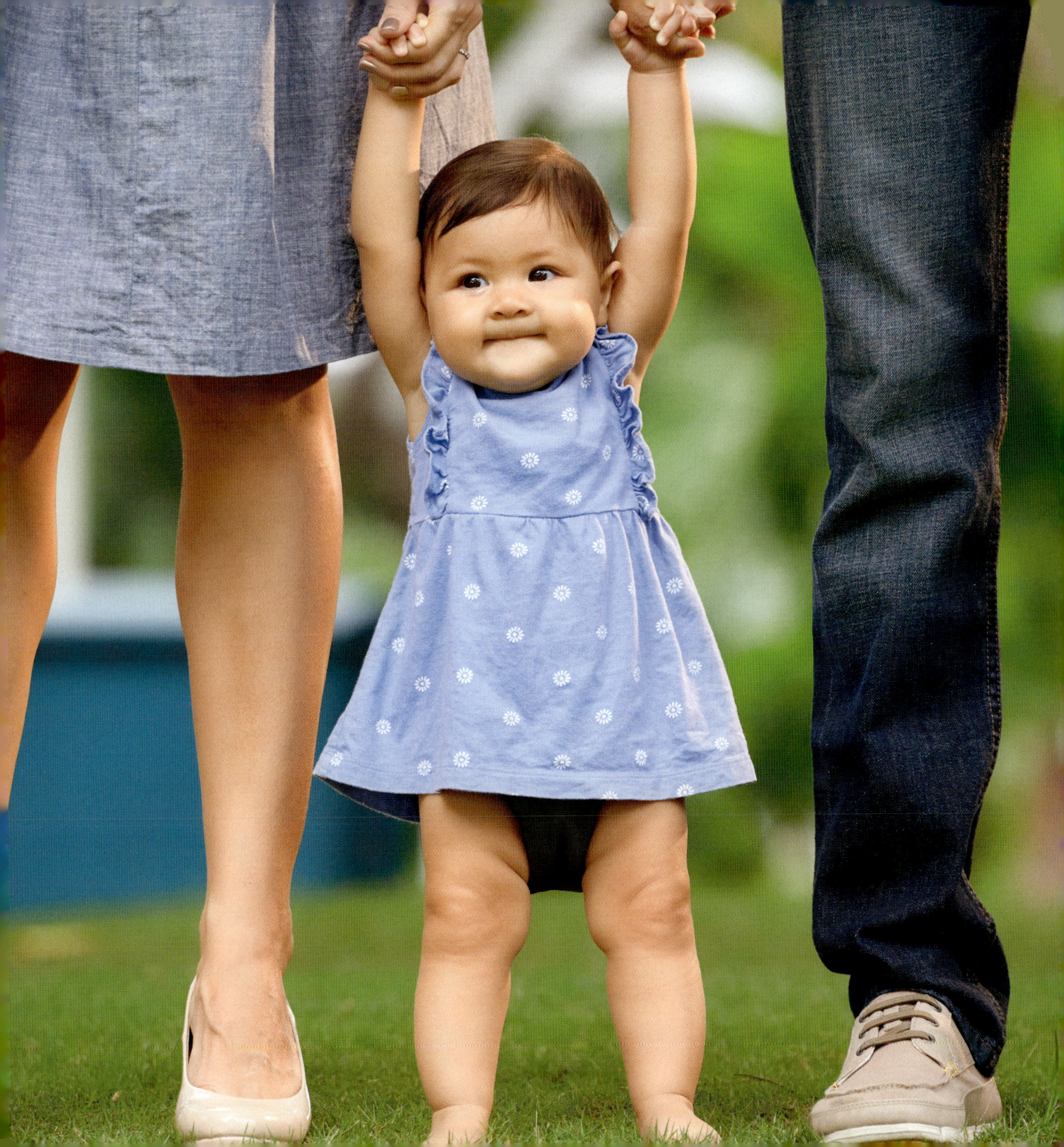

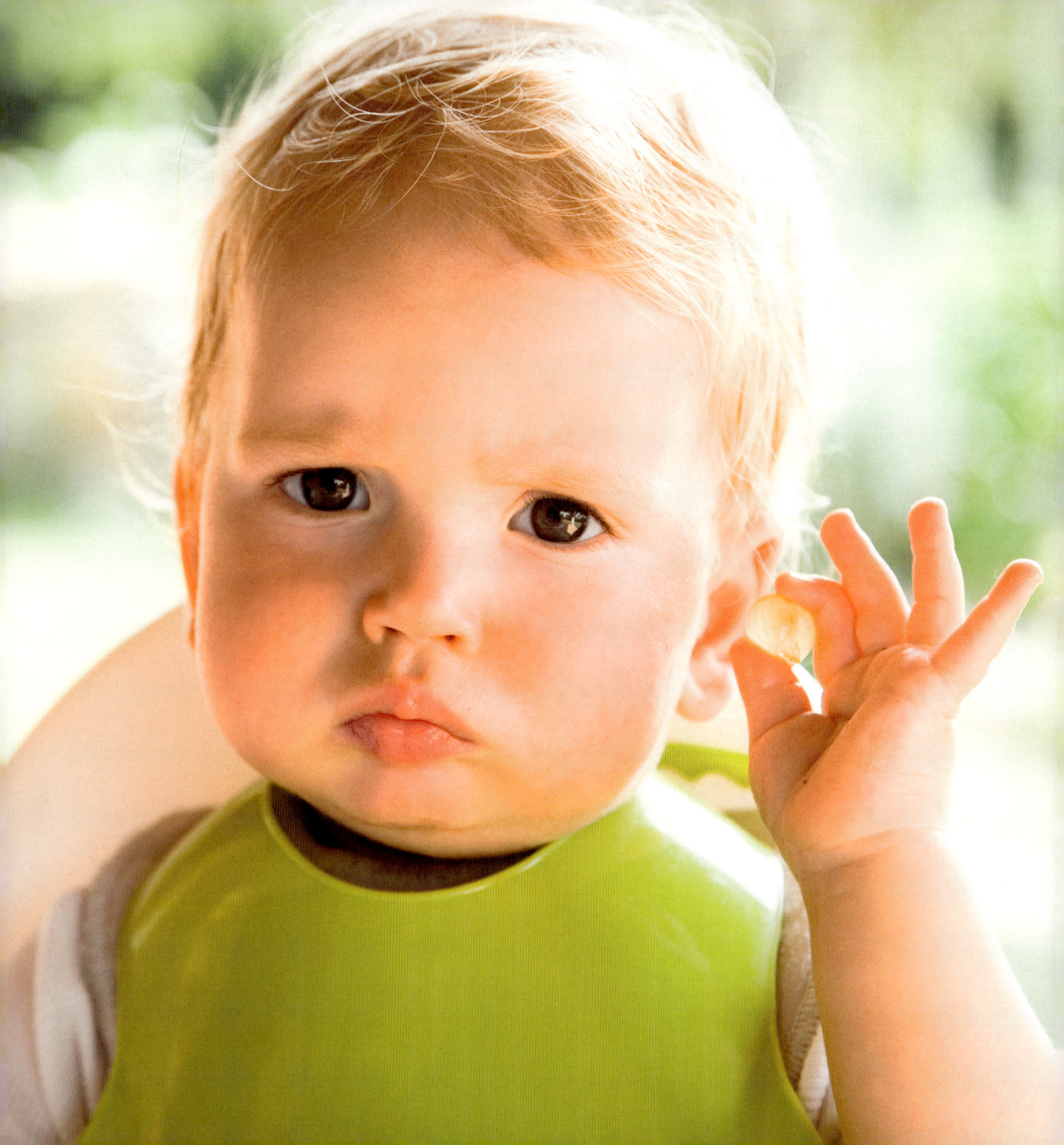

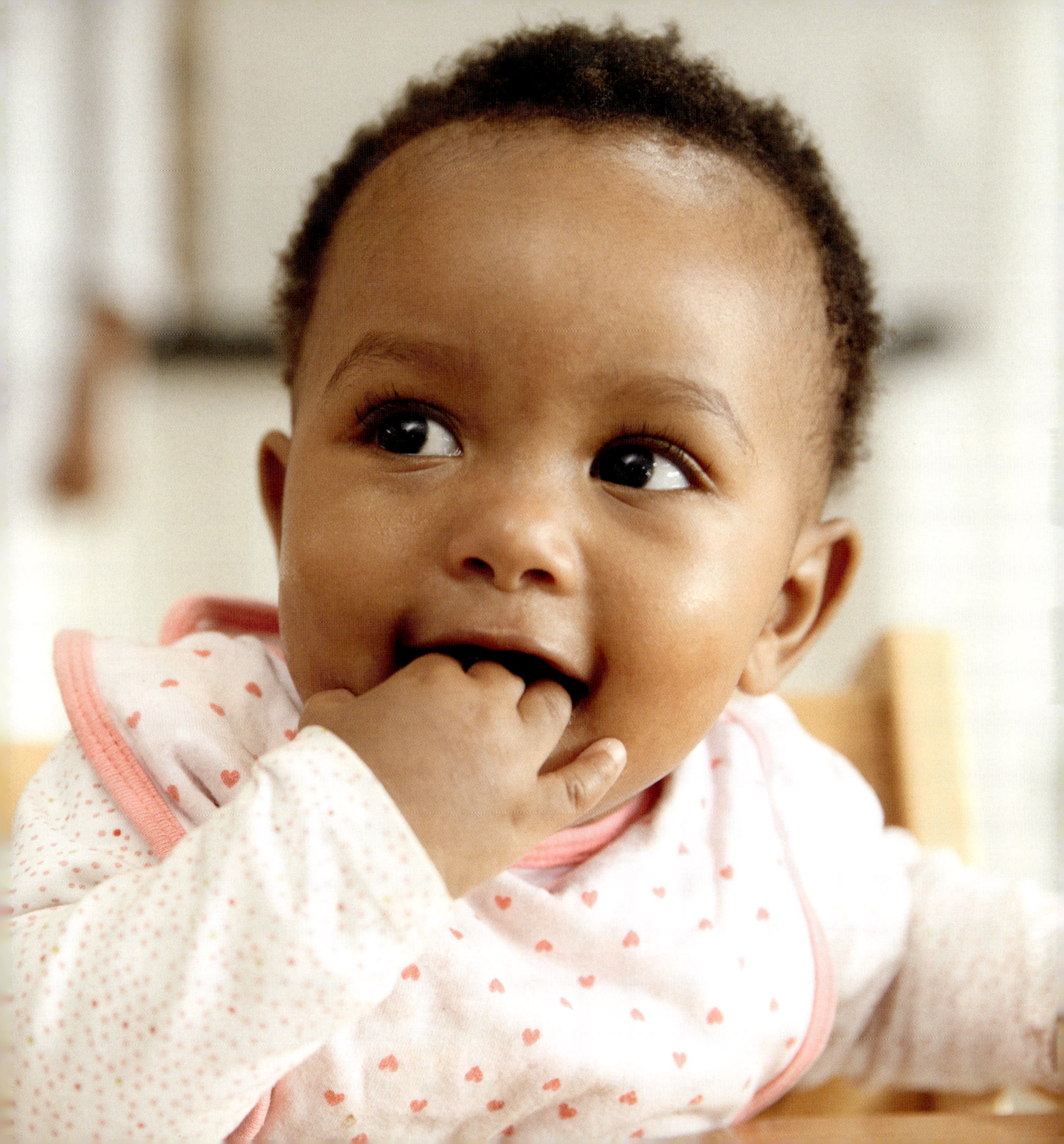

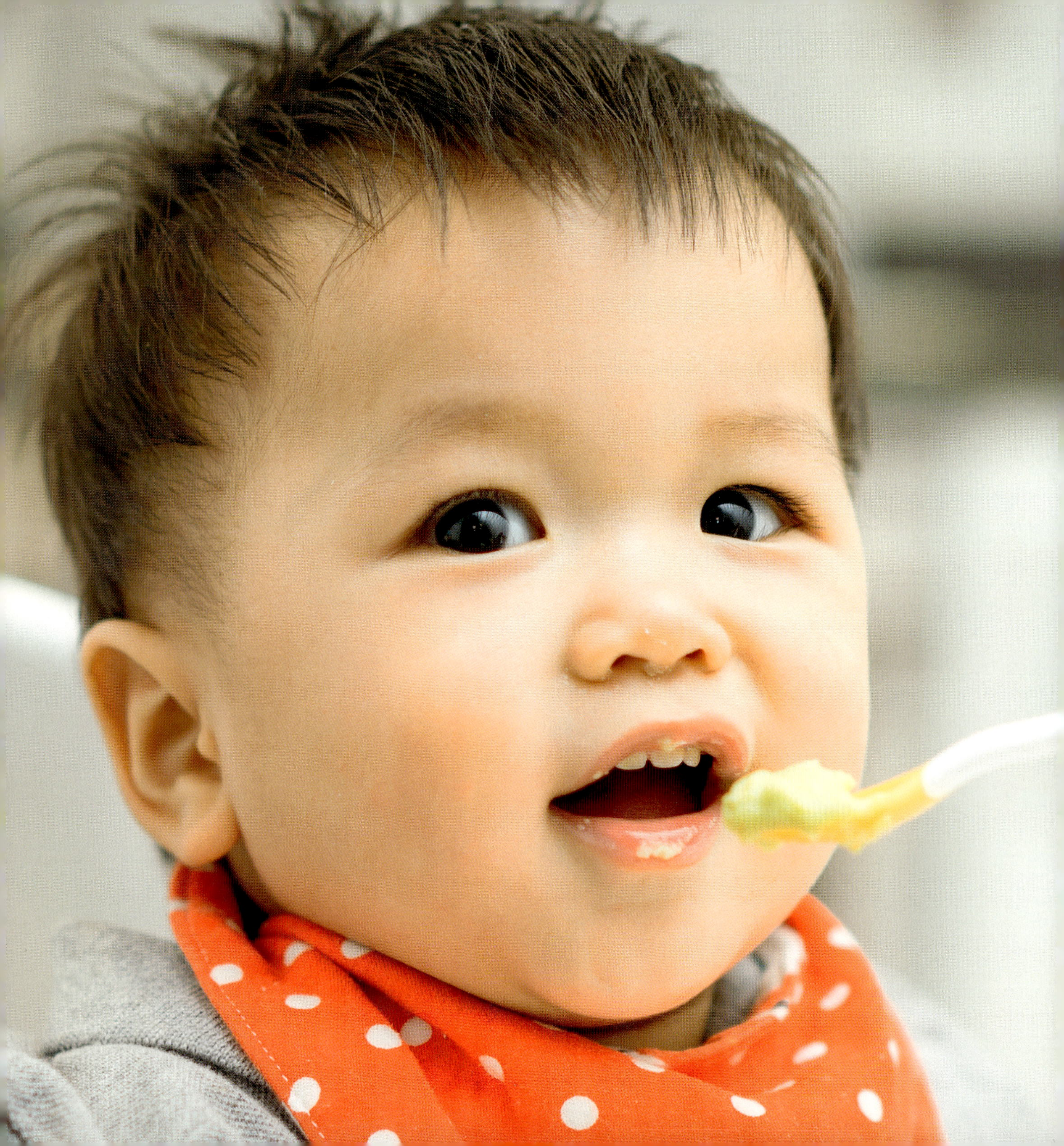

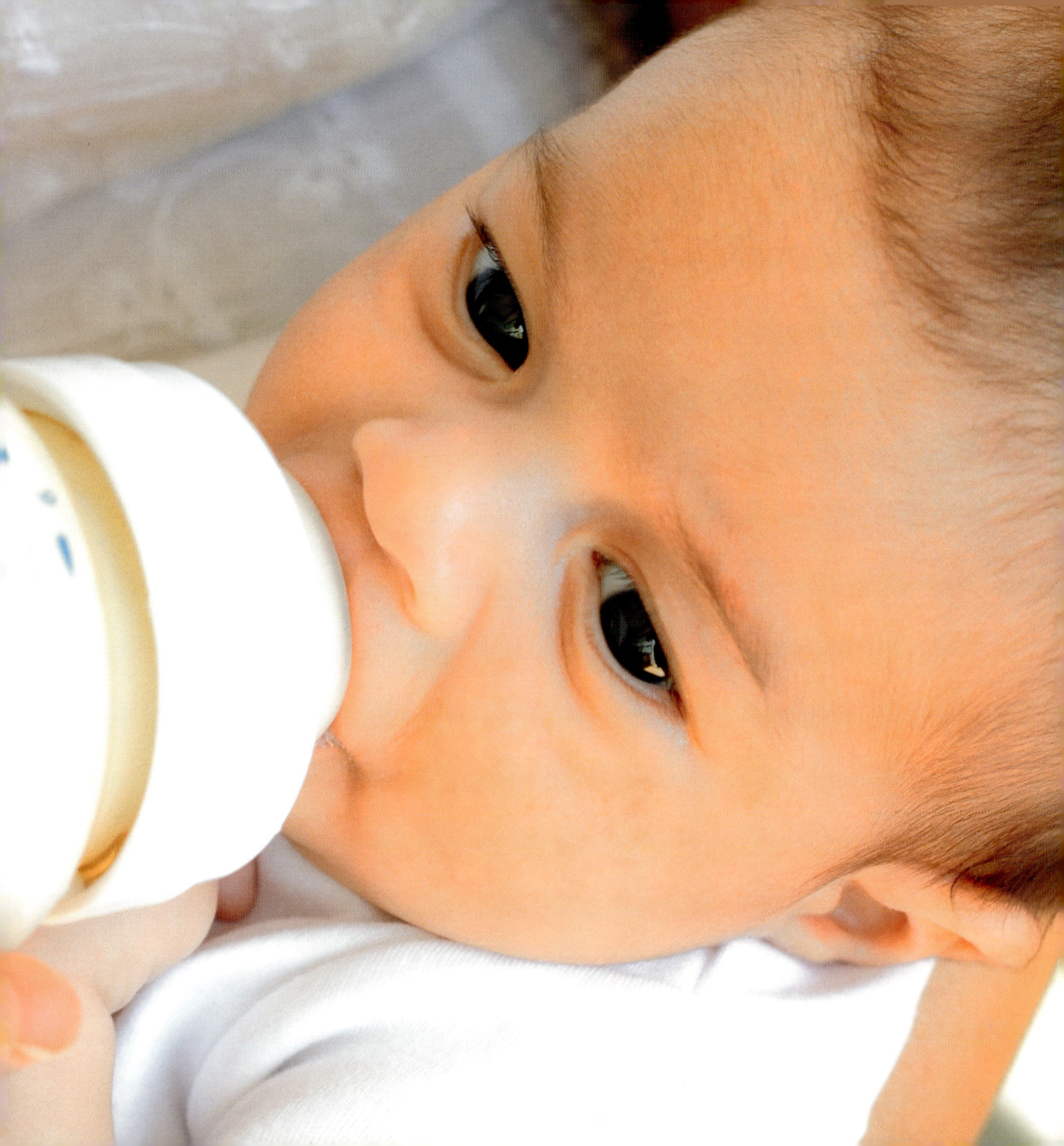

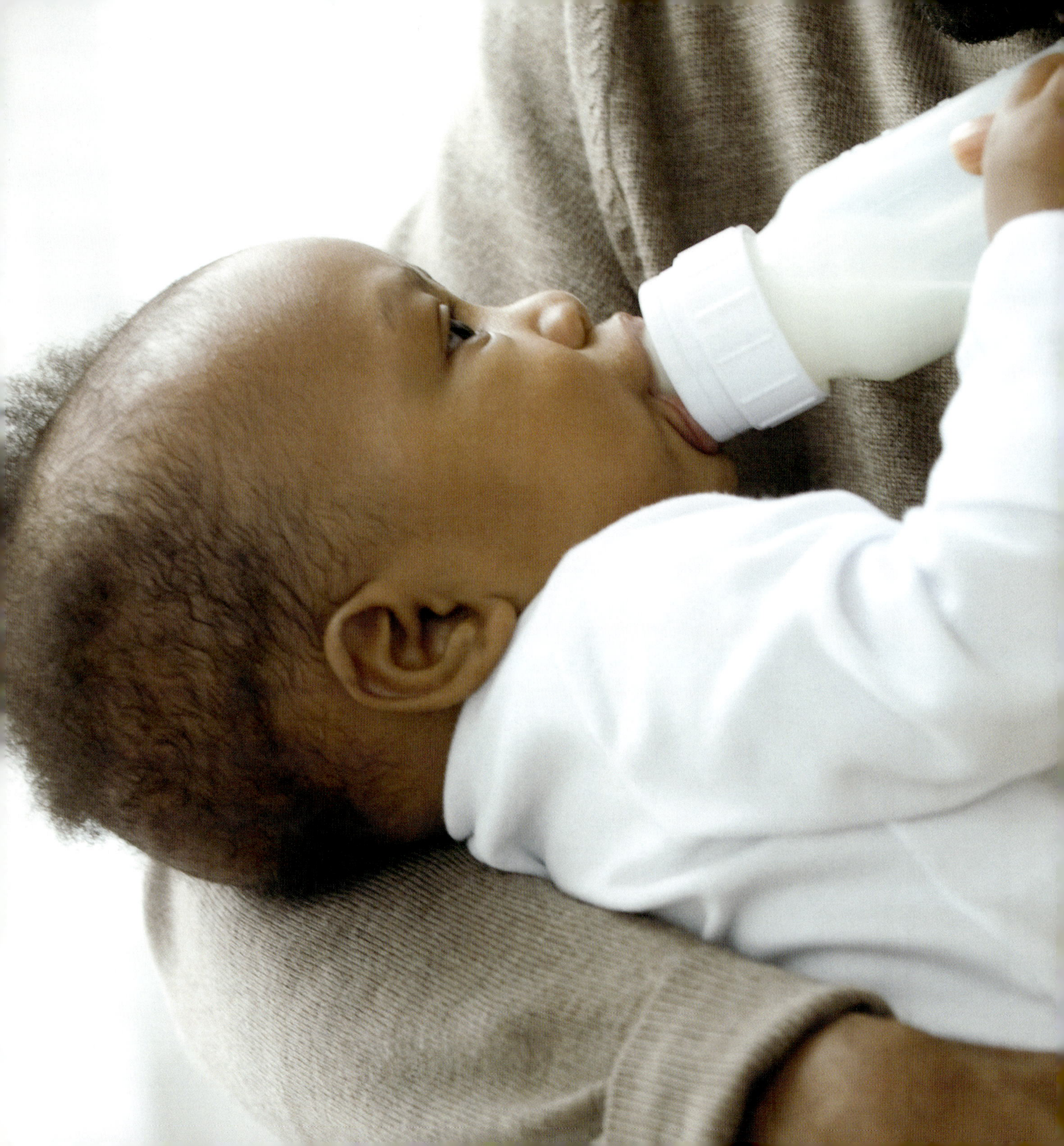

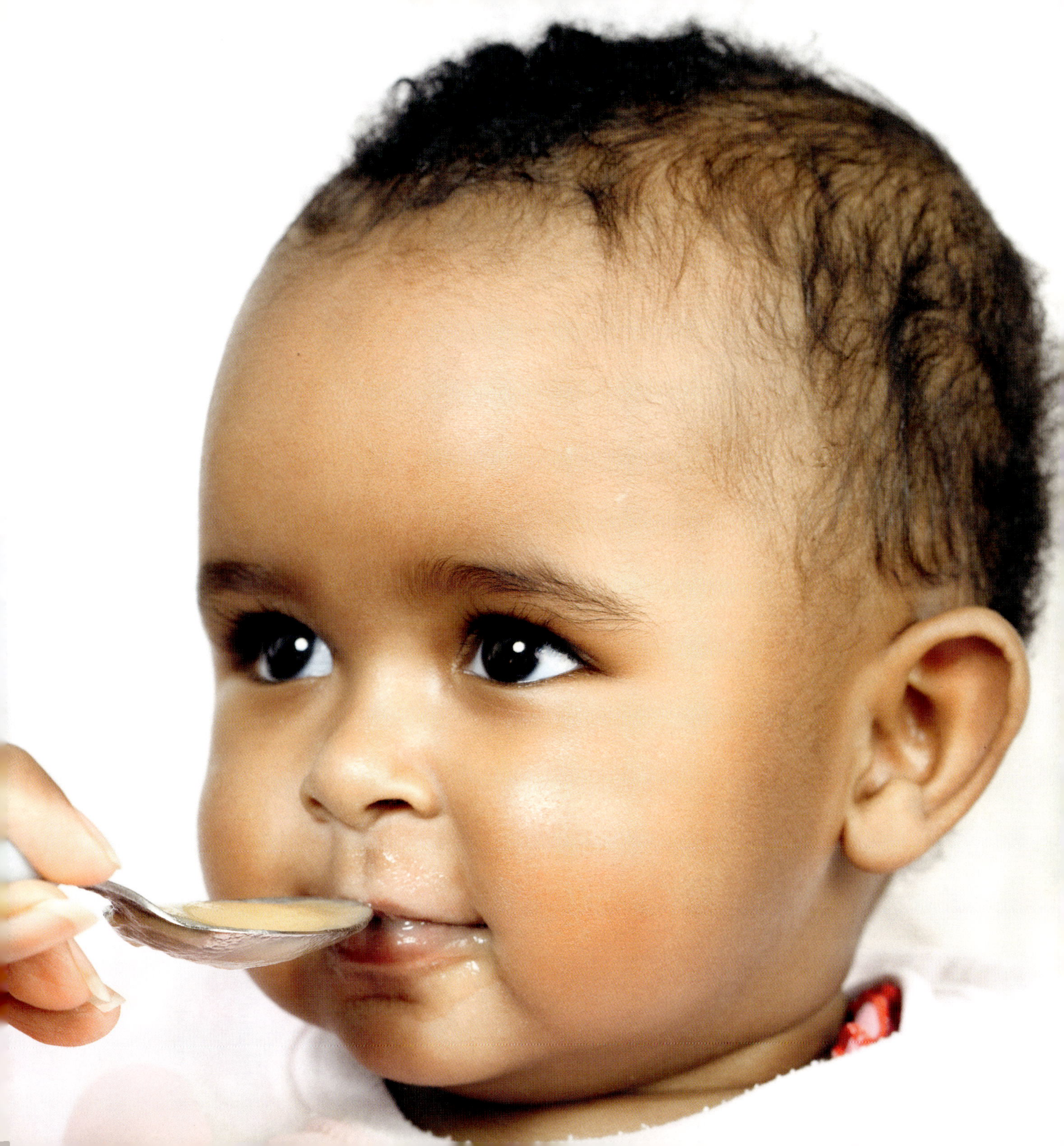

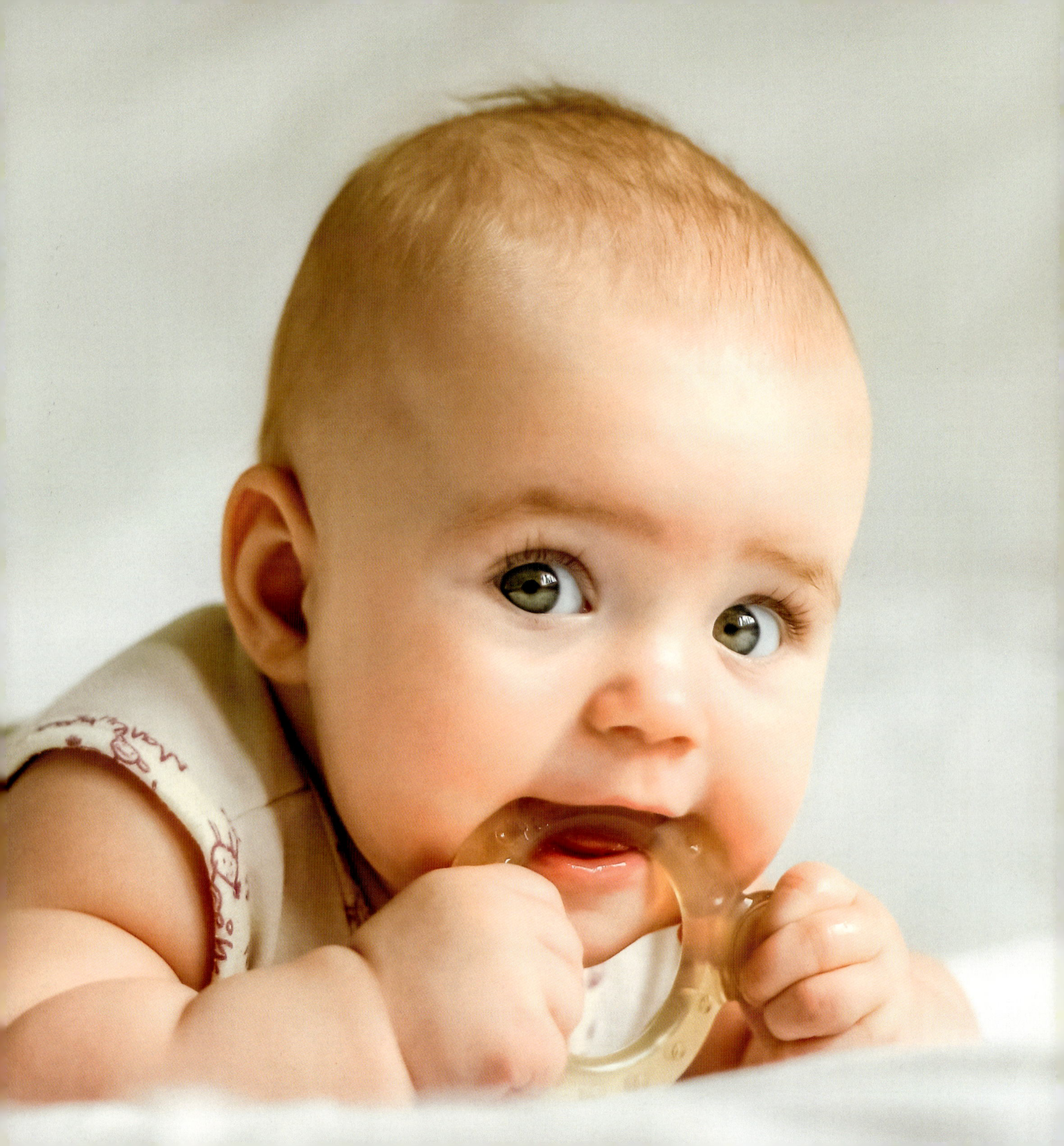

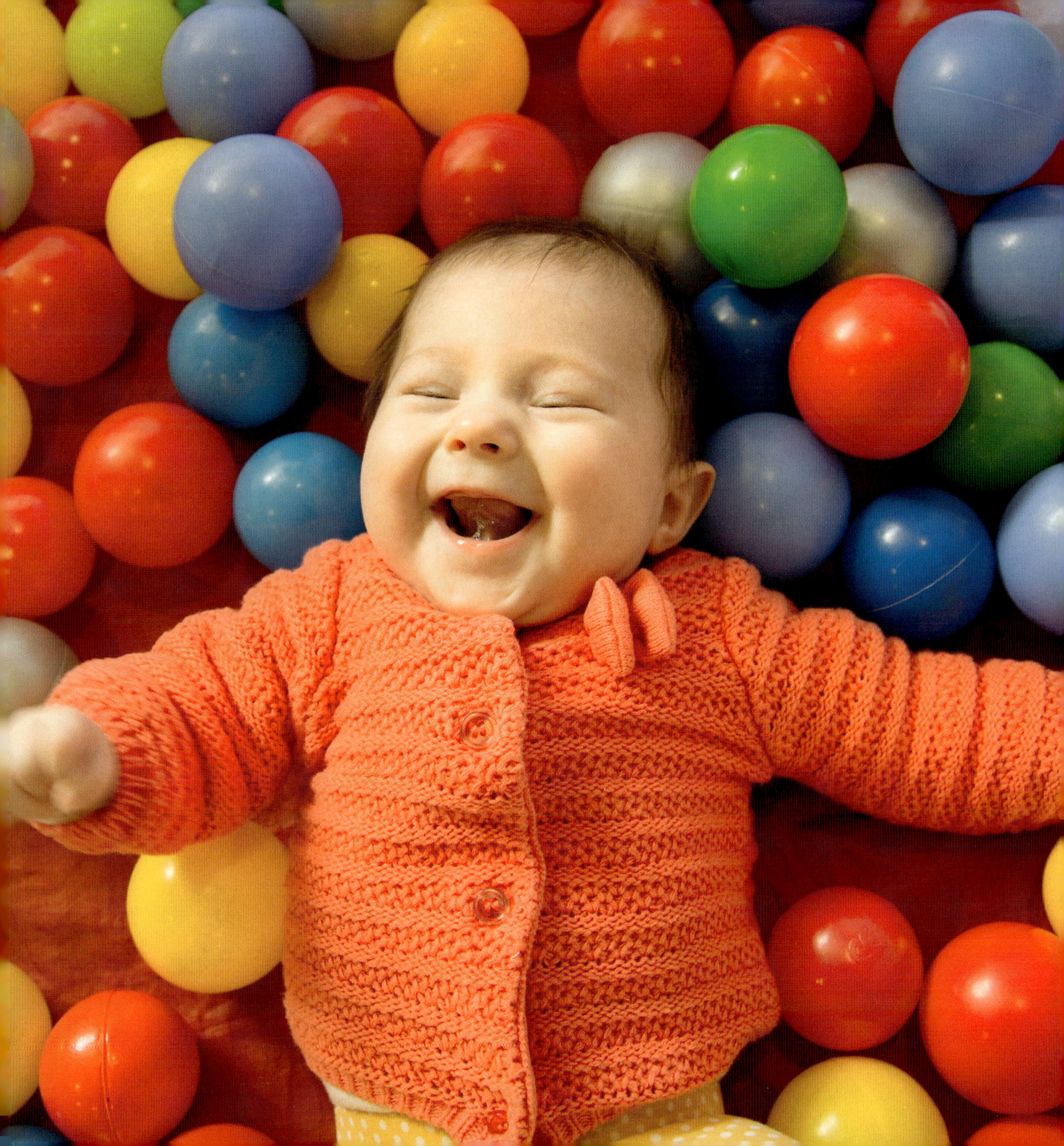

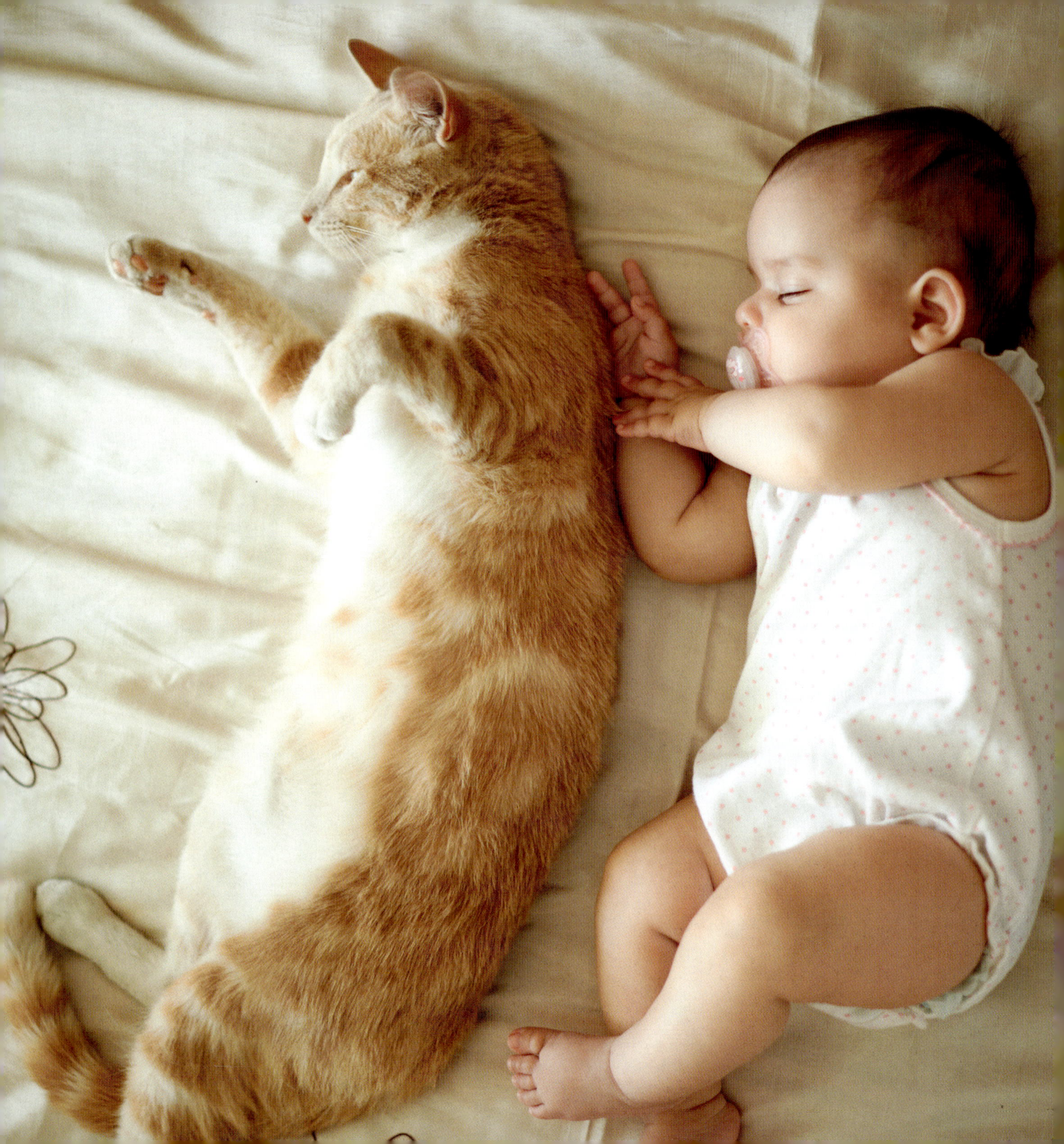

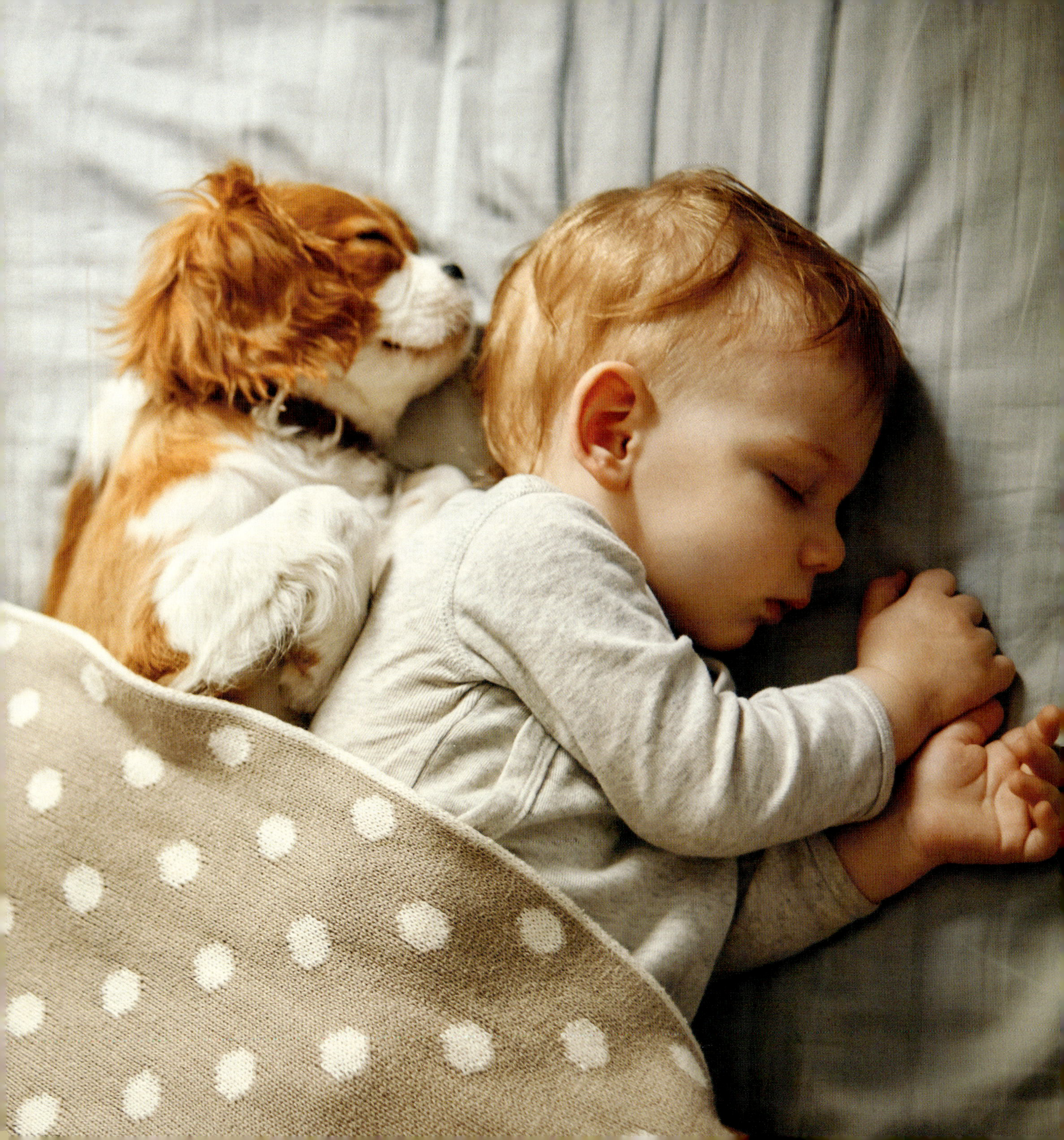

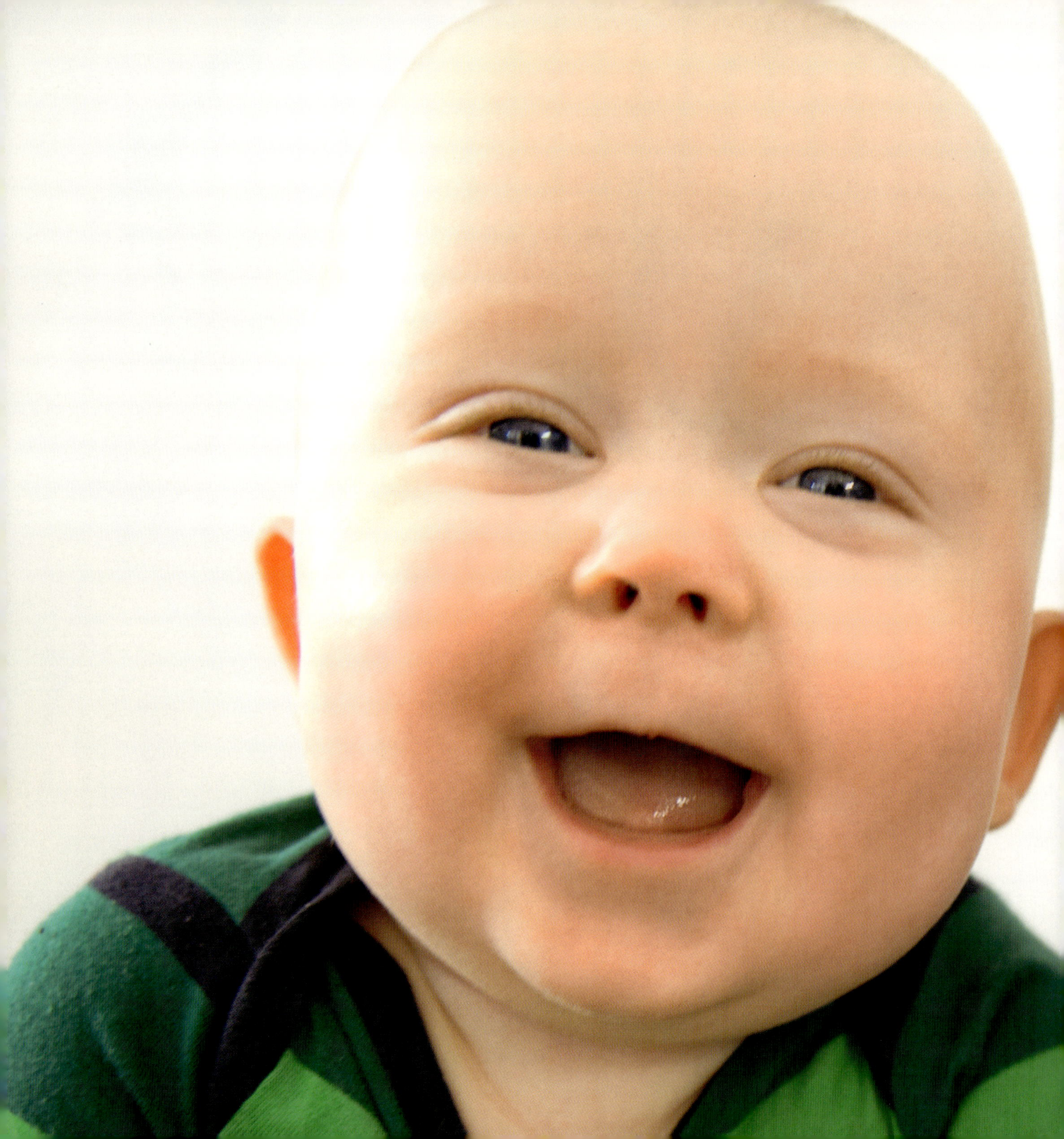

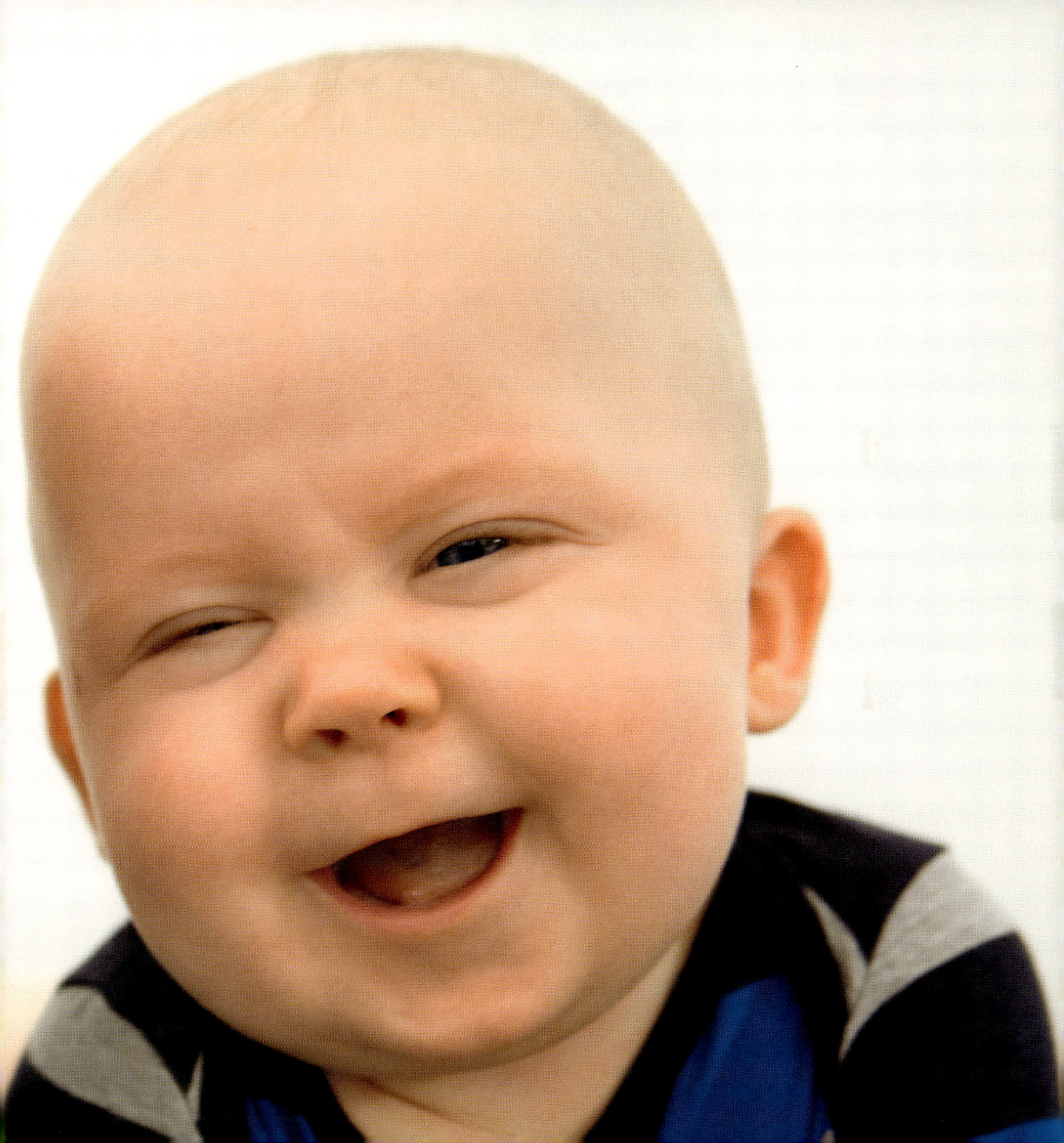

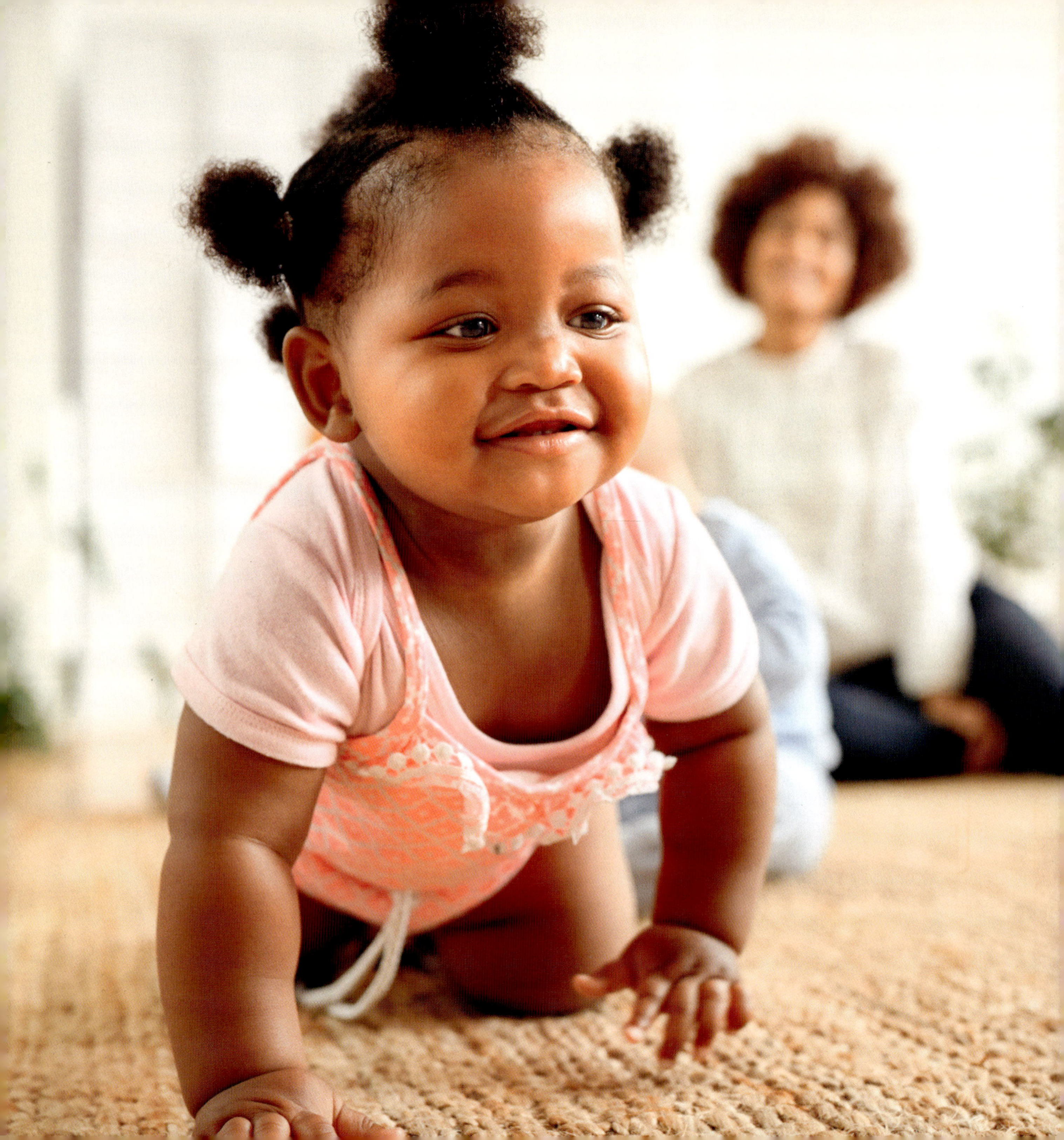